KIWIFRUIT
GROWING AND HANDLING

TECHNICAL EDITORS

JANINE K. HASEY, CO-CHAIR

R. SCOTT JOHNSON, CO-CHAIR

JOSEPH A. GRANT

WILBUR O. REIL

PUBLICATION 3344

UNIVERSITY OF CALIFORNIA
DIVISION OF AGRICULTURE
AND NATURAL RESOURCES

1994

FOR INFORMATION ABOUT ORDERING
THIS PUBLICATION, WRITE TO

ANR PUBLICATIONS
UNIVERSITY OF CALIFORNIA
6701 SAN PABLO AVENUE
OAKLAND, CALIFORNIA 94608-1239

TELEPHONE (510) 642-2431
FAX (510) 643-5470

Printed on Recycled Paper

ISBN 1-879906-04-X

Library of Congress Catalog Card No. 94-60052

© 1994 by The Regents of the University of California Division of Agriculture and Natural Resources.

All rights reserved.

No part of this publication may be reproduced, stored in a retrieval system, or transmitted, in any form or by any means, electronic, mechanical, photocopying, recording, or otherwise, without the written permission of the publisher and the authors.

Printed in the United States of America.

ACKNOWLEDGMENTS

The Technical Editors express appreciation to all the authors and reviewers for their contributions to their respective chapters. Thanks also to all those who supplied photographs, and especially Chet Fukushima, who provided numerous photographs, including some of those used on the front and back covers.

We sincerely appreciate the professional expertise provided by the ANR Publications personnel, including Franz Baumhackl, senior artist; Heidi Seney, senior editor; and Jason Joseph, senior publications coordinator. We especially thank JoAnn Coviello for her tireless efforts in putting this publication together and her many helpful suggestions.

> To simplify information, trade names of products have been used. No endorsement of named products is intended, nor is criticism implied of similar products that are not mentioned.

The University of California, in compliance with Titles VI and VII of the Civil Rights Act of 1964, Title IX of the Education Amendments of 1972, Sections 503 and 504 of the Rehabilitation Act of 1973, and the Age Discrimination Act of 1975, does not discriminate on the basis of race, religion, color, national origin, sex, mental or physical disability, or age in any of its programs or activities, or with respect to any of its employment policies, practices, or procedures. Nor does the University of California discriminate on the basis of ancestry, sexual orientation, marital status, citizenship, medical condition (as defined in Section 12926 of the California Government Code) or because individuals are special disabled veterans or Vietnam era veterans (as defined by the Vietnam Era Veterans Readjustment Act of 1974 and Section 12940 of the California Government Code). Inquiries regarding this policy may be addressed to the Affirmative Action Director, University of California, Agriculture and Natural Resources, 300 Lakeside Drive, 6th Floor, Oakland, CA 94612-3560. (510) 987-0097.

2.5m-pr-2/94-HS/FB

Contents

AUTHORS v

THE KIWIFRUIT INDUSTRY - AN OVERVIEW

1. History and Commercial Development **1**
   JAMES H. LARUE
2. Marketing **3**
   TOM SCHULTZ AND EMANUEL MCNEIL
3. Costs of Production **6**
   KAREN KLONSKY

THE KIWIFRUIT VINE AND FRUIT

4. The Genus *Actinidia* **9**
   FREDRICK A. BLISS
5. Vine Structure and Physiology **10**
   KAY RYUGO
6. Flower and Fruit Development **14**
   JOSEPH A. GRANT, VITO S. POLITO, AND KAY RYUGO

ESTABLISHING THE VINEYARD

7. Site Selection and Vineyard Development **18**
   MAXWELL V. NORTON
8. Propagation **21**
   GENE TANIMOTO
9. Vineyard Planning, Design, and Planting **25**
   WILBUR O. REIL
10. Training Young Vines **28**
    JANINE K. HASEY

CULTURAL CONSIDERATIONS

11. Dormant Pruning **30**
    JAMES A. BEUTEL
12. Summer Pruning **33**
    JANINE K. HASEY, WILLIAM H. OLSON, AND RACHEL B. ELKINS
13. Fruit Thinning **35**
    R. SCOTT JOHNSON AND JOSEPH A. GRANT
14. Irrigation Systems **36**
    RICHARD P. BUCHNER AND BLAINE R. HANSON
15. Irrigation Scheduling **43**
    RICHARD P. BUCHNER, DAVID A. GOLDHAMER, AND DAVID A. SHAW

16. Measuring Soil Moisture **50**
    HERBERT SCHULBACH
17. Pollination **53**
    ROBBIN W. THORP
18. Nutrition and Fertilization **58**
    JAMES A. BEUTEL, KIYOTO URIU, JOHN POST, AND JAMES PEARSON
19. Frost Sensitivity and Protection **61**
    RICHARD L. SNYDER

PEST MANAGEMENT

20. Weed Control **68**
    CLYDE L. ELMORE AND BILL B. FISCHER
21. Nematodes **70**
    MICHAEL V. MCKENRY
22. Diseases **80**
    W. DOUGLAS GUBLER AND KEVIN E. CONN
23. Insects and Mites **84**
    WILLIAM H. OLSON, RICHARD E. RICE, AND ROBERT H. BEEDE

HARVEST AND POSTHARVEST HANDLING

24. Postharvest Physiology and Causes of Deterioration **88**
    MARY LU ARPAIA, F. GORDON MITCHELL, AND ADEL A. KADER
25. Composition, Maturity, and Quality **94**
    F. GORDON MITCHELL
26. Harvesting and Preparation for Market **99**
    F. GORDON MITCHELL, MARY LU ARPAIA, AND GENE MAYER
27. Cooling, Storage, Transportation, and Distribution **108**
    MARY LU ARPAIA, F. GORDON MITCHELL, AND GENE MAYER
28. Postharvest Storage Diseases **116**
    NOEL F. SOMMER, J. EMILIO SUADI, AND ROBERT J. FORTLAGE

COLOR PLATES 75–78

INDEX 123

AUTHORS

Mary Lu Arpaia, Extension Subtropical Horticulturist, Department of Botany & Plant Sciences, UC Riverside

Robert H. Beede, Pomology Farm Advisor, Cooperative Extension, Kings County

James A. Beutel, Retired Pomology Extension Specialist, Department of Pomology, UC Davis

Fredrick A. Bliss, Pomologist, Department of Pomology, UC Davis

Richard P. Buchner, Plant Science Farm Advisor, Cooperative Extension, Tehama/Shasta Counties

Kevin E. Conn, Graduate Student, Department of Plant Pathology, UC Davis

Rachel B. Elkins, Plant Science Farm Advisor, Cooperative Extension, Lake County

Clyde L. Elmore, Extension Weed Scientist, Department of Agricultural Botany, UC Davis

Bill B. Fischer, Weed Control Farm Advisor Emeritus, Cooperative Extension, Fresno County

Robert J. Fortlage, Retired Staff Research Associate, Department of Pomology, UC Davis

David A. Goldhamer, Irrigation Extension Specialist, Department of Land, Air and Water Resources, UC Davis/Kearney Agricultural Center, Parlier

Joseph A. Grant, Pomology Farm Advisor, Cooperative Extension, San Joaquin County

W. Douglas Gubler, Plant Pathology Extension Specialist, Department of Plant Pathology, UC Davis

Blaine R. Hanson, Irrigation Extension Specialist, Department of Land, Air and Water Resources, UC Davis

Janine K. Hasey, Pomology Farm Advisor, Cooperative Extension, Sutter/Yuba Counties

R. Scott Johnson, Pomology Extension Specialist, Department of Pomology, UC Davis/Kearney Agricultural Center, Parlier

Adel A. Kader, Pomologist, Department of Pomology, UC Davis

Karen Klonsky, Economics Extension Specialist, Department of Agricultural Economics, UC Davis

James H. LaRue, Pomology Farm Advisor Emeritus, Cooperative Extension, Tulare County

Gene Mayer, Retired Staff Research Associate, Department of Pomology, UC Davis

Michael V. McKenry, Nematology Extension Specialist, Department of Nematology, UC Riverside/Kearney Agricultural Center, Parlier

Emanuel McNeil, Agricultural Economist, USDA Washington D.C.

F. Gordon Mitchell, Pomology Extension Specialist Emeritus, Department of Pomology, UC Davis

Maxwell V. Norton, Pomology Farm Advisor, Cooperative Extension, Merced County

William H. Olson, Pomology Farm Advisor, Cooperative Extension, Butte County

James Pearson, Retired Staff Research Associate, Department of Pomology, UC Davis

Vito S. Polito, Pomologist, Department of Pomology, UC Davis

John Post, Former Graduate Student, Department of Pomology, UC Davis

Wilbur O. Reil, Pomology Farm Advisor, Cooperative Extension, Yolo/Solano Counties

Richard E. Rice, Entomologist, Department of Entomology, UC Davis/Kearney Agricultural Center, Parlier

Kay Ryugo, Pomology Emeritus, Department of Pomology, UC Davis

Herbert Schulbach, Retired Soils and Water Specialist, Cooperative Extension, Colusa County

Tom Schultz, President, Chase National Kiwi Farms Inc., Marysville

David A. Shaw, Environmental Horticulture Farm Advisor, Cooperative Extension, San Diego County

Richard L. Snyder, Frost Protection Extension Specialist, Department of Land, Air and Water Resources, UC Davis

Noel F. Sommer, Pomologist Emeritus, Department of Pomology, UC Davis

J. Emilio Suadi, Former Graduate Student, Department of Pomology, UC Davis

Gene Tanimoto, Mike Tanimoto Nursery, Gridley

Robbin W. Thorp, Entomologist, Department of Entomology, UC Davis

Kiyoto Uriu, Pomologist Emeritus, Department of Pomology, UC Davis

History and Commercial Development

JAMES H. LARUE

The kiwifruit (*Actinidia deliciosa*) was relatively unknown several decades ago, but it has become a major worldwide fruit crop in recent years. There are now nearly 170,000 acres planted throughout many countries in both the northern and southern hemispheres. Acreage within the United States is only about 7,200 acres, almost all of which is found within California.

Indigenous to southeast Asia, the kiwifruit has been known to inhabitants of China and southeast Asia since ancient times. It is commonly found growing on forest margins of China's Yangtze Valley, where it grows naturally as a vigorous deciduous fruiting vine, often to a height of 30 feet or more. The 50 other species in the genus *Actinidia* are all native to Asia. Some are grown in other areas of the world as ornamental plants; only a few are grown for their edible fruits. *Actinidia deliciosa* has been found to be the most acceptable fruiting species for commercial purposes.

The kiwifruit plant was not exported until the turn of the 20th century, when Isabel Fraser, a native of New Zealand, visited China and returned home with kiwifruit seeds that she gave to Alexander Allison. Allison subsequently grew them successfully in Wanganui, and the vines from these seeds first fruited in 1910. It is now believed that all New Zealand kiwifruit varieties descended from those vines.

Years later, the first commercial crops were produced from plantings in the Bay of Plenty area on New Zealand's north island. Following World War II and initial success in early marketing, new plantings were added, resulting in a growth of export sales into the 1980s.

As New Zealand's success worldwide in marketing of kiwifruit was noted, other temperate-zone countries with the mild winters required for kiwifruit production began to import vines for trial plantings. From these early trials successful commercial kiwifruit plantings have developed in Australia, Chile, France, Greece, Italy, Japan, Portugal, South Africa, Spain, and the United States.

Kiwifruit was introduced into the United States in the early 1930s by the U.S. Department of Agriculture. The fruit was recognized as a potential new crop that seemed to be adaptable to the southern and western United States. Plants were distributed for trial throughout those areas, but the fruit was not immediately accepted by the public. Before long, most plants had disappeared from the gardens in which they had originally been planted.

At the USDA Plant Introduction Station in Chico, one of the plants originally introduced in 1934 thrived and served as the showpiece kiwifruit vine for the future California industry (Fig. 1.1). A cutting planted there in 1935 is still producing well and has been a source of propagating material for today's California kiwifruit vineyards.

Robert Smith, a research horticulturist of the now closed USDA Plant Introduction Station in Chico, became one of the first to demonstrate that kiwifruit could be grown and produced successfully in California. He provided seed and cuttings to growers establishing vineyards and offered advice on cultural practices.

The Tanimoto brothers of Gridley, California are credited with establishing the first commercial kiwifruit vineyard of any size in California. In 1965 they obtained some seed from Smith and later obtained scion wood for grafting. In 1968 these grafted vines were planted in an acre block in the

Fig. 1.1. Kiwifruit mother vine planted at the USDA Plant Introduction Station at Chico in 1934.

Sacramento Valley and produced their first commercial crop in 1971.

At about the same time, Judd Ingram also became interested in growing kiwifruit in the San Joaquin Valley's Delano-McFarland area. Ingram visited Smith and found that Chico had about the same weather year-round as Porterville. In the early 1960s Ingram's attempt to grow plant material obtained in northern California was not successful, but in 1966, with the help of the California Department of Food and Agriculture (CDFA), he obtained a permit to import 20 plants from New Zealand. Once in McFarland, they were immediately potted in 5-gallon cans. When Ingram saw their successful growth, he ordered 200 more plants which he planted directly in the field in 1967. He admits he did everything wrong, beginning by placing plants too far apart in the row. Due to a nursery mistake, he later found, about four or five other varieties were mixed throughout his Hayward vines, the variety preferred now in almost all California kiwifruit vineyards. But as Ingram says, "It didn't matter then because we could sell anything with fuzz on it."

Ingram started his own nursery and for many years sold plants throughout the San Joaquin Valley. He also packed his own fruit from the beginning because "there was no one else to do it." He started with an egg sizer that took two fruit at a time and packed them into fig flats.

Frieda Caplan, owner of the Los Angeles distribution firm, Produce Specialties, Inc., began importing and selling New Zealand kiwifruit in California around 1970. Shortly after the first New Zealand imports arrived, Caplan began selling fruit grown by the Tanimoto brothers, Judd Ingram, and another grower, John Heinke, who farms in Paradise (Butte County). With Los Angeles wholesale market prices for California-grown fruit at $1.50 per pound, interest in planting kiwifruit increased rapidly.

Calchico, Inc., a pioneer in the kiwifruit nursery business, began extensively promoting kiwifruit plants in 1971. Before it filed for bankruptcy in 1976, Calchico had grown and sold thousands of seedlings and grafted plants throughout California. Demand for vines seemed always to exceed supply in those early expanding years. Large and small plantings by farmers, family-type growers, and retired persons increased eac year. Many plantings were supported by investors seeking tax shelters or groups eager to become early producers to take advantage of the high prices being received in wholesale markets.

During the 1960s and 1970s, when little was known about the cultural practices necessary to produce kiwifruit successfully in California, failures were common. Substandard nursery plants, poor soil conditions, improper planting site preparation and irrigation, inadequate trellising and training, along with a general lack of knowledge concerning commercial kiwifruit culture in California's diverse climates, gave many growers a shaky start. Some vineyards required many replacement plants; a few vineyards were abandoned or removed. The many growers in the San Diego area who enthusiastically planted kiwifruit obtained low yields (mainly due to inadequate winter chilling) and found that it was not economically sound to grow this crop in that area. With experience, increasing knowledge, and good management, many vineyards planted in the 1970s became highly productive.

New plantings leveled off in the 1980s as production increased and wholesale market prices decreased. Production from plantings elsewhere in the northern (and southern) hemisphere was in competition with California. By this time, however, California growers were supplying kiwifruit to well established markets. In addition, thanks to a decade or more of experience, kiwifruit production practices were becoming more sophisticated, and fruit quality had become competitive with other areas of the world.

Few new vineyards have been planted in California in the 1990s. The main production is concentrated in the northern Sacramento Valley counties of Butte, Sutter, and Yuba and in the southern San Joaquin Valley counties of Tulare, Kern, Kings, and Fresno (Fig. 1.2).

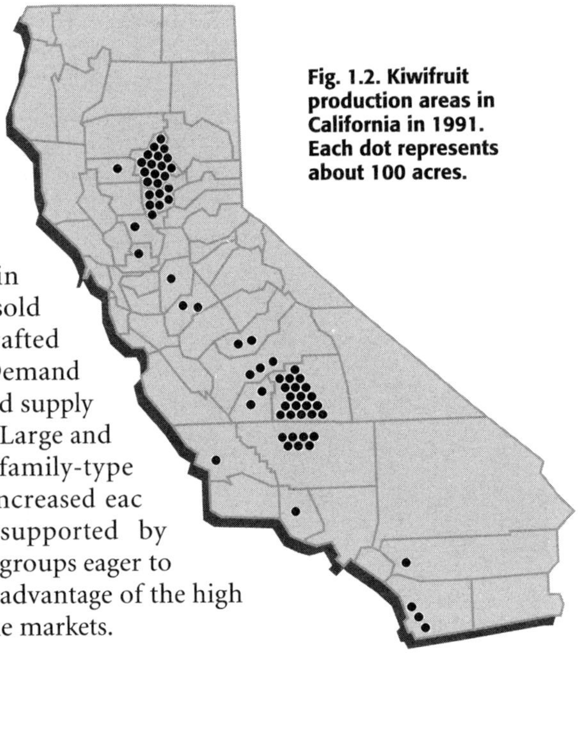

Fig. 1.2. Kiwifruit production areas in California in 1991. Each dot represents about 100 acres.

California Kiwifruit Acreage Estimates as of 1991

County	Harvested Acreage 1991
Butte	1,460
Fresno	310
Glenn	56
Kern	731
Kings	244
Madera	189
Riverside	136
San Diego	317
San Luis Obispo	105
San Joaquin	149
Solano	105
Stanislaus	237
Sutter	319
Tulare	1,936
Ventura	92
Yolo	100
Yuba	417
Sum of others	329
	7,232

THE KIWIFRUIT INDUSTRY - AN OVERVIEW

2

Marketing

TOM SCHULTZ AND EMANUEL MCNEIL

Marketing kiwifruit has come a long way since the early 1950s, when the first commercial shipment of kiwifruit arrived in Europe from New Zealand. Now it is marketed throughout the world by numerous countries including New Zealand, Chile, and Australia in the southern hemisphere and Italy, Japan, France, Greece, and the United States in the northern hemisphere.

Italy has recently passed New Zealand as the world's largest producer of kiwifruit. Because of the rapid growth in kiwifruit production in other major producing countries such as Chile, France, Japan, Greece, and the United States, competition for international markets is increasing.

Table 2.1 shows the 1989 and 1992 planted acreage, total production, and exports worldwide. Kiwifruit production and trade have increased dramatically. Production has risen from 54,000 U.S. tons in 1982 to more than 644,000 tons in 1989. Total world production in 1992 exceeded 927,000 tons. Total area planted to kiwifruit in the eight countries in 1992 was estimated at nearly 166,000 acres (67,000 hectares), up 11 percent from 1989. In general, northern hemisphere producers market their crop during the first half of the year; southern hemisphere producers, primarily New Zealand, market their crop during the second half.

Kiwifruit markets continue to expand to new countries throughout the world as consumption increases. Table 2.2 shows the principal countries importing kiwifruit, the quantity imported in 1987 and 1991, and the country of origin of the fruit.

Table 2.1. Kiwifruit production and trade in major producing countries, calendar years 1989 and 1992*

Country	Year	Total area	Production	Exports
		(acres)	(U.S. tons)	
Southern Hemisphere:†				
New Zealand	1989	43,737	231,000	185,000
	1992	42,748	309,000	231,000
Chile	1989	19,768	15,000	14,700
	1992	24,710	63,500	59,500
Australia	1989	2,842	12,100	550
	1992	4,942‡	16,500	1,100
Northern Hemisphere:§				
Italy	1989	44,651	231,000	74,000
	1992	47,443	320,000	121,000‡
Japan	1989	12,602	48,200	—
	1992	13,343	77,200	—
France	1989	12,852	53,700	15,000
	1992	13,096	61,700‡	22,000‡
Greece	1989	6,178	13,000	8,500‡
	1992	12,355	40,800	24,300
United States	1989	7,200	40,000	10,800
	1992	7,166‡	38,600‡	8,300‡
GRAND TOTAL	1989	149,830	644,000	308,550
	1992	165,803	927,300	467,200

* 1992 data are estimates.
† Southern Hemisphere crops are harvested mostly in April-June, marketed mostly from May to December.
‡ FAS estimate.
§ Northern Hemisphere crops are harvested mostly in October-November, marketed mostly from December to May.
— = Not available.

Source: U.S. Agricultural Counselor and Attache Reports; USDA, National Agricultural Statistics Service; and U.S. Department of Commerce, Bureau

WORLDWIDE KIWIFRUIT PRODUCTION

New Zealand

New Zealand, the largest exporter of kiwifruit, exports approximately 75 percent of its production, but this output has begun to level off as vines planted in the early 1980s reach full production. Some kiwifruit producers are unable to market fruit economically at current export prices. In response to the growing flood of kiwifruit onto world markets, the Kiwifruit Marketing Board (KFMB) has opted to emphasize higher quality fruit and larger sizes. New varieties are being researched and tested, but none is commercially available. In 1989, the KFMB experimented with packaging fruit in bulk bins or tri-pack (three loosely packed layers in one box). The new pack was successful, except in some markets that require repacking fruit into single-layer trays, including New Zealand's biggest market, Europe.

Italy

Italy is now the world's largest producer but is still second to New Zealand in exports. The area planted to kiwifruit in Italy expanded from slightly more than 14,800 acres (6,000 hectares) in 1985, to nearly 45,000 acres (18,000 hectares) in 1989, and it is estimated to have exceeded 47,000 acres (19,000 hectares) in 1992. Italian kiwifruit acreage now exceeds that of New Zealand, and plantings are projected to continue increasing through 1995. The rapid increase in kiwifruit production has caused a significant decline in grower prices, despite increasing kiwifruit consumption in Italy. Germany and other European countries represent more than 80 percent of the market for Italian exports.

France

French production of kiwifruit in 1992 was forecast to reach about 62,000 tons. Acres planted to kiwifruit in 1989 totaled 12,800 (5,200 hectares). According to the French Kiwifruit Industry Association, production of kiwifruit in 1988 was 29,700 tons. French kiwifruit production is forecast to reach 88,000 to 110,000 tons by 1995. New Zealand remained France's leading supplier of kiwifruit imports in 1991, although imports from Italy and Chile continue to rise as a result of increased production in the two countries. European competition has driven U.S. shipments of kiwifruit to the French market from 386 tons in 1987 to an insignificant level in 1991.

Chile

Chileans have invested heavily in the production of kiwifruit in recent years. Production has grown from 4,200 tons on 3,900 acres (1,600 hectares) in 1985 to 63,500 tons on about 25,500 acres (10,000 hectares) in 1992. As production increased and domestic and international prices fell, return to growers has declined. Low grower returns have reduced interest in expanding planted areas. Reportedly, even if planted area does not increase substantially in the next few years, total kiwifruit production from the already planted area could reach about 220,000 tons by 1995. Chile's exports of kiwifruit have been directed primarily to the western European market. Exports are expected to become proportionately more important in the future. However, a greater marketing effort will be necessary to export the rapidly increasing crops. Reportedly, Chilean export prices have been depressed due to low quality and large market supply. The Chilean harvest is from March through July; much of the harvest occurs during April.

Greece

Kiwifruit production in Greece has increased dramatically. Total acreage has doubled since 1989 so production will continue to rise as young vineyards come into bearing. Most of the expansion is taking place in Macedonia.

United States

Essentially all U.S. production of kiwifruit is from California. Total production for California's kiwifruit crop in 1992 was a record 45,020 tons, up 56 percent from 1991. Production is forecast at about 34,000 tons for 1993. Total area planted to kiwifruit in 1992 was 7,111 acres (2,878 hectares). In recent years, U.S. kiwifruit has lost market share, especially in western Europe and Japan. On the other hand, U.S. export performance to other Far Eastern markets and Canada has improved.

Table 2.2. Kiwifruit imports by country, showing major countries of origin, 1987 and 1991 (U.S. tons)

Country/Origin	1987	1991	Country/Origin	1987	1991
West Germany*:	49,584	126,771	Netherlands:	25,186	34,736
			Chile	1,156	11,836
Japan:	59,447	48,502	Belgium-Lux†	482	11,270
New Zealand	57,056	48,502	Italy	478	5,792
United States	2,391	0	France	2,048	2,557
			Greece	486	2,375
France:	17,607	34,079	New Zealand	18,422	415
New Zealand	13,917	14,871			
Italy	2,237	12,205	Sweden:	5,980	8,999‡
Chile	390	5,688	New Zealand	4,237	2,700
Greece	139	927	Italy	308	4,909
United States	386	—	Chile	139	998
			United States	807	—
United States:	19,435	31,969			
New Zealand	18,954	28,267	United Kingdom:	6,143	—
Chile	394	3,415	New Zealand	4,413	—
Italy	0	252	Italy	625	—
			France	180	—
Italy:	10,018	22,909	Chile	101	—
Chile	538	7,000	Belgium-Lux†	13	—
Belgium-Lux†	0	5,826	United States	591	—
New Zealand	7,596	4,231			
France	556	3,754			
Netherlands†	481	1,101			
Austria:	11,244	16,535			
New Zealand	6,834	6,614			
Italy	2,205	7,716			
Chile	110	1,433			
Greece	331	772			
United States	1,433	—			

* 1991 German kiwifruit imports include East and West Germany data; 1987 imports include only West Germany. Country of origin data not available at time of publication.
† These countries are re-exporters of kiwifruit.
‡ Jan.-Sept. imports only.
— = Indicates zero, not available, or included in "others" not identified.

Source: U.S. Agricultural Counselor and Attache Reports, and U.S. Department of Commerce, Bureau of the Census.

Japan

Kiwifruit production in Japan in 1989 is estimated at 48,000 tons, down 15 percent from the previous season despite an estimated 11 percent increase in total harvested area. Kiwifruit is harvested in November and marketed December through April. Japan's kiwifruit production for 1992 was forecast to reach 77,000 tons. New Zealand supplies virtually 100 percent of the kiwifruit imported into Japan. To date, Japan has only imported kiwifruit from New Zealand and the United States. Its plant quarantine authorities consider kiwifruit to be a host of the Mediterranean fruit fly, and therefore prohibit the importation of kiwifruit from Italy and other countries with this pest. However, in view of the increasing availability of a wide variety of fresh fruit on the Japanese market, both domestic and imported, Japanese demand for imported kiwifruit is not expected to grow, at least for the next several years. Japan has exported small quantities of kiwifruit in recent years, mainly to Hong Kong and Europe.

Australia

In 1989, production of kiwifruit in Australia totaled 12,000 tons on 2,800 acres (1,150 hectares), up from 550 tons on 1,090 acres (440 hectares) in 1983. It is anticipated that overall production will continue to rise as vineyards mature. Australia's kiwifruit season begins in Queensland in March, and a month or so later in the south. Australia consumes almost all of its own fruit. Additionally, Australian imports of kiwifruit totaled 5,300 tons in 1989, up 9 percent from 1988.

MARKETING CALIFORNIA KIWIFRUIT

More than 100 marketing firms in California sell kiwifruit. Most kiwifruit is marketed in approximately 7-pound trays by California growers. Other packs are volume-fill and boxes containing individual 1-pound bags. The average sales commission charged to growers by handlers is between 6 and 10 percent of the f.o.b. sales price. The marketing season for California kiwifruit extends from October through May, when exports by southern hemisphere producers begin. California producers still look to the U.S. as their largest potential market.

California Kiwifruit Commission

The California Kiwifruit Commission is administered by kiwifruit growers and shippers elected from kiwifruit production districts. According to section 68003 of the California Food and Agricultural Code, the commission "is necessary for the efficient development and management of a national and industrial advertising program and essential to ensure that the California kiwifruit industry can compete successfully in the marketplace." California producers are assessed each year to pay for a generic promotion and advertising campaign. In 1986-1988 matching funds were obtained from the USDA Target Export Assistance Program to conduct an export marketing program for California kiwifruit. In 1986 the California Kiwifruit Commission received $500,000 for promotion in Japan. In 1988 these same funds were used in Japan, Hong Kong, and Taiwan. Since 1990, funding at this same level or higher has been used in Hong Kong, Taiwan, Korea, and Canada.

Kiwifruit Administrative Committee

In 1985 kiwifruit growers in California voted to create a federal marketing order to establish minimum quality standards for all kiwifruit grown in California. The Kiwifruit Administrative Committee, which regulates the marketing order, is composed of producers representing California districts where kiwifruit are grown. The committee has set minimum standards for grades U.S. 1, U.S. 2, and U.S. Fancy. Each year the board meets to set standards for the upcoming season. The federal marketing order, like the California Kiwifruit Commission, is periodically subject to a grower referendum to determine whether the program should continue or be terminated.

3

Costs of Production

KAREN KLONSKY

Per capita consumption of kiwifruit in the United States is one-fifth of a pound, a tiny fraction of the average 90 pounds of fruit eaten annually by each American. Although U.S. kiwifruit production is small compared with other fruit crops, it has increased dramatically since 1975.

Virtually all of the kiwifruit grown in the United States is grown in California. Bearing acreage has increased from 105 acres in 1975 to 7,300 acres in 1990. The heaviest planting took place between 1979 and 1982, averaging about 800 new acres per year. Planting slowed to only 256 new acres in 1985. Most plantings are of the Hayward variety with Chico male vines used for pollination.

Establishing a kiwifruit vineyard is a capital-intensive investment: 4 years must pass before any returns are realized. See Table 3.1 for per-acre costs to establish a kiwifruit vineyard and Table 3.2 for costs of operation after establishment in the Sacramento Valley area. Industry averages have not been used. In particular, trellis, irrigation systems, and fertilizer practices vary widely.

The example gives the per-acre costs for 20 acres of kiwifruit spaced 15 feet × 18 feet. A pergola trellis is used. Irrigation employs a dual system: solid-set sprinklers for frost control and supplemental irrigation and drip/microsprinklers to irrigate vines. Frost is controlled with from one to six applications per season (spring and fall). Drip irrigation applications are made twice weekly (at least) from April to October.

Vineyard floor management in the example consists of mowing the middles and spraying the strips with herbicide. Cultivating the middles, instead of mowing, costs about the same.

Fertilizer is generally applied in February, April, May, June, and July. Additional nutrients are often applied through the irrigation system. Costs vary according to materials used and application methods.

EQUIPMENT COSTS

In allocating equipment costs per acre, the following calculations are made:

1. Original cost of equipment is new cost including sales tax.

2. Depreciation is cost per acre divided by years of life. New cost per acre is figured as cost divided by the number of acres on which the equipment will be used.

3. Interest on investment is figured as half of the new cost per acre multiplied by the interest rate. Half of the new cost is the average value of the equipment during its useful life.

4. Investment per acre is calculated at 60 percent of the depreciation and interest costs for all new equipment to reflect a mix of new and used equipment. Equipment, buildings, and costs are listed in Table 3.3.

INCOME

Income from production in the fourth year is subtracted from total costs as a reduction in establishment costs. Although receipts are listed in the same year in which the crop is harvested, payment is not usually received until the following year.

Total costs of establishment are sensitive to interest rates and methods of financing. If no money is borrowed to establish the vineyard, then there is no cash interest cost on investment. In the example shown this would reduce cash costs by $2,614 over the 4-year establishment period. This number is the sum of the

Table 3.1. Sample costs per acre to establish a kiwifruit vineyard, Sacramento Valley, 1991

Labor: $5.50 per hour

Item	1st Year	2nd Year	3rd Year	4th Year
Yield per acre:				
7.6-lb trays				333
23-lb volume-fill containers				55
Preharvest costs:				
Contract land level	$ 100			
Contract ripping	400			
Strip weed control: material & application		$ 100	$ 100	$ 100
Stake & layout	100			
Vines: 160 in yr 1, 7 in yr 2 @ $8 each	1,280	56		
Vine stakes: $.50/vine	80			
Contract plant: $.50/vine	80	4		
Dormant prune	73	147	220	366
Dormant tie	73	73	147	176
Summer train, tie, sucker	220	220	293	325
Pruning and training materials	16	16	24	32
Brush removal (rake, chop)				13
Mow	52	52	52	52
Irrigation, frost control				
Pumping power @ $35/ac-ft	70	105	140	140
Labor	28	28	28	28
Fertilize: materials, application		34	57	80
Bees: 2 hives @ $10 each				20
Misc. labor, materials, repairs	70	70	70	70
Total preharvest costs	$2,642	$ 905	$ 1,131	$ 1,402
Harvesting costs:				
Pick and haul				$ 139
Pack				971
Store				316
Forklift				33
Selling charges:				
Marketing Commission 8.5% of gross FOB				226
California Kiwifruit Commission				100
Federal Marketing Order				20
Repack 80% of fruit				88
Total harvest costs				$ 1,893
Overhead costs:				
Office, business costs	200	200	200	200
County taxes	90	90	90	90
Total overhead costs	$ 290	$ 290	$ 290	$ 290
Total cash costs	$2,932	$1,195	$1,421	$3,585
Accumulated cash costs	$2,932	$4,127	$5,548	$9,133
Depreciation:*				
Building, equipment	319	319	319	319
Irrigation system	176	176	176	176
Trellis	200	200	200	200
Total depreciation	$ 695	$ 695	$ 695	$ 695
Interest on investment at 12%:				
Building, equipment*	170	170	170	170
Irrigation system*	194	194	194	194
Trellis*	180	180	180	180
Land @ $5,500/acre	660	660	660	660
Interest on accumulated cash costs	353	497	667	1,097
Total interest on investment	$1,557	$1,701	$ 1,871	$ 2,301
Total cost for the year	$5,184	$3,591	$ 3,987	$ 6,581
Credit for fruit @ $5.37/tray, $15.80/volume-fill container				$ 2,657
Net cost for year	$5,184	$3,591	$ 3,987	$ 3,924
Total accumulated net cost	$5,184	$8,775	$12,762	$16,686

* Refer to table 3.3 for details.

Table 3.2. Kiwifruit production costs per acre, Sacramento Valley, 1991

Labor: $5.50 per hour
Yield per acre is:
7.6 tons or
1,334 trays (7.6 lb each) and
220 volume-fill containers (23 lb each)

Item	Hours per acre	Labor cost	Fuel and repair	Custom/ material	Total cost per acre
Preharvest costs:					
Strip weed control	1.0	$ 5.50	$ 4.30	$90.20	$ 100.00
Pest control:					
Custom app. 2x @ $20 ea.				40.00	
materials				55.00	95.00
Fertilize: materials, application	1.0	5.50	5.30	92.80	103.60
Dormant prune	106.7	586.85			586.85
Dormant tie	40.0	220.00			220.00
Summer prune, tie	71.0	390.50			390.50
Pruning, training materials				36.80	36.80
Fruit thinning	16.6	91.12			91.12
Brush removal (hand rake, chop)	2.2	12.00	1.00		13.00
Mow	3.0	16.50	22.20		38.70
Irrigation, frost control	5.0	27.50			27.50
Power: pump 4 ac-ft @ $35/ac-ft.					140.00
Bees: 2 hives @ $10				20.00	20.00
Misc. repairs, labor, materials					75.00
Total preharvest costs					$1,938.07
Total preharvest costs per ton					$ 255.01
Harvesting costs:		$/tray	$/volume fill		
Pick and haul		.25	1.00		$ 553.50
Pack		2.25	4.00		3,881.50
Store		.75	1.20		1,264.50
Forklift		.02	.05		33.00
Selling charges:					
Marketing Commission 8.5% of gross FOB		.46	1.34		904.36
California Kiwifruit Commission		.20	.60		398.80
Federal Marketing Order		.05	.07		78.33
Repack 80% of fruit		.18	.50		350.12
Total harvest costs		$4.16	$8.76		$7,464.11
Total harvest costs per ton					$ 982.12
Overhead costs					
County taxes					100.44
Office, business costs					200.00
Interest on operating capital, 12% for 6 months					116.28
Total overhead costs					$ 416.72
Total cash costs					$9,818.90
Total cash costs per ton					$1,291.96
Investment costs:		Depreciation	Interest @ 12%		
Land, $5,500/acre			660.00		660.00
Vines, $16,690/acre 30 yr life*		556.33	1,001.40		1,557.73
Building, equipment†		319.00	170.00		489.00
Irrigation system†		176.00	194.00		370.00
Trellis†		200.00	180.00		380.00
Total depreciation, interest		$1,251.33	$2,205.40		$ 3,456.73
Total cost per acre					$13,275.63
Total cost per ton					$ 1,746.79

*Refer to table 3.1 for details.
†Refer to table 3.3 for details.

interest on accumulated cash costs over the 4-year period (table 3.1). Realize, however, that even when interest is not paid on borrowed funds, tying up capital in a nonproducing vineyard is a cost. Money that could be earning interest in other kinds of investments is not generating any income for 3 years. Consider the value of foregone earned interest in making any investment decision.

Tax laws can also influence the investment decision. Vines are considered depreciable property under the Internal Revenue Service Code. Investments in the irrigation systems, trellises, machinery, and buildings are also depreciable. Land itself is not depreciable.

DEPRECIATION "BASIS"

Before figuring the depreciation deduction for vines, determine the "basis" in the vines—your investment in them up to the income-producing stage 4 years later. Your costs can be recovered through depreciation. When you depreciate the vines, a certain percentage of your basis is deducted from your taxable income each year. The basis, in other words, is the costs incurred during the years before the first marketable crop.

The basis must be decreased by the amount of any Section 179 deduction taken. The Section 179 deduction allows you to deduct part of the vineyard's establishment as an operating expense rather than as a capital expenditure. The maximum allowed for 1991 returns was $10,000. You cannot take depreciation on costs you elect as operating expenses.

Once income is reported from the vineyard, depreciation begins. The amount of depreciation allowed each year is determined by the tax laws in effect when the vineyard reaches the income-producing stage and by the depreciation method chosen. Any vine coming into production after 1988 must be depreciated under the modified accelerated cost recovery system (MACRS), using the straight line method with a no salvage value and a recovery period of 10 years or 20 years under the alternative MACRS method. The tax laws concerning vineyards are somewhat complex and subject to change. Consult a tax advisor specializing in agriculture and, preferably, in permanent crops.

Table 3.3. Kiwifruit vineyard equipment and building list, Sacramento Valley, 1991

Item	New cost	Annual use (acres)	Cost per acre	Life (years)	Overhead Depreciation	Overhead Interest @ 12%	Fuel & repair cost/hr
Building and equipment:							
Tractor, 50 HP 2 WD	$18,500	20	$ 925	12	$ 77	$ 55	$3.80
Mower, rotary	9,000	20	450	10	45	27	3.60
Weed sprayer, attachment	900	20	45	10	4	3	.50
4-wheel, all-terrain motorcycle	4,000	20	200	5	40	12	
Front-end forklift attachment	5,200	20	260	12	22	16	1.60
Tape guns, 4 @ $33.50 each	134	20	7	5	1	0	
Picking bags, 12 @ $22 each	264	20	13	5	3	1	
Farm shop	30,000	20	1,500	20	75	90	
Pickup	16,500	20	825	5	165	49	
Misc. equipment	10,000	20	500	5	100	30	
Subtotal	$94,498		$4,725		$532	$283	
60% of new cost*	$56,699		$2,835		$319	$170	
Irrigation system:							
1. Sprinkler (solid-set frost control system) PVC, mainline, etc. (installed)	$23,200	20	$1,160	20	$ 58	$ 70	
Pump 40 HP turbine (installed)	12,000	20	600	20	30	36	
Well	10,000	20	500	25	20	30	
2. Drip/microsprinkler	7,526	20	376	10	38	22	
Booster pump 40 HP	12,000	20	600	20	30	36	
Subtotal	$64,726		$3,236		$176	$194	
Trellis: Pergola system	$60,000	20	$3,000	15	$200	$180	

*60% of new costs are used in the cost studies to represent a mix of new and used equipment.

4

The Genus *Actinidia*

FREDRICK A. BLISS

Commercial cultivars of kiwifruit are large-fruited selections of *Actinidia deliciosa* (A. Chevalier, C.F. Liang et al., A.R. Ferguson), a recent change in nomenclature from the former classification, *A. chinensis* Planch. The genus *Actinidia* is solely of Asian origin; plants are found ranging from northeast India through China to tropical Java and into the cold climates of Manchuria, Japan, and eastern Siberia. All kiwifruit cultivars grown commercially in California were introduced primarily from New Zealand by the USDA Plant Introduction Station at Chico in the 1930s.

In addition to *A. deliciosa*, there are other species of interest because of their edible fruits: *A. chinensis*, *A. arguta*, *A. kolomikta*, *A. polygama*, and *A. eriantha*. Perhaps the best known is *A. arguta*, plants of which are often sold in the U.S. as hardy kiwifruit, since the vines are winter hardy to severe below-freezing temperatures. Issai is a widely available cultivar of *A. arguta*. Most of these lesser-known species bear fruits that are smooth skinned and about $\frac{1}{10}$ to $\frac{1}{20}$ the size of the fruits of common kiwifruit cultivars (**plate 1**). Although winter hardy, *A. arguta* appears to tolerate high temperatures, if there is adequate soil moisture. Not all clones of *A. kolomikta*, native to eastern Siberia, appear to thrive in the Central Valley's high temperatures. The fruits of the small-fruited species are usually consumed at a more advanced stage of ripeness. The berries have a pleasant, sweet flavor, and there is a wide range of subtle differences among the various cultivars.

Because kiwifruit is functionally dioecious, successful fruit production requires both the female cultivar and a suitable male pollenizer to supply a large quantity of viable pollen, beginning slightly before and continuing throughout the flowering period of the female. Hayward, the most widely grown commercial cultivar, is usually considered the standard fruit prototype. It is a high-chill cultivar requiring from 600 to 850 hours below 45°F (7°C); therefore, it is best suited to northern areas. It is late flowering and the fruit shape is a flattened oval. Other high-chill cultivars are Monty and Kramer. Low-chill cultivars requiring from 50 to 250 hours below 45°F include Bruno, Abbott, Allison, Vincent, Tewi, Elmwood, and Blake. Bruno is early flowering with long, oval, dark brown fruits. Abbott and Allison are similar early flowering cultivars that have oval, brown fruits with long hairs. The fruit flesh color of all current cultivars is a vivid green; however, some newly developed Japanese cultivars have fruits with light red, yellow, and orange flesh.

The most common of the named male cultivars are Matua, a long-flowering type unable to withstand cold temperatures, and Tomuri, long flowering but producing fewer flowers and able to withstand cold temperatures. The males used by California growers include several selected from clones introduced early into California, such as Cal Chico No. 3, Chico Early, and Chico Extra Early. A series of male clones have been selected in New Zealand, and the more popular ones are M51, M52, M54, and M56. These have not been tested or grown extensively in California, but are worthy of consideration.

Both male and female cultivars usually are propagated asexually to assure trueness of type. Dormant wood is usually grafted onto 1-year-old seedling rootstocks rather than self rooted. Seedling rootstocks are the most commonly used, with the source of seed being the female cultivar, Bruno; thus, the common reference to "Bruno rootstocks." Because the genetically heterozygous female vine is pollinated by a heterozygous male, often of unknown origin, resulting seedlings are expected to be genetically variable. More attention should be given to selecting improved uniform rootstocks, either seedlings or clonal, with disease and nematode resistance.

the kiwifruit vine and fruit

5

Vine Structure and Physiology

KAY RYUGO

The kiwifruit vine's growth habit relies on another plant or structure to support it. Unlike the grape shoot, the kiwifruit shoot lacks tendrils; upon contact, however, its terminal portion will entwine another shoot or a wire for support. In its native China, this evolutionary adaptation enables vines to grow over adjacent trees and shrubs to compete for sunlight.

Southern China differs climatically from California's central valleys. It is characterized by high rainfall evenly distributed throughout the year. Kiwifruit are found in dense forest or scrub vegetation. Many of their leaves are shaded for much of the day and relative humidity remains consistently high. Organic matter content of the soil is high. Kiwifruit are seldom found in sites with little moisture.

SHOOT AND CANE GROWTH

In California, budbreak generally occurs for the principal variety, Hayward, in early March. Reproductive buds are mixed, possessing flowers either singly or in small inflorescences. They are borne in axils of leaves between the second and seventh nodes. The number of buds that emerge in spring and their distribution along a cane depend on the cane's orientation. If a cane is kept in an upright position after dormant pruning, two to three buds near the cut will break first and the basal buds on the cane will emerge later. However, if the cane is tied horizontally, four to eight evenly spaced buds will break almost simultaneously along the entire length.

Basal portions of vigorous shoots are hairy and develop small buds. As shoot extension proceeds, the bristles disappear, the epidermis becomes relatively smooth, and the buds become knobby. The pith is initially solid, but it becomes septate.

Shoots grow to varying lengths, depending on their vigor and position. Basal buds that break late in spring tend to be unfruitful and vigorous. As shoots elongate and come into contact with other shoots or trellis wires, their internodes shorten and the shoot terminals begin to twist and entwine about them. Commercial growers head back such entwining shoots in summer because they are too time-consuming to remove at the dormant pruning period. Terminal shoots induced by summer pruning do not exhibit the entwining characteristic.

The kiwifruit vine's trunk and branches are not rigid enough to adequately support the vine and its crop. A large, mature vine may bear more than 200 pounds of fruit. Hence, all commercially grown kiwifruit vines require rigid trellising. The trellis serves not only to support the vine and crop, but it also allows the manipulation of the canopy so as to maximize the exposure of foliage to sunlight and thereby optimize photosynthesis and transpiration.

PHYSIOLOGY OF LEAVES

Photosynthesis

Consider the entire vine or foliar canopy as a solar collector and the leaves as cells that convert radiant energy from the sun into chemical energy by photosynthesis, a process that combines carbon dioxide (CO_2) and water

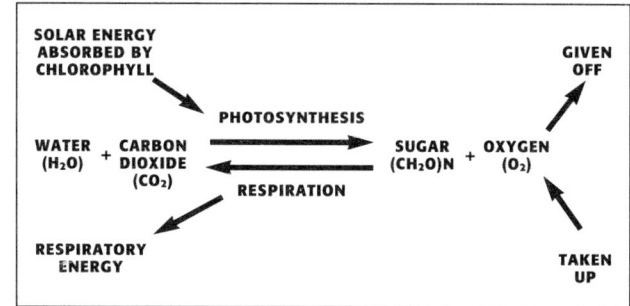

Fig. 5.1. Use of solar radiant energy to convert carbon dioxide and water into energy-rich sugars and oxygen is called photosynthesis. In the reverse reaction, respiration, sugar is utilized by living cells to release chemical energy, yielding carbon dioxide and water.

to form sugars in the presence of light and chlorophyll, the green pigment found in leaves and other green tissues (Fig. 5.1). Carbon dioxide of the air enters the leaf through microscopic pores known as stomates located on the hairy, lower epidermis.

Whereas only green cells carry on photosynthesis, all plant cells continuously utilize the products of photosynthesis for respiration. The light intensity at which the photosynthetic rate equals that of respiration so there is no net CO_2 uptake is known as the compensation point. Shaded leaves remain barely above the compensation point for much of the day (Fig. 5.2).

Photosynthesis (Pn) measurements on light-exposed leaves taken from sunup to sundown reveal that the mean photosynthetic rate follows a bell-shaped trend, reaching a maximum rate at 2 p.m. (Fig. 5.2). The stomates open shortly after daybreak; they begin to close in early afternoon so the rate of photosynthesis decreases. Pn rate of light-exposed leaves diminishes after 2 p.m. because:

1. Photosynthesis in morning hours may be great enough to substantially increase sugar concentration in mesophyll cells, resulting in deposition of starch and feedback inhibition of photosynthesis.

2. The ambient temperature may exceed the optimum range for photosynthesis. Maximum photosynthesis for kiwifruit leaves occurs at about 70° to 80°F (21° to 27°C) and drops rapidly as temperatures approach 100°F (38°C).

3. The relative humidity of the atmosphere decreases so the transpiration rate surpasses the rate of water uptake by roots. This leads to water stress in leaves and partial stomatal closure.

Photosynthetic rates of exposed leaves increase rapidly as light intensifies in the morning. Like leaves of most deciduous fruit tree species, maximum photosynthesis occurs between one-fourth and one-half full sunlight, depending on the natural light exposure of the leaf (Fig. 5.3).

This ability of the photosynthetic apparatus to be saturated at relatively low light intensity is attributed to the surroundings in which the species evolved. Species with a vine-type growth that evolve in forested areas have many leaves that grow in a dimly lit environment during their juvenile years and even when mature.

Transpiration and mineral nutrient accumulation

In transpiration, water vapor is lost from the plant through the stomates. It is controlled by the degree of opening of the stomates and the environmental conditions which affect water evaporation: temperature, humidity, wind speed, etc. Water vapor is primarily lost through the same stomates through which carbon dioxide enters the leaf, although a small amount of water is lost through the cuticle, a waxy covering on the epidermal cells. Transpiration allows water to be "pulled" from the roots to the leaves. Because most water is lost through the stomates at the same time that carbon dioxide is being fixed in the leaves, most water in the transpiration stream is lost during the daylight hours. However, kiwifruit lose more water at night than do many other plants because their stomates remain partially open. Even during the day, kiwifruit do not appear to regulate their stomates well to use water efficiently. Perhaps having evolved in an environment with high rainfall, high relative humidity, and good soil water-holding capacity, there was never selection pressure to conserve water.

In drawing water extracted from the soil by roots through the xylem tissue of the vine, mineral nutrients dissolved in the water are also transported upward to

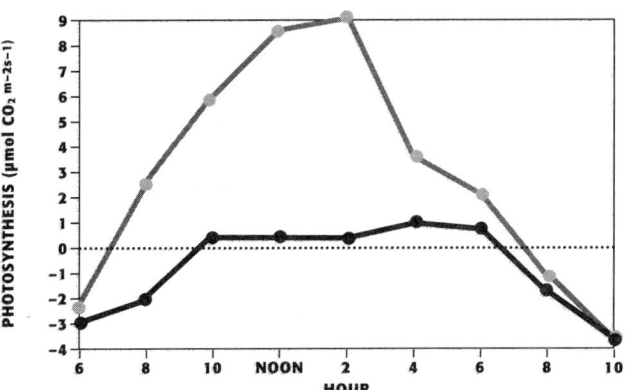

Fig. 5.2. Net photosynthesis of light-exposed (○) and shaded (●) leaves is depicted.

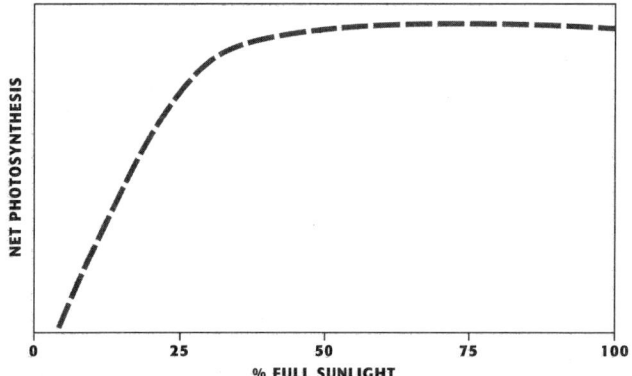

Fig. 5.3. Typical photosynthetic response of kiwifruit leaves to light.

the leaves. Naturally, leaves exposed to the sun transpire more water and accumulate more nutrients than do shaded leaves. Such mobile elements as potassium, however, are retranslocated out of leaves with carbohydrates; hence, their levels fluctuate more within leaves than do less mobile elements such as calcium and iron.

DISTRIBUTION/STORAGE OF CARBOHYDRATES

Primary and secondary products of photosynthesis, such as sugars, organic acids, and amino acids, are partitioned or diverted to (1) the structural components of the vine, the trunk, cordons, shoots, and roots, (2) the reproductive organs, the flowers that eventually develop into fruits, and (3) temporary storage products that serve as reserves, such as starch, hemicellulose, mucilages, oil, and proteins.

In nearly all temperate-zone woody species, cells in bark and wood tissues store starch reserves. Starch content fluctuates throughout the year according to the demand by various developing organs or in response to changing climatic conditions. The annual curve usually manifests two maxima and minima. Kiwifruit shoots begin to store starch as the basal leaves reach one-half to three-fourths of full size. As the rate of shoot elongation diminishes in late fall, the starch level usually reaches a maximum value (Fig. 5.4).

The amount and pattern of starch storage depends on cropping and sunlight exposure. Kiwifruit accumulate starch, like such pome fruits as apples and pears. The demand for current photosynthates by the crop is reflected in the pattern of shoot and root growth and the rate of deposition of starch in these organs. Because of this internal competition, bark and wood starch content in heavily cropped vines may be minimal. Nonbearing or lightly cropped vines accumulate more starch and use more sugar for vegetative growth.

As with other perennial woody species that evolved in the world's temperate zones, starch stored in summer and early fall in the kiwifruit shoot is converted to sugar in late September and early October as nights become cooler (Fig. 5.4). The interconversion of starch to sugar proceeds so that minimum starch and maximum sugar levels are attained by January in most fruit tree species. The increase in sugar concentration in cells is considered an evolutionary adaptation to avoid or minimize freezing injury.

The duration of this late winter sugar maximum may extend for 2 months, after which starch is resynthesized. In kiwifruit canes, starch reaches the second maximum at budbreak. Both starch and sugar contents are at a minimum by full bloom because the soluble carbohydrates are consumed for growth and for respiratory substrates.

If the temperature drops rapidly to below freezing in fall, vines can suffer injury. Damage is usually confined to the lateral cambium near ground level because (1) the tissue may still be actively dividing at the base of the trunk and (2) the temperature is coldest next to the soil when the air is still. Fall frost injury can be alleviated by cutting off irrigation early to force vines into dormancy and by removing the cover crop that absorbs light energy and prevents the soil from becoming warm. Wrapping the trunks with an insulated material and pruning off low branches that tend to block air movement may also be helpful.

As temperate-zone plants are subjected to freezing temperatures, water in the living part of the cells is secreted into the intercellular air spaces, thus

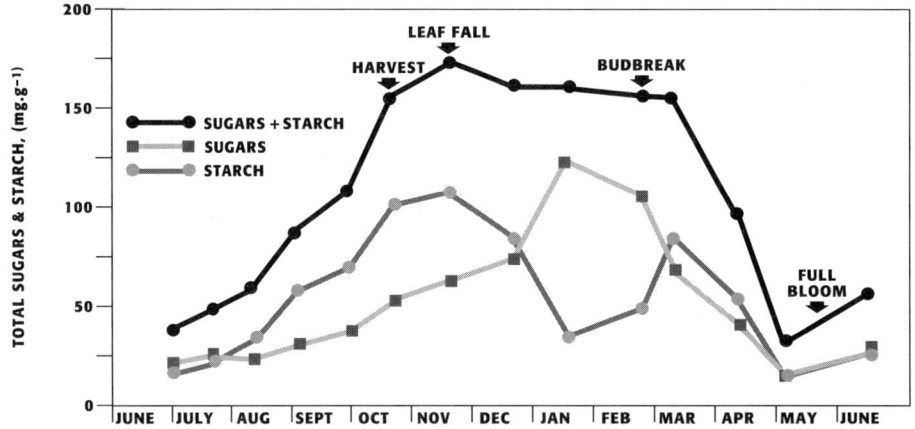

Fig. 5.4. Seasonal fluctuations in total sugar and starch content in kiwifruit branches. (From Grant, J. A. 1983. Influence of within-canopy shading on photosynthesis and fruit characteristics of kiwifruit. Masters Thesis, University of California, Davis.)

increasing sugar concentration in the cells. Water in the intercellular spaces may freeze, but the cells' increased sugar concentration lowers their freezing point by several degrees, thereby affording some protection. If vines are gradually exposed to freezing temperatures, fully dormant kiwifruit vines are cold-hardy down to about 14°F (−10°C).

Mineral nutrients, such as nitrogen and phosphorus, are also stored in the wood and bark during winter. These elements are remobilized from the leaves in fall before leaf abscission occurs. This process has not been studied extensively in kiwifruit, but other fruit trees are able to recover about 50 percent of the total nitrogen and phosphorus in leaves before they abscise. These elements are then available to support the first flush of shoot growth in early spring. Some nutrients, such as potassium and calcium, are not recovered efficiently from senescing leaves. Therefore, the majority of the plant's needs for these elements must come from soil uptake. A more detailed discussion of nutrient distribution during the growing season is covered in chapter 18, *Nutrition and Fertilization*.

ROOT GROWTH AND FUNCTION

Based on research on apple trees, root growth is thought to alternate with shoot growth in kiwifruit vines. However, data on the cyclic nature of root growth in kiwifruit vines are meager. One study of 5-year-old vines in New Zealand showed that peak root growth occurred in midsummer.

Roots tend to grow laterally and downward from the crown of the vine, especially if the soil is sandy, deep, and fertile. The distribution of roots depends on irrigation practices and soil type. A fairly even distribution with depth can be found in deep, sandy soils that have not been irrigated too frequently. However, when frequent irrigations are applied to maintain high soil moisture, roots are often found more abundantly near the soil surface.

Roots perform the following functions: (1) anchor plants to the soil, (2) take up water and mineral nutrients, (3) synthesize hormones and other compounds, such as amino acids, and (4) store reserve food.

Kiwifruit vines are normally supported by a trellis so that anchorage is not as important as it is with free-standing fruit trees. Uptake of water and absorption of mineral nutrients from the soil solution are the two other principal functions of roots. Care must be exercised in managing a kiwifruit plantation because poor management of irrigation, fertilization, cultivation, and other cultural practices can interrupt or disturb these biological processes.

The synthesis of amino acids from nitrate absorbed from the soil solution is thought to occur in the primary roots, probably in the cells of the root hairs. The rate that nitrate ions and other elements are absorbed by root cells is decreased if the soil becomes saturated with water for a long period, leading to an anaerobic condition. Kiwifruit roots appear to be particularly sensitive to anaerobic conditions, leading to rapid closing of stomata under waterlogged conditions.

Kiwifruit vines may exude more than 15 gallons (60 liters) of xylary sap if they are pruned during late winter and early spring. Appearance of the sap, a result of root pressure, may indicate that root growth has begun. The exudate contains nitrate, free ammonia, amino acids, mucilages, and hormones.

Dormant pruning should be done soon after leaf fall and before the sap begins bleeding so reserve carbohydrate and nitrogenous substances can be conserved. Vines that bleed profusely exhibit yellower leaves and fewer flowers than do vines pruned in mid-December before bleeding begins. Vines pruned in early winter do not bleed as much and theoretically have a greater potential to produce a higher yield.

Xylem exudates play a detrimental role in vine propagation. If vines are grafted while they are exuding sap, callus formation is inhibited and scions often fail to heal and grow. This failure is attributed to the presence of an inhibitory constituent in the sap that prevents callus formation and to the washing away of some growth-promoting substances transported from the scion buds to the graft union.

6

Flower and Fruit Development

JOSEPH A. GRANT, VITO S. POLITO, AND KAY RYUGO

The male and female flowers on kiwifruit vines are borne on separate plants. Both types of flowers have male (stamens) and female (pistils) parts, but the pollen fails to fully develop on female flowers and the flowers on male plants have only rudimentary pistils that never fully develop. Because it is the female flowers that develop into fruits, this chapter focuses on the development of these flowers in the Hayward variety, the only variety grown commercially in California.

FLOWER DEVELOPMENT

Kiwifruit flowers are borne on inflorescences arising from axils of leaves. Flowers may form on up to six of the first basal nodes on a current season's shoot. In the Hayward variety, the number of flowers produced per inflorescence varies at each node along a shoot. On heavily cropped vines, many nodes bear inflorescences with up to three flowers. On lightly cropped vines, one or both of the lateral or side flowers on many of the inflorescences abort some time before bloom, leaving mostly single fruits at each node.

As a shoot elongates during the growing season, a bud forms in the axil of each leaf. By leaf fall, each bud contains a compressed shoot enclosed within several thick protective bud scales (Fig. 6.1). Each shoot may have as many as 15 microscopic leaf primordia. Buds closer to the base of the shoot begin to form earlier, and by the end of the season have more leaf primordia than buds near the end of the shoot.

The first sign that a flower is going to form occurs in the axils of leaf primordia some time in midsummer. A single small inflorescence primordium forms in each fruitful axil (Fig. 6.1). At this time, the primordia are merely undifferentiated protrusions without any form (Fig. 6.2a). They remain in this condition until just before budbreak the following spring.

As new shoots begin to elongate in spring, individual parts of flowers form rapidly from the primordia. The green sepals of the flower form first, followed by petals, stamens, and pistil (Fig. 6.2b-d). By the time shoots have grown 4 to 6 inches long, all parts of the flower have formed. These continue to expand until bloom. (Kiwifruit flower structure is discussed in chapter 17, *Pollination*.)

FACTORS AFFECTING BUD FRUITFULNESS

The number, vigor, fruitfulness, and uniformity of buds that break into growth in spring are thought to depend on the amount of winter chilling—that is, the cumulative exposure to cold temperatures—that a vine receives. The chilling requirement of other fruit and nut species is expressed as the number of hours of temperatures below 45°F (7.2°C) needed before the plant can resume growth with the return of warmer temperatures.

Kiwifruit vines have a chilling requirement of around 600 to 850 hours. Vineyards located in areas receiving less than this amount of chilling have not produced as consistently as those in colder areas.

Bud fruitfulness also depends on the degree to which leaves are exposed to sunlight as the shoots grow during summer. Studies show that shoots well exposed to sunlight during summer survive better through winter and initiate more flower buds the following spring than shoots growing in shade.

Almost all dormant buds on a cane contain flower

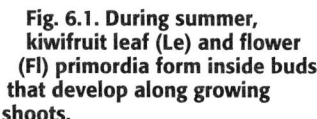

Fig. 6.1. During summer, kiwifruit leaf (Le) and flower (Fl) primordia form inside buds that develop along growing shoots.

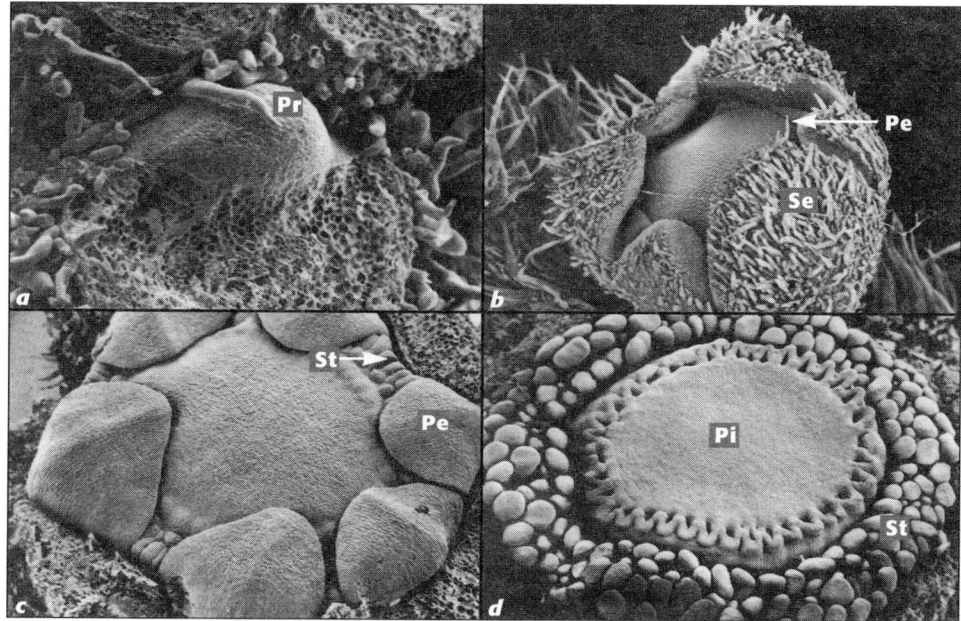

Fig. 6.2. Scanning electron micrograph shows stages of kiwifruit flower differentiation:

(*a*) undifferentiated floral primordium (Pr) in axil of excised leaf primordium;

(*b*) developing sepals (Se) and petals (Pe);

(*c*) beginning of petal (Pe) and stamen (St) formation, sepals removed, and

(*d*) developing pistil (Pi) and stamens (St), sepals and petals removed.

primordia and, therefore, have the potential to flower. However, as buds begin to enlarge and grow in spring, those that break into growth after the first main period of budbreak lose the potential to flower. Why this happens is not well understood. The flowering stimulus may be only weakly imparted to buds at first and may be withdrawn from dormant buds by adjacent ones that begin growing first. Buds in the initial flush could be depleting some chemical compound(s) necessary for flowering, causing late-breaking buds to develop into vegetative shoots. Another possible explanation is that early breaking buds may be exporting some flowering inhibitor to adjacent buds, preventing them from flowering.

These interactions among buds make it necessary to guard against wind, frost, or other influences that could damage or kill early breaking fruitful shoots. Most or all of the shoots that develop to replace damaged ones would be unfruitful and vigorous, thus reducing yield.

POLLINATION

Male kiwifruit flowers produce numerous, tiny, pollen grains that insects transport to the stigmas of female flowers. A pollen grain germinating on a stigma forms a pollen tube that grows through the style, carrying the male germ cells deep inside the pistil (Fig. 6.3). Within the pistil are numerous ovules, each potentially a seed. Each stigma and style is associated with one locule containing two rows of ovules. For an ovule to develop into a seed, it must be fertilized by a male germ cell carried by a pollen tube. Each pollen tube can fertilize only one ovule.

Pollination and subsequent seed formation strongly influence final fruit size (Fig. 6.4). Seeds are thought to produce hormones that promote the growth of fruit cells around them. The more ovules pollinated, the more seeds the fruit will have, and the bigger the fruit will be. In addition, each of the many stigmas is associated with a sector of the pistil. If pollination is uneven, irregularly shaped fruit may develop.

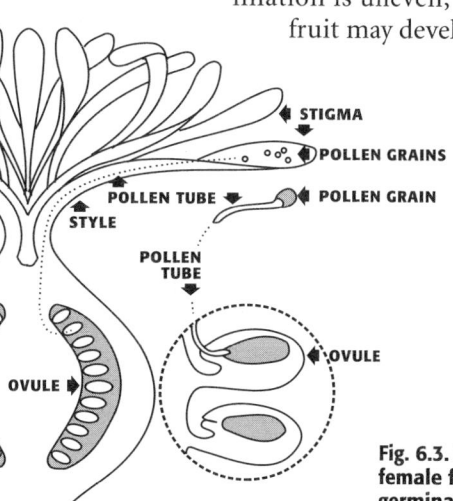

Fig. 6.3. Line drawing of female flower shows germinated pollen grains and pollen tubes penetrating pistil toward ovules.

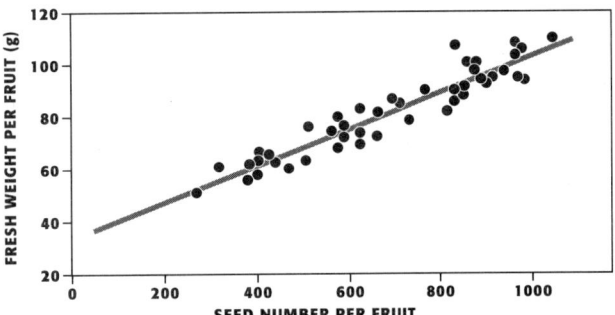

Fig. 6.4. Fruit fresh weight and seed number are closely correlated.

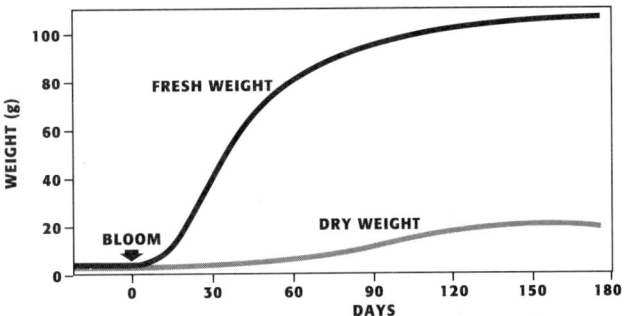

Fig. 6.5. Seasonal growth of kiwifruit occurs in at least three distinct stages.

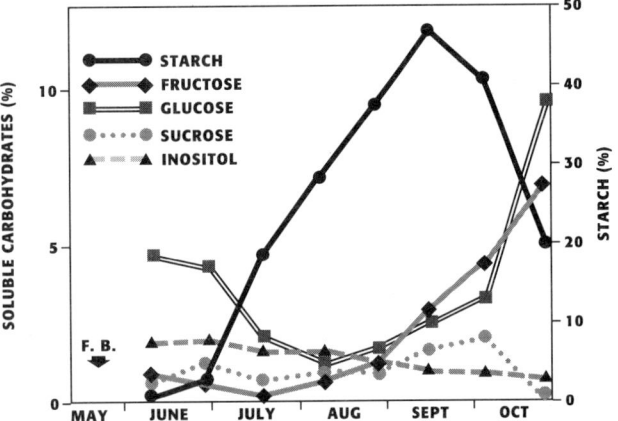

Fig. 6.6. Starch accumulates rapidly in immature fruit and is converted to fructose and glucose as fruit matures. (Starch percentage is measured on right-hand scale; all other values are measured on left-hand scale.)

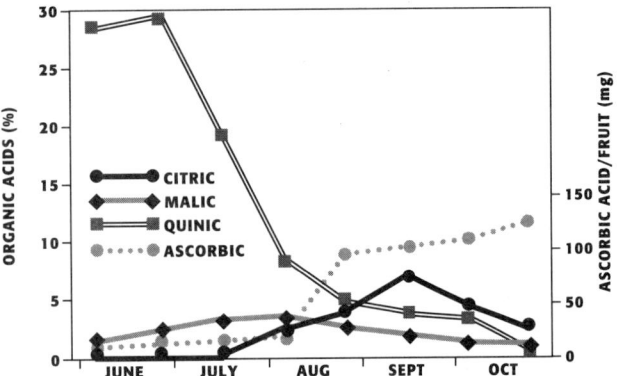

Fig. 6.7. Seasonal changes in organic acids found in developing kiwifruit. (Ascorbic acid values are measured in milligrams on right-hand scale; other values are measured in percentage on left-hand scale.)

FRUIT SET AND GROWTH

Fully developed flowers rarely, if ever, abscise. Even those that are poorly pollinated will form a few seeds and develop into small fruit. After a flower is pollinated, the petals turn brown and the pistil begins to enlarge.

Although dry matter accumulates in fruit at a fairly constant rate from bloom to harvest, growth in fresh weight occurs in cycles or stages (Fig. 6.5). Studies aimed at characterizing growth patterns of kiwifruit have yielded conflicting results, probably because they were conducted on different varieties and under varying fruit loads and environmental conditions. Three general stages of fruit growth are common to most of these studies, however. Following successful pollination, fruit growth rate increases rapidly for 30 to 40 days. It then continues at a less rapid but steady rate for another 30 to 40 days. These initial rapid growth states are followed by a third and prolonged period of slower growth lasting until harvest.

Fruit grow by virtue of two processes that occur simultaneously—cell division and cell enlargement. Most of the early and rapid increase in size is due to increases in cell numbers; late season growth is due mainly to cell enlargement.

A factor known to affect fruit size is the exposure of shoots to sunlight. Fruit on a vine compete with each other for sugars and other products of photosynthesis within leaves. Fruit located on shoots well exposed to sunlight are better supplied with these photosynthates and size better than fruit from shaded shoots, all other factors being equal.

Kiwifruit contain about 80 percent water and 20 percent dry matter. In young fruit undergoing rapid cell division, dry matter consists mostly of structural materials comprising cell walls and cytoplasm, or cell contents. As fruit enlarge, carbohydrates, nitrogenous compounds, and other products of photosynthesis are imported from leaves into fruit. These substances are converted into additional cell wall and cytoplasmic components as well as a multitude of compounds whose metabolic roles are yet unknown.

Starch is deposited in immature fruit cells from July until mid-September, at which time starch levels reach around 50 percent of fruit dry matter (Fig. 6.6). As fruit begin to mature, this starch is converted to the sugars glucose and fructose. Sucrose and the sugar-alcohol, inositol, are found in smaller quantities.

The principal organic acids present in developing kiwifruit are quinic, citric, malic, and ascorbic or vitamin C. Their seasonal trends are shown in Figure 6.7. Fruit borne on shoots with good exposure to light have been found to contain more vitamin C than those growing in shade. Oxalic acid is present in trace amounts in

Fig. 6.8. Fruit that are wider than long are considered fans under current grade standards and are handled as culls by most kiwifruit growers and packers.

Fig. 6.9. Flowers that will become fasciated fruit (*center, right*) have more sepals, petals, stamens, and styles than normal flowers (*left*).

Fig. 6.10. Lateral flowers in clusters with fasciated "king" flowers usually abort before bloom. Occasionally, however, they are retained and develop into normal or slightly flattened "side" fruit.

Fig. 6.11. Fasciated (*bottom*) and normal (*top*) flower buds are shown just before bloom.

kiwifruit. However, kiwifruit have specialized cells called raphides, which contain fairly large quantities of small needlelike crystals of calcium oxalate.

The green flesh color of kiwifruit is due to the presence of the pigment, chlorophyll. Several yellow carotenoid pigments are also present, but their color is masked by the chlorophyll present. Unlike those of leaves, green cells of fruit do not use appreciable amounts of carbon dioxide from the atmosphere in photosynthesis but may assimilate the carbon dioxide given off by respiring cells within the fruit.

FLOWER AND FRUIT ABNORMALITIES

Some flower buds at nodes along the base of bearing shoots develop into fasciated or "fan"-shaped fruit (Fig. 6.8). Most kiwifruit vineyards produce a small number of these fruit each year, and there can be considerable variation from site to site. Fasciated fruit that are wider than long are unsalable under current federal grade standards and are therefore thinned off early, left unpicked at harvest time, or sorted out as culls by packing sheds. Fasciated fruit have abnormally large numbers of sepals, petals, stamens, and styles (Fig. 6.9). Because of this, fan formation is thought to begin very early during flower differentiation in early spring.

The number of fasciated fruit produced varies from shoot to shoot, cane to cane, vine to vine, and year to year. In general, more fans are borne on vines or shoots of high vigor. Among canes on a vine, some tend to produce predominantly fan-bearing shoots; others have few or none. Among individual fruit on fan-bearing shoots, there tends to be a gradation in the size and degree of fasciation with fans at the base, slightly flattened fruit ("flats") next, and normally shaped fruit at more distal nodes.

Little is known about how fasciated fruit are formed. It has been suggested that they may originate from the fusion of lateral and terminal flowers of the kiwifruit's compound inflorescence, during flower differentiation. However, the frequent occurrence of three-fruit clusters having fasciated terminal fruit and flattened or normal lateral fruit would seem to contradict this theory (Fig. 6.10).

Because flowers that give rise to fans are distinguishable before bloom (Fig. 6.11), some growers remove these flower buds at or just before bloom, or as small fruitlets shortly after bloom. This is thought of as thinning by most growers, but there is no evidence that removing the small numbers of fasciated fruit typically present benefits the sizing of the fruit remaining on vines. Flower and fruit thinning are discussed more fully in chapter 13, *Fruit Thinning*.

ESTABLISHING THE VINEYARD

7

Site Selection and Vineyard Development

MAXWELL V. NORTON

Proper soil selection, preplant preparation, site improvement, irrigation system design, and planting guarantee successful plant growth and fruit production. Conduct each step at the right time. Leveling, ripping, or fumigating when the ground is too wet can adversely affect the entire life of the planting. Permitting noxious weeds to build up or employing improperly designed irrigation systems, trellises, or plantings can cause high management costs or poor production. Rather than farm a series of mistakes, take the time to eliminate major problems before planting to ensure success.

SITE SELECTION

Kiwifruit require a temperate climate of mild winters and a long, warm growing season of 225 to 240 frost-free days. During the dormant season (November to February) they require 600 to 850 chilling hours at or below 45°F (7.2°C) to bloom and set reliably. Spring frosts below 30°F (−1.1°C) kill shoots and severely damage the crop. Fall frosts below 27°F (−2.8°C) before leaf fall can injure trunks and canes. Vines can be killed by temperatures below 10°F (−12.2°C). The growing season begins in March when the vines leaf out; bloom occurs in May, and fruit is harvested in October and November.

Winds over 20 miles per hour can damage kiwifruit by breaking shoots, scarring fruit, and even blowing over vines if the trellis system is not adequate. Most locations require windbreaks.

A kiwifruit vineyard site must have available a plentiful supply of good quality water. A fully canopied vineyard requires approximately 40 to 48 acre-inches of water per year. Peak water use during summer when temperatures exceed 100°F (38°C) is about 10,000 gallons per acre per day. Your water supply must be able to supply 13,000 gallons per acre per day to account for breakdowns and other interruptions.

To achieve top production, kiwifruit require deep, well-drained soils similar to those required by peaches and other fruit crops, preferably Class I soils. Kiwifruit vines are sensitive to high pH (over 7.2) soils or those containing high levels of salt. Soils should contain little sodium, less than 0.5 ppm boron, and have an electrical conductivity (EC) of 1.0 or less. Yellow vines caused by iron chlorosis occur in most California soils, even with a pH only slightly above 7.2.

PREPARATION FOR PLANTING

Cleanup

Crop residue of any type must be thoroughly disked in and decomposed, especially if releveling is planned. Even dead and dry residues can cause major problems; if buried, they decompose anaerobically, producing gases that damage roots. Because old roots host nematodes and diseases, dig up as many as possible and remove them from the field. This often involves deep tillage, followed by crews handpicking any roots that have surfaced, a process that often needs repeating until all but the smallest roots are removed.

Leveling or releveling

Before installing drip or sprinkler systems, level the site to ensure good surface drainage during the wet season and to prevent puddling in low spots while sprinkling. If flood irrigating, precision level to facilitate uniform water distribution. Most leveling operations result in differing degrees of compaction, so ripping or subsoiling 18 to 20 inches deep is often required after leveling.

Slipplowing and ripping

Unless the soil is uniform to 6 to 7 feet (and such soils are rare), it is beneficial to slipplow or backhoe. Ripping can effectively shatter a cemented hardpan, but it does little to mix the soil. Even when there are no pans of any type, water and roots can be impeded by changes in texture, such as a clay loam over a sand. Mixing the soil improves the environment for roots to explore. Generally, the more soil is mixed, the larger the root system that can develop. The first ripping should be down the vine row itself.

Studies show that ripping at 45-degree angles is much more effective than ripping at 90-degree angles. Ripping at a 45-degree angle shatters the hardpan for a longer distance from the shank. Rip deep enough to penetrate all the way through the hardpan.

Planting a rotation crop

Properly developing a vineyard, with all the steps undertaken in an unhurried manner, takes two seasons. A grain crop planted in November in an old orchard or vineyard site can generate extra cash and reduce nematode populations and other problems associated with these sites. Small grains are the best rotational crops as they are poor hosts for the kinds of nematodes that attack trees and vines.

Fumigating

Vineyards with sandy soil or previously planted to nematode hosts, such as orchards or grapes, probably benefit from preplant fumigation. Any evidence of oak root fungus also justifies fumigating. During summer, after the soil settles and after discing up the grain stubble, touch-up level before fumigating. Remember, do not move any soil between treated and untreated areas after fumigating; doing so recontaminates fumigated soil.

New information on how nematodes migrate shows they can move farther and faster than previously thought. For this reason, when developing a whole block or even a few rows, it is best to solid fumigate. Because fumigation cannot be repeated after planting, do it properly before planting.

Normally, the fumigant shanks should be set no farther than 18 inches apart, and the fumigant should be injected between 12 and 18 inches deep, ideally at 18 inches. The soil needs to be as dry as possible. Unless the soil has been repeatedly deep-tilled through summer, it is hard to get the soil too dry.

When selecting rates, consider that you need to treat as deep as where the roots of the previous crop were located. This could be 5 feet deep or down to an impervious pan.

Preplant weed control

Weeds, especially such perennials as bermudagrass and johnsongrass, must be eradicated with herbicides the summer and fall before planting. Eliminate annual weeds from the berm or vine row by discing or with herbicides before planting. A clean strip makes it easy to lay out and mark the field and to eliminate weeds that rob young vines of vigor. Use preemergent herbicides after planting or the soil will be disturbed, reducing the herbicide's effectiveness. Also, roots are harmed by herbicide-treated soils packed around them.

PLANTING AND EARLY CARE

Planting bare root

From the time the new vines are dug at the nursery to when they are planted in the ground, never allow them to dry out, even for a couple of hours. Store them in a cool, shaded area with roots well protected from drying out.

Vines planted in mid-January have a head start on vines planted in March or April. Even when properly maintained in cold storage, vines kept past April or May may deteriorate. Keep the soil moist enough to supply moisture for early growth. However, waterlogged soils will suffocate the root system and cause root rots.

Some tips on planting:

1. Make the planting hole large enough to accommodate the roots without bending them. Trim roots only enough to fit into the hole.

2. Hand-digging holes is best, but augers can give good results if used correctly and without glazing the sides. Do not dig the hole deeper than needed or settling may be excessive. Plant vines deep enough to cover the top roots and to allow for minor settling. Cave in the sides of the holes when backfilling if they are glazed. Planting on top of a mound or berm facilitates drainage and reduces chances for root rot to develop. Never throw up a berm or mound after planting.

3. Do not add any kind of fertilizer, including manure or mulches, to the hole when planting. The value of Vitamin B_1 dips has never been demonstrated.

4. Tamp the soil in firmly around the roots while backfilling, taking care not to cause compaction. Newly planted vines should be tank-watered or lightly irrigated immediately after planting to settle the soil and fill air pockets.

5. Trunks should be painted with a 1:1 mixture of water and interior white latex paint to prevent damage from borers and sunburn. Milk cartons or wraps also can help prevent sunburn and rodent

damage, while protecting plants from such phytotoxic materials as contact herbicides.

6. Carefully mark and personally supervise placement of male plants. Plant all male plants first; then fill in with females. Inspect all vines as they come from the nursery and replace any that are damaged or dried out, show signs of disease, or do not look true to type.

Container-grown plants

As with bare-root plants, keep container plants moist. The hole must be as deep as the container is tall. Place the plant in the hole and backfill immediately after removing the container. Do not add anything to the hole except native soil. Promptly water the new plants with enough water to fill in any air pockets. Add more soil to bring up to ground level. As with bare roots, do not plant too deep.

The advantage of container-grown plants is that they can be planted anytime of the year except during hot summer months. Planting during the growing season requires especially careful moisture monitoring of the root ball and usually frequent but light irrigations.

Postplant weed control

After planting, treat vine rows with a safe preemergent herbicide. Competitive weeds can rob young vines of much or all of their vigor. Postemergent weed control around young vines, whether with herbicides or hoes, is more difficult and carries the risk of vine damage.

Irrigating new plants

By the time vines are planted, the irrigation system must be fully installed, tested, and operational. An early, warm spring following a dry winter may necessitate an irrigation earlier than usual. You may want to use the system to water the newly planted vines or for frost protection. When scheduling irrigations, monitor the moisture in the root zone of the plant, where the moisture is depleted.

The trick with irrigating young plants is to apply enough water to wet the root zone without keeping the crown too wet; otherwise, crown or root rot will be induced. With young plants, the range between too wet and too dry is very narrow.

8

Propagation

GENE TANIMOTO

Kiwifruit do not grow true to type from seed. That is, unlike many annual crops, kiwifruit seedlings may not grow into satisfactory adult plants with consistent and desirable plant and fruit characteristics (correct bloom time, cane growth, fruit shape and size, or edibility). Genetic variability in the seeds, not unlike the differences in human siblings, causes these characteristics to be changeable. Therefore, propagation of kiwifruit plants is done through vegetative or clonal propagation of adult plants—grafting, budding, or cuttings.

Because the preferred kiwifruit variety is the Hayward, this chapter describes procedures that have succeeded in commercial kiwifruit nurseries supplying this variety.

PROPAGATION METHODS

The preferred method of propagation is grafting varieties to seedling rootstock. Occasionally, plants are obtained from softwood cuttings of the preferred variety. Budding, considered less efficient, will not be discussed here. The need for clonal propagation of rootstock has not been demonstrated. Unlike apples or almonds, where climatic or soil variations or soil pathogens demand development of a more tolerant rootstock, no difference in the performance of kiwifruit plants has been attributed to rootstock variability. Normal genetic variation in the rootstock has not caused noticeable differences in plant growth or fruit yield in kiwifruit planted on well-drained soils.

Propagation from cuttings made from roots instead of shoots is not considered practical, but it has been reported in the literature. Tissue culture techniques have been reported in scientific literature, but in California few plants have been raised commercially. Somatic embryogenesis from anther-derived callus, tissue culture of nodal segments, and *in vitro* organ culture have been described, but they, too, are not considered commercially practical.

Differences in crop yield, fruit size, postharvest physiology, plant growth, or longevity between cutting-grown or grafted-seedling-grown plants have not been found. Container-grown or dormant, bare-root kiwifruit plants are available in California.

STARTING SEEDLINGS AND CUTTINGS

Preparing and planting seeds

Seeds for kiwifruit rootstock are harvested from ripe mature kiwifruit in November. Most nurseries use seeds from the Bruno variety. There is little research on the use of Bruno seed, but Bruno is commonly thought to have superior rooting characteristics.

Seeds are separated from the pulp of peeled kiwifruit by macerating the flesh; substantial quantities of seed can be obtained by using a food blender. The blender-pureed pulp and seed are separated by pushing the seed through a screen mesh just large enough to allow seed to pass through. After thorough rinsing, seeds are dried at room temperature (moisture content estimated at 4 to 10 percent). Dried seed can be stored in a sealed container at 40°F (4°C) for more than 1 year.

Before planting, seeds are stratified in sterilized, moistened sand to improve germination. Dry seeds are placed in wet sand at 34°F (1°C) for at least 2 weeks. In most cases, low germination rates can be attributed to seed coat inhibition. Scarification of the seed coat or gibberellic acid treatments (GA_3—10 ppm—soaked overnight) can increase germination, but they will not shorten the time necessary for germination. Stratified seeds can be sown directly in 4-inch potting cups or in starting trays and then transplanted into the cups. Any sterilized, well-draining potting mix is effective. Seeds are planted ⅛ inch deep (3 mm) and watered. Greenhouse temperatures should be maintained between 60° and 80°F (16° and 27°C). Seeds germinate in 10 to 14 days at 70°F (21°C). Seeds can be successfully germinated anytime of the year. Slow-release fertilizers work well; adjust amounts according to the potting mix used. Overwatering, which causes fungal damping off, is a potential problem best controlled by careful soil water management.

Growing cuttings

Softwood cuttings root more easily and uniformly and are, therefore, preferred over hardwood. Current season growth (3 to 4 feet) is selected in late April and May. Shoots are firm with much secondary growth, but they are still green. Cut shoots into segments of one to three leaf nodes. Make the bottom or basal cut just below a leaf node. Remove all but one leaf and dip the basal end into a root-promoting chemical. Plant in a 4-inch pot filled with well-draining sterilized potting mix (depth is variable). Maintain soil temperature at 70°F (21°C). Intermittently mist plants. Rooting time is variable and can be visually followed. Transfer the rooted cuttings to a lath house for hardening in 6 to 8 weeks before transplanting to the nursery.

TRANSPLANTING TO THE NURSERY

Preparing nursery ground

Careful preparation is necessary to achieve uniform growth on nursery vines. Fumigate the soil as described in chapter 7, *Site Selection and Vineyard Development*. After fumigation, add phosphate and zinc to the soil to lessen chances of fumigant-induced nutrient deficiencies.

Hardening seedlings

To avoid shock, harden greenhouse seedlings before transplanting. A shade house covered with 50 percent shade screen netting can be used for hardening. Hardening requires about 2 weeks. Take care to water plants adequately during this stage. Transplant potted plants from the greenhouse to raised nursery beds (furrows on 4-foot centers) during spring and fall when they are 3 to 4 months old.

Growth of seedlings

Plant seedlings in nursery rows, the spacing depending on individual needs for equipment and employees, and the final sizes of the plants before they are sold. Train plants vertically and stake, using ¾ × ¾-inch × 5-feet clear redwood or equivalent.

Plant seedlings on raised beds or on flat ground, depending on the soil's drainage characteristics. If the soil is to be cultivated when the plants are in the nursery, raised beds may not be convenient. Train the rootstock to assure that a selection of straight, graftable stems will be available the next spring. Two or three stems are usually trained to a height of 15 inches. Subsequent top growth can be allowed to grow untrained, but keep suckers and watersprouts from growing below 15 inches. Only one stem is grafted; the other(s) are used to control the plant from growing too large in diameter and to divert the xylem sap and prevent excessive bleeding during grafting.

Containerized growth

Soil mixtures for container-grown plants vary; usually the choice of a peat, sand, and perlite mixture is preferred over one that contains only loam. Consider adding phosphorus and zinc. Fumigate all potting soil and sterilize all preplant containers for container-grown plants. Polyethylene bags with holes punched in the bottom are typically used. Irrigate containers with overhead sprinklers or drip emitters; the latter make fertilization easier to accomplish. Root damage can occur from cold during winter, if frost protection is not provided.

Containerized kiwifruit plants commonly become root bound, if the container is too small or if plants are allowed to grow too long before sale. An improperly designed container may cause roots to wrap in circles within the container. Plant roots often retain this pattern and never form a healthy system after transplanting to the vineyard.

Irrigation requirements

Supply adequate water. In areas prone to spring and autumn frosts, overhead sprinklers can be used primarily to irrigate and secondarily for frost protection. In nonfrosted areas, drip, modified drip, and trickle irrigation are preferred to flood or furrow irrigation. In California's Central Valley, kiwifruit nursery stock can use as much as 4 acre-feet of water per year. On a summer day, larger nursery stock (½ inch in diameter, 5 feet tall) can use .8 to 1 gallon (3 to 4 liters) of water per plant each day.

Kiwifruit chronology

Most bare-root kiwifruit nursery stock is grown for 2 years before being sold as cuttings or grafted seedlings. Seedlings are grown 1 year in the nursery; the rootstock is grafted during spring of the second year. The rootstock is considered to be 2 years old, but in California the clock is reset and the new 2-year-old transplant is called the first leaf. In New Zealand, age is determined by the rootstock's real age.

GRAFTING

Kiwifruit plants are easily grafted. Excessive sap bleeding and warm temperature (above 90°F [32°C]) of the scion wood frequently prevent successful union of scion and rootstock. Excessive sap flow during grafting is taken up by the extra foliage left on the rootstock. Making cuts below the graft to draw off root pressure, as is done with other fruit trees, is not advised. Most areas of California have sufficient amounts of foliage by April 15. Average daytime temperatures above 90°F (32°C) are not conducive for adequate healing of the new graft union.

Select scion wood the previous winter from vigorous productive plants. Cut it from the previous season's mature growth. It should have well-developed buds and be reasonably straight. Select a variety of sizes from $\frac{1}{4}$ inch to $\frac{5}{8}$ inch in diameter and cut into 15-inch lengths. Protect the wood from desiccation by packing it in damp (but not wet) material, such as peat moss, redwood shingletoes, or kiln-dried softwood (fir or pine). Store in cold storage at 32° to 34°F (0° to 1°C). (Use of nonkiln-dried softwood or any type of hardwood shavings can damage graftwood.)

Most nurseries use a modified whip graft technique (Figs. 8.1, 8.2, 8.3). Select the most straight and most convenient stem to train. The diameter should not be greater than $\frac{5}{8}$ inch. Make a fresh cut at the top of the rootstock (below 15 inches on a trained stock). If excessive bleeding occurs, delay grafting. Select a scion of approximately the same diameter (one bud and 2 inches of internode). Make reciprocal diagonal cuts on both the rootstock and matching scion wood (Fig. 8.1); the length of the cut should be approximately two to three times the diameter of the wood (make sure the bud is not upside down). Make a tongue in both cut faces half way down the length of one and one-third the length of the other, so that when joined the tongues groove into each other and the cut surfaces' cambium mates and does not protrude over the edges at the bottom or top (Fig. 8.2).

Make sure the sides are aligned; if the diameters are slightly different, align one side and the bottom edge. The graft is secured in an airtight seal of grafting rubbers of $\frac{1}{2}$-inch diameter and 10-inch length (Fig. 8.3). Do not overtighten the band; a loose fit is preferable. Seal the top transverse cut of the scion with a water-soluble graphite graft-sealing compound. The graft should callus within the week and the band should fall off on its own in about a month; if it does not, remove it at that time.

Alternatively, grafting can be done on the current season's suckers that are old or hard enough to be grafted. This is usually a late-season event (May) and dependent on rootstock vigor. Nevertheless, complete most grafting by mid-May to insure adequate time to grow. In some warmer areas, adequate adhesion and healing ("take") of the graft do not occur if done much later.

The new shoot should sprout in 2 weeks and the growth should look normal; that is, it should be growing vigorously 1 to 2 inches per day and have a compact shoot tip with leaves that do not expand immediately. Keep plants well watered during this time. Start training after the shoot is 5 to 10 inches long and continue weekly.

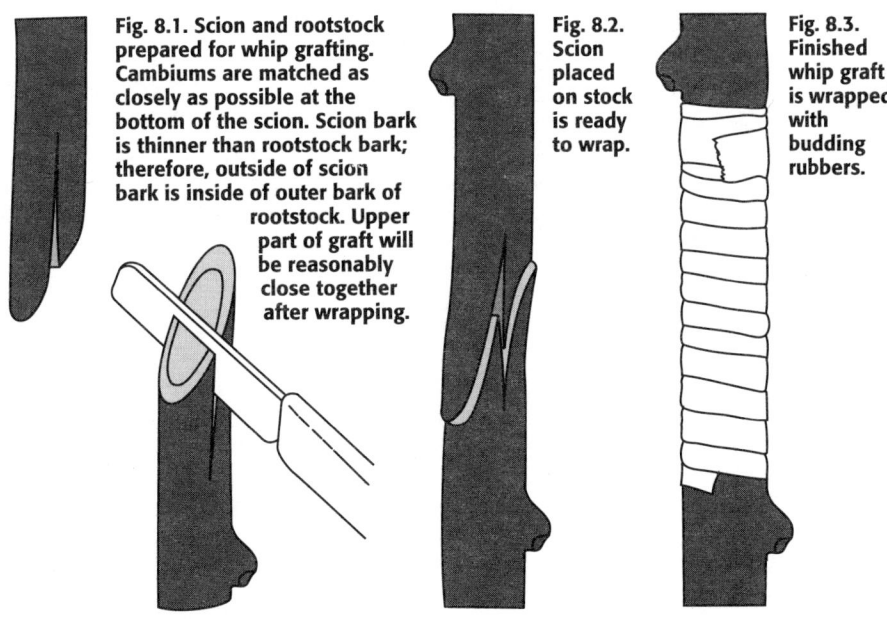

Fig. 8.1. Scion and rootstock prepared for whip grafting. Cambiums are matched as closely as possible at the bottom of the scion. Scion bark is thinner than rootstock bark; therefore, outside of scion bark is inside of outer bark of rootstock. Upper part of graft will be reasonably close together after wrapping.

Fig. 8.2. Scion placed on stock is ready to wrap.

Fig. 8.3. Finished whip graft is wrapped with budding rubbers.

TRANSPLANTING TO THE FIELD

Digging nursery stock

Nursey-grown vines are generally dug when they are 2 to 3 years old and have about ½ to ¾ inch of stem diameter (measured at the graft union or 10 inches above the soil level). Plants must be completely dormant. Most plants that were trained still need trimming and topping to facilitate digging. Plants that are too tall or with excessively long lateral branches are likely to get damaged.

Use a shovel to dig out bare-root plants, although less root length is preserved with this method. The goal is to save about 10 to 12 inches of root length and to not damage the fibrous lateral roots. Shoveling is a labor-intensive way to dig bare-root plants, and most operations use commercial nursery cutting bars mounted on track-layer tractors that cut below the roots and lift out the root mass and dirt so that the root can be shaken free from dirt. Understandably, the sandier and looser the soil, the less damage will occur to the roots using either method.

Palletize plants horizontally on cold-storage racks (4 feet wide × 6 feet long × 6 feet high) in cold-storage facilities that can maintain 100 percent humidity and water misting at 34°F (1°C). This is a safe method to store plants for 2 to 3 months. Most tree crops and kiwifruit plants are susceptible to crown and root rot if they are stored for prolonged periods on open racks in a misted room. If your situation demands longer storage, heel bare-root kiwifruit plants in moistened kiln-dried softwood shavings. During January and perhaps part of February, this can be done outdoors. Shavings should be moist but not saturated. When the weather warms up in February and root movement can be detected, place plants in cold storage.

For ease in handling, most plants are heeled into bins with the shavings and taken to storage. At most, the shavings are remoistened at 5- to 6-week intervals. Take plants directly from cold storage to the field through April. After that, acclimate the plants in a shaded environment outdoors for a few days. Usually, these plants have been stored in bins with their roots heeled in shavings, so this should not create undue hardship. If they were not stored in bins, they can be heeled under shade in moistened sand or soil. Avoid enclosed environments that can get hot.

Transporting to the field

The advantage of bare-root delivery is that more bare-root plants than container-grown plants can be loaded onto tarped flatbed or pickup trucks or enclosed vans. Usually, the weight and size of containerized plants prohibit transportation over long distances. Avoid excessive heat during delivery. Usually, this is not a consideration for spring plantings. Bare-root plants do not need to be kept continually wet, but avoid excessive drying (1 to 2 hours in the sun). The advantage of containerized plants is that they are easier to handle in the field.

Transplanting nursery stock

Never plant either container-grown or dormant, bare-root stock so that the resultant soil line after initial watering and settling is above the plant's original soil line. Because roots are so close to this line (usually within a fraction of an inch), the tendency is to plant deeper. This and the overwatering that usually follows are the most common mistakes made. Water the plant to settle the soil; do not rewater dormant bare-root plants until the shoots start to grow or unless the soil becomes excessively dry.

Water containerized plants, if green, with a drip emitter to keep the root ball moist. The root ball–new soil interface often resists water penetration, and overwatering outside the root ball to keep the plant growing is not advised. Fertilize after new growth begins, never before, and never in excess. Transplants do not tolerate being "pushed." To prevent heat shock, apply a whitewash of diluted interior white latex paint to trunks of late spring plantings.

In areas with early autumn frosts below 28°F (−2°C), whitewash on trunks reflects the heat of the sun and allows the trunks to go dormant earlier. This may help prevent bark damage to young vines from frost. Three- to 4-year-old plants seldom need whitewash.

9

Vineyard Planning, Design, and Planting

WILBUR O. REIL

Mature kiwifruit vines are vigorous and fast growing, with canes that grow 6 to 12 feet a year and, occasionally, over 20 feet. Allow for this vigor when planning a vineyard. While higher density plantings may be more productive the first few years, plant vigor can soon create overgrowth and shading that will require extensive summer pruning.

VINEYARD LAYOUT

Row spacing and plant spacing between vines are usually about 15 to 16 feet. Growers can modify spacing down the row, depending on the potential vigor expected. On excellent soil, vine rows can be widened to 18 or even 20 feet; on poor soil they can be narrowed to 14 feet.

The standard male-to-female ratio is one male plant to eight female plants, a ratio achieved by planting a male every third vine in every third row (Fig. 9.1). This pattern has generally gained acceptance, although some growers have increased the number of male-to-female plants to improve pollination. Planting every second vine in every third row or every third vine in every other row changes the ratio to 1:5 (Fig. 9.2). Adequate pollination is a key to producing large fruit as fruit size is directly correlated to number of seeds.

TRELLIS SYSTEMS

Kiwifruit are grown on one of two types of trellis systems, the T-bar trellis or pergola. Growers have modified these systems or combined certain features of each. The crossbars and vines are generally trellised at 6 feet.

Both trellis systems are designed with a support post placed down the row at the same spacing as the vines (15 or 16 feet in standard plantings). Generally, it is not advisable to have either the vine or the irrigation system next to the post in case the post has to be removed or the cross arm needs repair.

T-bar trellis

T-bar trellis has a 6-foot cross arm extending across the top of the post (Fig. 9.3). This cross arm usually consists of a 2 × 6-inch board bolted into a cut notch on the pole, thus providing a 3-foot arm in each direction perpendicular to the direction of the row. The top of the cross arm is 6 feet from the ground. Usually, a wire is stapled on the top middle and wires are stapled on each side of the cross arm. The kiwifruit canes are tied to the three wires on top of the cross arm.

Pergola trellis

Pergola trellis is a solid lattice frame with the cross arm extending across the middle between the rows from one post to another and with wires extending down the row spaced about 3 feet apart (Fig. 9.4). The cross arms used have generally been made of 1 x 6 or 1 x 4 lumber bolted together double thickness for added strength. More recently, wire has been used instead of wood cross arms. Usually, the normal high tensile no. 12 wire is doubled to form

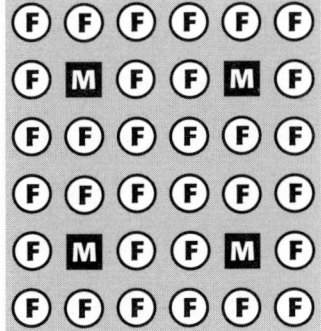

Fig. 9.1. Traditional kiwifruit planting employs a 1:8 ratio: one pollenizer male plant (M) to eight fruiting female plants (F).

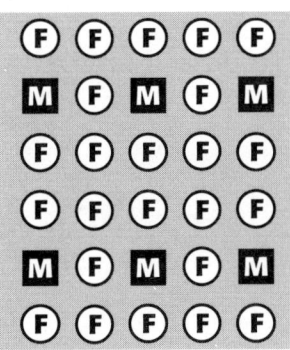

Fig. 9.2. Increasing the pollenizer to every third vine in every other row changes the ratio of male (M) to female (F) plants to 1:5.

the cross arms and is used as single strands down the row.

A few growers have used the pergola for a four-row planting with the T-bar on the outside of each four rows to allow a drive row for moving equipment. This system works well with wooden cross arms, but it cannot be used with wire cross arms.

System supports

Trellis systems must be strong to support a heavy crop load. There are many different ideas on what is the best system, and probably there is no best system for all areas and soil types. Usually, pressure-treated, lodgepole pine poles, 5 or 6 inches in diameter and 9 feet tall, are the best to use for maximum life. These poles, treated with chromated copper arsenate, can be driven vertically 3 feet into the ground with the taper down. End posts should be at least 6 inches in diameter and driven at an angle with the top of the post leaning 1 foot from perpendicular away from the row. End support braces can be of several types. Usually, the most effective has been the same type of pole used for posts that are driven into the ground as deeply as possible, 6 feet from the end pole (preferably 7 feet) and slanted at 30 degrees away from the last pole (Fig. 9.5). Rebar eyes or earth anchors usually set in concrete or dead-man anchors have also been used. Wire or cable is then tightly stretched from near the ground on the support brace to the top of the end post.

Horizontal brace end assemblies (Fig. 9.3), reportedly used in New Zealand, have not been used much in this country. The assembly allows vines to grow to the end of the trellis. The system is made by two posts, 9 feet apart, with a third post placed horizontally between the tops of these posts. Wires are then wrapped diagonally from the top of the inside post to the outside post at ground level and tightened.

Galvanized, high-tensile, 12-gauge wire is used to support the vines. On pergola systems, where wire is used for both the cross arm and the support, a plastic clip or support is usually used between the wires to prevent undue rubbing and stress on the wire and to prevent slippage.

Wire tension is an important consideration. Kiwifruit vines support up to 200 pounds of fruit plus leaves, canes, and cordon arms. Wires, therefore, must be tightened well to support the crop and to prevent undue sag or collapse of the vines and trellis system. Tighten wires initially to a tension of 225 pounds or less. More tension will be needed later under heavy loads to prevent excessive sag between cross arms. No more than 4 inches of sag should occur between posts. Although slightly more sag can be tolerated on T-bar systems, it is not recommended.

Fig. 9.3. T-bar trellis system uses a horizontal brace and assembly for the end post. This system provides support without a deep anchor. Poplar windbreak is in the background.

Fig. 9.4. Pergola trellis has double strands of no. 12 wire used as cross arms and single-strand wire extending down vine row, spaced about 3 feet apart.

Fig. 9.5. End support brace uses a post driven 7 feet into ground to support the outside post of a pergola system.

Fig. 9.6. Kiwifruit vines are bordered by a poplar windbreak in background.

WINDBREAKS

Windbreaks are needed in kiwifruit vineyards, except in the most sheltered areas (Fig. 9.6). Although they are costly to plant and maintain, wind damage to kiwifruit vines can be disastrous, breaking newly developing canes, scarring fruit, causing loss of canes and crop from limb breakage, and decreasing vine growth. Plant windbreaks to form a continuous hedge as perpendicular to the wind direction as possible.

Windbreaks of many different tree species have been tried successfully (Table 9.1). Base your choice on the vineyard's need, experience from nearby plantings, and experience of local experts. Table 9.2 lists anticipated height, spacing, benefits, and possible problems of commonly used windbreaks. Artificial shelters, used in some foreign countries, are extremely costly to build and maintain and have not been used in California.

Determine the distance between windbreaks by the anticipated height of the tree species to be planted and the estimated intensity of the wind. Damage from wind has been observed to start increasing at a distance about five times the height of the windbreak, and the effect of the windbreak is minimal at ten times the height. For example, in a vineyard with poplars 80 feet high, full protection will extend about 400 feet and marginal protection 800 feet. For maximum protection, more windbreaks will then be needed every 400 to 800 feet, preferably every 400 to 600 feet.

Windbreak trees must be fast growing and planted at the same time or ahead of the vineyard's planting. Considerable cane breakage can occur in early establishment, even when windbreaks are planted at the same time. The trees require excellent care (particularly frequent irrigation and fertilization) in the first few years to maximize growth.

Before planting a windbreak, set up an irrigation system independent of the vineyard. Consider both the width or spread of the tree and the care and maintenance pruning needed to confine the top to the narrow hedge desired. For trees that may need topping, provide adequate space between the kiwifruit vines and the windbreak for large pruning towers.

Also, consider the invasiveness of the windbreak's root system. Many species used for windbreaks, such as poplar, have shallow roots that spread far from the trunk. Growers have effectively decreased these competitive roots with trenching or backhoeing but only where irrigation system piping and trellis systems have been designed to not interfere with this operation.

Both deciduous and evergreen trees have been used for windbreaks. In areas where spring frosts occur, take care that natural air drainage is not stopped and cold pockets caused. Under these conditions, deciduous trees probably work best. Also, select trees that will not be killed by the extreme cold that occasionally occurs.

Table 9.1. Trees commonly used as windbreaks

Common name	Genus species
Lombardy poplar*	Populus nigra 'Italica'
Poplar hybrids*	Populus deltoides x nigra
Bluegum	Eucalyptus globulus
Redgum	Eucalyptus camaldulensis
Willow	Salix matsudana and hybrids
Arizona cypress	Cupressus glabra
River she oak	Casuarina cunninghamiana
Horsetail tree	Casuarina equisetifolia

*Poplars had been planted the most in the past because of their quick growth and their inexpensive propagation. Many poplar windbreaks have since been removed because of invasive roots.

Table 9.2. Factors influencing proper selection of commonly used windbreaks

Tree genus	Anticip. height (feet)	Planting spacing (feet)	Benefits	Problems
Populus (poplar)	80–100	3–6	Inexpensive; ease of establishment; columnar tree shape; deciduous	Late leafing in spring; invasive roots; severe suckering
Poplar hybrids	80–100	3–8	Same as poplar, plus roots less invasive than poplar	Occasional-to-severe suckers; late leafing
Eucalyptus	80–100	4	Roots are not invasive; evergreen	Occasional freeze damage occurs; tree canopy spreads, especially toward south
Salix (willow)	40–50	4	Fast growing; deciduous	Tree canopy spreads; is killed by Armillaria
Cupressus	40	6	Evergreen	Slow growing
Casuarina	60–70	6	Fast growing; moderately upright; evergreen; tolerates poor soil conditions	Fine leaves; spreads so needs side pruning; occasional freeze damage occurs

10

Training Young Vines

JANINE K. HASEY

Developing young kiwifruit vines into a simple, bilateral cordon structure allows easier management of mature plants. Close attention is required to train vines properly as they are developing. In the first few years, vines are trained the same way on both pergola or T-bar trellis systems.

FIRST SEASON

During the first growing season, the main objective is to develop a single, straight trunk. After planting nursery grafted or rooted vines in early spring, prune them back to a large, robust bud that may be a few buds above the graft union or higher. Paint vines with white latex paint to prevent sunburn damage.

After growth begins in spring, select a vigorous shoot to train upward as the trunk. Place a light stake beside the plant and attach it to the trellis wire. As an alternative, use a shorter stake and tie tree rope from the stake to the wire. To provide support and to prevent wind breakage, tie vines to the stake or rope at frequent intervals. Do not allow the trunk to twist around the stake.

Concentrate growth in one shoot to encourage strong development of the trunk. There are two

Fig. 10.1. Kiwifruit vine shows growth at end of first growing season. Notice several side shoots on trunk that were pinched back.

Fig. 10.3. Closeup shows bilateral cordon development originating 6 to 8 inches below wire.

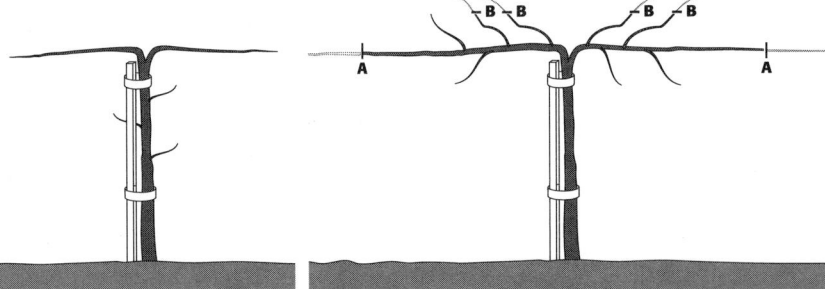

Fig. 10.2. End of first growing season with bilateral cordon established.

Fig. 10.4. Dormant pruning marks end of second growing season. (*A*) Head back cordons. (*B*) Head back lateral canes to force buds to produce fruiting canes.

schools of thought on how to accomplish this objective: Some growers remove most shoot growth from the trunk, forcing maximum growth into the main shoot; others leave shoots above the graft for 1 or 2 years, keeping them pinched back to 6 to 10 inches long. These shoots provide surface area for carbohydrate production and shade the trunk. Remove all suckers below the graft union (Fig. 10.1). If the main shoot loses vigor and begins to twist tightly around the stake, head back the terminal growth to a good bud to stimulate strong growth. Continue to tie the trunk to the stake until the shoot grows 2 to 3 inches above the top wire. If the main shoot is a few inches over the wire before the end of the growing season, cut it just to the wire to harden the shoot and to force production of new branches.

Select two new shoots growing in opposite directions and train them along the center wire to form the two main arms called cordons (Fig. 10.2). Cordons must be symmetrically balanced to achieve maximum fruit production. An alternative method to cordon formation is to train the trunk leader one way along the wire and wait for a well-placed shoot to train as the opposite cordon. This, however, may result in cordons of unequal size. During the first dormant period, prune the cordons back to $\frac{1}{4}$ inch in diameter or to larger wood. If vines do not make adequate growth to form cordons the first season, head the trunk back about 2 inches below the trellis wire, to force new buds early the following growing season.

SECOND SEASON

The objective is to develop two permanent cordons along the center wire from two vigorous shoots growing in opposite directions from the trunk. Hang cordons over the center wire and tie them to it. As each cordon grows, wrap it around the center wire about every 18 to 24 inches so that the vine is securely supported. The cordon crotch should be no more than 6 to 8 inches below the wire, so that potential fruit production near the trunk is not lost (Fig. 10.3). A system of temporary fruiting canes is trained perpendicular to the cordon on both sides at about 10- to 12-inch intervals. Prune back all spindly growth before it tangles and twists around the desirable cane growth. Carefully tie canes down to the outer trellis wires to hold them in position. The first crop of fruit will form on these canes. In the dormant season, prune both the main cordons and lateral canes back to large, round buds on wood $\frac{1}{4}$ inch in diameter or larger (Fig. 10.4). Remove any new growth on the trunk.

THIRD AND FOURTH SEASON

Continue to extend the cordons by encouraging the strongest shoots down the center wire until they are within about 1 foot from adjacent vines. Do not allow them to twist tightly around the wire; this could restrict sap flow later, weakening the vine at that point. Continue to train lateral canes perpendicular to the cordons. Do not train fruiting canes along the outer trellis wire parallel to the permanent cordons; shoots from them will compete with the fruiting canes originating directly from the cordon, and the resulting dense growth can adversely affect overall vine growth.

Fruit and new shoot growth require large amounts of carbohydrate. Direct the vine's energy toward building the supportive framework, rather than toward fruit production.

Fruit produced in the third year often sunburn because of inadequate canopy cover. It may be advisable to remove some early fruit because of their inferior quality and their competition with strong vine development. Allowing the vine to overfruit at this stage will inhibit fourth-year growth, long-term vine development and, ultimately, fruit production.

In dormancy, cut back the cordon and canes to wood $\frac{1}{4}$ inch in diameter. Prune so that 15 to 20 well-spaced canes remain on the vine, depending on vigor (Fig. 10.5). Remove any suckers or side growth from the trunk.

By the fourth year, the permanent vine structure is established. Future pruning in productive years centers around renewing fruiting canes while maintaining structural strength and crop support.

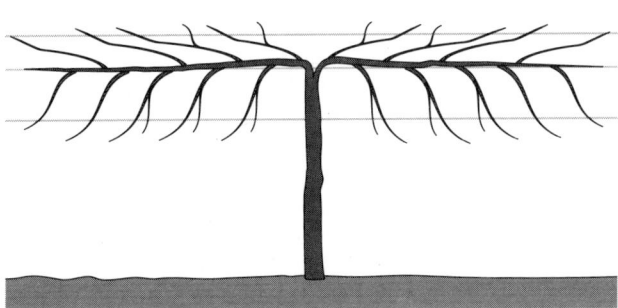

Fig. 10.5. Dormant pruning marks end of third growing season. Fifteen to 20 well-spaced canes remain after pruning.

CULTURAL CONSIDERATIONS

11

Dormant Pruning

JAMES A. BEUTEL

Pruning old fruiting wood of kiwifruit maintains production of strong annual cane growth and regulates the next season's crop yield and fruit size. Unpruned vines become a tangled mass of canes that produce fewer and smaller fruit each year.

Annual pruning is essential to profitable fruit production. Prune male plants each year to maintain good flowering shoots; unpruned male vines can provide male flowers for 2 or 3 years but not after that. (Unpruned vines shade out older wood.) Pruning allows the light penetration needed by fruiting canes to mature the following season.

TIMING

Dormant pruning of female vines is generally timed for December and January in California. Start pruning as soon as cold weather freezes leaves in November or early December. Complete it before sap flow in February. Pruning after sap flow does not seem desirable, although there is no evidence available that damage results from sap bleeding from the plant.

Prune male plants in the dormant period, December and January, and/or after flowering ends in May.

Pruning twice each year restricts male vine growth, confines the vine to a small space, and minimizes overgrowth into producing plants. Pruning too severely in May can result in sunburn damage to the vine. It is often necessary to whitewash the vine after pruning in May.

VINE AND PRUNING TERMS

To clarify pruning procedures, certain terms are defined here (Fig. 11.1).

Buds. The structure at the base of leaves on shoots. When the leaves fall, they appear as flat, round vegetative buds at the base of most canes. The large, raised structures on canes are the fruitful buds; these bear hidden, tiny shoots that will develop into fruiting shoots the following year.

Cane. A 1- or 2-year-old shoot bearing buds that will develop into next year's fruiting shoots.

Cordon. A large arm of the vine generally tied to the center wire of the trellis. A second arm grows in the opposite direction (180 degrees) of the first arm. Cordons

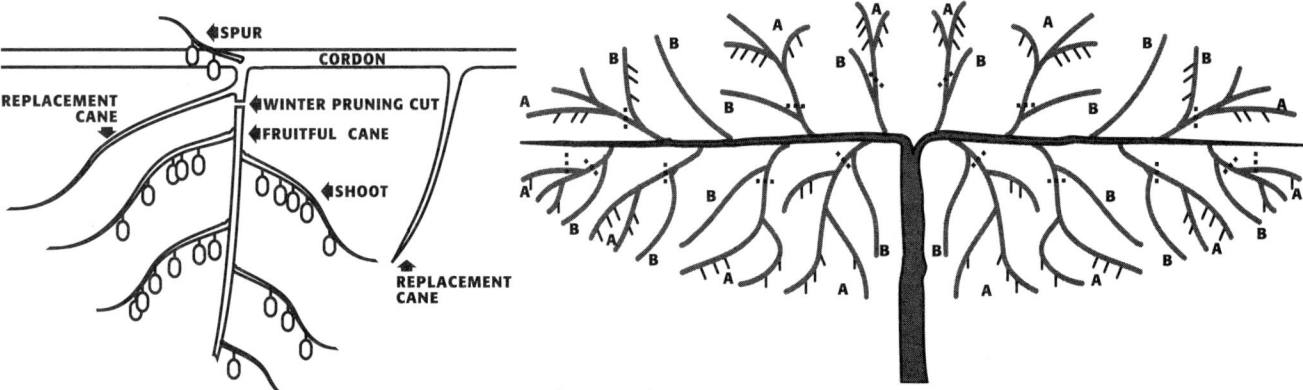

Fig. 11.1. Vine and pruning terms illustrated.

Fig. 11.2. The one strong cane left at the base of an old fruiting cane becomes the replacement cane to bear fruit the following season. A = old fruiting cane; B = replacement cane; ⋯ = winter pruning cut; / = stem from harvested fruit.

bear the fruiting canes of the kiwifruit vine. Kiwifruit vines perform best when they have two large cordons, each 7 to 8 feet long.

Fruitful cane. A 1-year-old cane with stems that bore fruit last year at its base and flower-bearing buds that will produce next year's fruiting shoots and crop.

Replacement cane or vegetative cane. A 1-year-old cane without fruit but with both leaf buds and flower-bearing buds that will produce next year's crop.

Shoot. The current season's growth, bearing leaves, flowers, and fruit.

Spurs. Short, self-terminating shoots arising from 1-year-old wood.

PRUNING MATURE VINES

Prune kiwifruit vines in winter in three steps:

1. Cut off most of the canes that fruited during the previous season. Leave one strong cane at the base of each old fruiting cane; it becomes the replacement cane to bear fruit for the current season (Fig. 11.2). Usually this basal cane is near (6 to 15 inches) the cordon and is about as long as the old fruiting cane from which it arises. By using a replacement cane near the cordon, fruiting will begin near the cordon and spread to outer edges of the vine. Normally, start pruning at one end of the vine or row and proceed down the side of the vine, until all old canes are cut out. Then proceed to the next vine.

2. After the old fruiting canes have been cut out, count the remaining canes to determine whether any more can be removed. Normally, 30 to 40 canes are left per vine over 7 years old; approximately equal numbers are left on each side of the vine's cordon. Younger vines have 8 to 12 canes for the first good crop year (at age 4); 14 to 18, the second crop year (at age 5); 20 to 24, the third and often heavy crop year (at age 6), and 30 to 40, crop years 7 or 8. Only the most vigorous vineyards should leave 40 canes per vine. Too many canes results in overcropping with smaller fruit and poor renewal cane growth for the next year.

Where adequate or excessive cane numbers exist, remove the least desirable canes: small-sized canes (less than ½ inch in diameter); weak canes growing in the lower part of the vine canopy; very strong, upward-growing canes that are hard to tie down to the trellis; canes originating on one side of the vine and crossing over the cordon to the opposite side; and canes originating on old wood more than 18 inches from the cordon.

Canes originating a long way from the cordon tend to extend into adjacent vines on a pergola or to hang too far down on a T-bar for proper cultivation. Leaving canes of this type creates a woody vine with fruit only on the extremities.

Canes growing under more vigorous vines usually have been shaded during the summer and have weaker flower buds that will result in small fruit the following year. Small canes usually produce smaller and sometimes fewer fruit than do large-diameter canes. The vigorous, upright-growing canes ¾ inch in diameter often break when tied to the trellis; they also tend to have many vegetative buds near the cordon that create excessive growth and shade in the next year. The vigorous canes also have flower buds far from the cordon. Vigorous canes can bear good, large fruit, but they are not more desirable than the less vigorous, flatter growing canes that are ⅝ inch in diameter and generally well supplied with fruitful buds.

3. In the final operation head or cut the remaining canes so that they will produce an adequate number of new shoots for next year's crop but not too many shoots or the fruit will be too small. The decision to head the shoots is based on vine vigor, shoot diameter, last year's crop, winter chilling, and the experience of the kiwifruit grower and pruners. Vines and smaller canes, weakened previously by a heavy crop, poor soil, and inadequate nitrogen fertilizer and irrigation, need to be cut more severely than vigorous growth.

One basis for pruning is to head all canes where they are ⅜ inch in diameter. This procedure leaves vigorous canes 6 to 7 feet long and medium to small canes 2 feet long with most good canes 4 to 5 feet long. If the previous crop was light, the next year's crop is expected to be heavy, so heading canes more severely than normal to ½-inch diameter wood or a foot shorter than usual will result in fewer, but larger, fruit. In contrast, canes following a heavy crop may be left longer than normal. Avoid severely pruning the vine following a heavy crop with small-sized fruit; severe pruning will decrease the next year's crop.

Another system to follow is to count fruitful buds and leave 10 to 14 per cane. Usually about 50 percent of the fruitful buds will produce shoots with four to six fruit or fruit clusters. If ten buds are left and five grow with five fruit each, then 25 fruit (about 5 pounds) of large size may develop on each cane. At this rate, each vine can potentially yield 150 to 200 pounds of kiwifruit. With packout at 70 percent, 100 to 140 pounds per vine will be available for packing. This number translates into 14 to 20 trays of 7 pounds each per vine and a 2,000- to 3,000-tray-per-acre crop. This assumes well-timed irrigation, culture, and thinning of vigorous vines and fruit of mostly 30 to 39 size.

In areas with warm winters, like southern California, poor budbreak occurs, and only 20 to 25 percent of buds or only the two or three buds behind the heading cut bear shoots with fruit. In these situations leaving more canes per plant may be desirable.

When old canes are removed and no replacement cane is available, pruners are encouraged to leave a 1- to 2-inch stub or spur. This results in new shoots growing from these stubs 50 to 65 percent of the time. Cut out old, dead stubs the next season.

Pergola and T-bar pruning

The principles of pruning are the same for pergola and T-bar trellises. Two cordons, growing in opposite directions, are better in pergola trellises than four cordons because there are fewer canes crossing over each other. Pergola vines should not overlap and create too much shade.

T-bar pruning encourages 30 to 40 canes, but restricts the length of the canes to prevent them from touching the ground. Heading canes 3 to 4 feet aboveground permits the mowing of cover crops and weeds; at the same time, the canes are long enough to sustain adequate crops of large fruit. Generally, the more the canes extend over the outrigger wires, the smaller the fruit.

Taping, tying, or clipping canes

Tape or clip the replacement canes to the trellis wires about 1 foot apart, without crossing, to intercept light and to give each cane space to grow fruiting shoots. The most convenient time for doing this is in February when warmer weather begins. Also, in warmer weather canes tend to bend better and break less. Some bending with the fingers near the point of attachment will minimize cane breakage. There are several types of hand-held taping and stapling equipment available to help speed this process.

During the growth period before bloom, shoots grow from the cordon, from stubs along the cordon, and from the tied-down canes. If growth is excessive during May and June, shading of fruit and canes can become a problem. (See chapter 12, *Summer Pruning*.)

Cordon maintenance

To be the most fruitful, cordons should be allowed to grow long and strong with fruiting canes well spaced along them. Canes should cover the entire trellis and fill spaces between vines. Cordon development is a continuous process. When vines are young, the best cane is tied on top of the vine and cut to about 2 feet long to force at least half of the buds to become strong growing points along the cane, one of which will become the cordon. Do not twist the cordon around the center wire of the trellis, because twisted cordons often become stunted.

Even with proper pruning, cordons often lose vigor and fail to continue to elongate. In these cases, tie strong canes to the center wire, headed 2 or 3 feet long, to encourage them to become strong cordons. Often these canes fruit heavily, stunting their growth and necessitating selection of another cane as a cordon replacement for the next year. If the replacement cordon appears weak, lay a second potential cordon on a wire to the left or right of the center cordon wire. Next year the better cordon cane can be established. If a heavy crop develops on canes off the potential cordon, thin the fruit. Tie cordons to the wire to encourage vigorous growth and development; sagging cordons tend to decline. Canes crossing over or wires cutting into a cordon can damage it. As necessary, use strong canes to replace weaker cordons.

PRUNING MALE VINES

In dormant season pruning of male vines, compared with pruning female vines, growers generally leave more canes so there are more flowers for pollination. Leave canes long but cut the tip of the cane to encourage flowers over a longer blooming period, thereby enhancing pollination of female plants. Another technique in pruning male vines: Cut out most twisted canes or, at least, the tangled ends, and leave the rest of the canes for flower production. Also, cut the male vines back so that the ends of their canes are 3 to 4 feet away from the ends of female canes. This permits light into the vineyard and allows maximum space for the fruiting vines.

Annual winter pruning prevents male vines from becoming dense, shaded, and immense. It is not as necessary as winter pruning of female vines because male vines not pruned in the dormant season can be pruned in May after flowering ends.

In May, cut back tall canes of male plants to within 3 feet of the cordon. Also, canes higher than 2 feet above the cordon are best headed at 2 feet above the trellis. Do not overprune male vines in May as temperatures over 90°F (32°C) will severely sunburn the cordons, causing damage that may necessitate replacing them and retraining. Whitewash cordons, if necessary.

Maintaining perfect cane spacing and cordon development is less necessary in male than in female vines, because their purposes in kiwifruit vineyards differ. However, if no attempt is made to let light reach the cordons in winter or May, excessive dead wood will develop in male vines.

CULTURAL CONSIDERATIONS

12

Summer Pruning

JANINE K. HASEY, WILLIAM H. OLSON, AND RACHEL B. ELKINS

The objectives of summer pruning mature, full-canopied kiwifruit vineyards are to:

1. Maintain light intensity within the vine but not to the extent that fruit become sunburned.

2. Maintain the order and space between vines attained by dormant pruning.

3. Retain an adequate leaf canopy to support fruit growth.

Summer pruning is done during the growing season by hedging along the sides of vines, removing canes and excessive growth from within the canopy, or a combination of both.

Summer pruning eliminates shade and introduces the light needed to influence fruitfulness. Flowers for the next season's crop are initiated during late summer and early fall of the current season, and if developing buds are shaded during this period, floral initiation is reduced. More dead, dormant, and vegetative buds are found on shaded canes. Canes exposed to sun have up to three times more fruitful buds than do shaded ones.

Excessive shading can adversely affect fruit size. Fruit from sun-exposed canes are consistently larger than fruit from shaded canes, despite having equal seed counts. However, removing excessive leaf canopy at any given time can upset the vine's carbohydrate balance and result in smaller fruit size. With kiwifruit, maintaining a sound carbohydrate balance in the vine is vital to ensuring production of quality fruit.

Other points favoring summer pruning:

1. Research indicates that fruit from sun-exposed canes stay firmer after 3 months in cold storage than do fruit from shaded canes. Reports that fruit from shaded areas of the vine have a lower soluble solids content (SSC) than fruit from sun-exposed areas have not been substantiated.

2. Research on summer pruning demonstrates that fruit is firmer after 1 month in cold storage, when vines were summer pruned in June and/or July, compared with fruit from unpruned vines.

3. Summer pruning may help facilitate better spray coverage, increased air movement, and decreased humidity resulting in reduced disease incidence.

4. Summer pruning methods may vary, depending on the trellis system in use. Whatever method is used, try to reduce situations where the canopy is more than three layers thick. Most sunlight is absorbed by the outer layer of leaves. The second layer receives about 10 percent of full sunlight; the third layer receives only about 1 percent of full sunlight. The goal of summer pruning is to maintain filtered sunlight throughout the entire vine canopy. As a general rule, approximately one-third of the vineyard floor should show sunlight.

SUMMER PRUNING METHODS

Inasmuch as summer pruning practices are not well established in California, the method outlined here is offered as a guideline only. During June, unfruitful canes, not required for fruit production the next year, can be removed or cut back to a short stub. This stub will contain buds for the growth of future fruiting canes.

Cut back excessive growth on lateral branches to three or four leaves beyond the fruit. Prune these fruiting shoots back to a number of leaves equal to the number of fruit on the shoot. Remove any twisted and tangled growth. Hedging all growth beyond the outer wire will significantly increase light access to the vine. This practice, however, is better suited to T-bar trellis systems and should only be practiced where little fruit loss will occur. Hedge two to four times during the season to keep an open alleyway at all times. Regardless of the method used, do not prune off too much leaf area at any one time, creating a carbohydrate imbalance that will adversely affect fruit size.

Prune back male vines to new growth near the permanent cordon branches in May immediately after they have flowered. (Pruning male vines is discussed in chapter 11, *Dormant Pruning.*) It may be necessary to cut canes on male vines back again in August or September, if growth is excessive.

Any pruning performed from 1 to 7 weeks after petal fall should be done carefully to avoid touching the fruit; touching can lead to scarring.

It may be necessary to prune again by the end of July to remove tangles or any excessive growth blocking light penetration through the canopy. This second pruning may not be justifiable because summer pruning is costly. Summer pruning, however, will slightly reduce dormant pruning costs and may make dormant pruning easier. Determining whether summer pruning is economically feasible and necessary requires evaluating the vineyard's vigor, fruit quality, and extent of shading.

CULTURAL CONSIDERATIONS

13

Fruit Thinning

R. SCOTT JOHNSON AND JOSEPH A. GRANT

Fruit thinning, long practiced on fruits destined for fresh market consumption, reduces the crop load so the remaining fruit can reach the minimum size accepted for market. In fruit thinning, also, damaged or misshapen fruit that would be unmarketable at the time of harvest are removed—a practice annually required for most varieties of apples, peaches, apricots, and plums. It is questionable whether fruit thinning of kiwifruit is economically feasible. There are two reasons why:

1. A significant amount of thinning can be achieved by proper pruning during the dormant season (see chapter 11, *Dormant Pruning*). Generally, with no additional fruit thinning and unless the vines are stressed or pollination is poor, most fruit will reach an acceptable minimum size for marketing.

2. Research shows that fruit thinning with moderately heavy crop loads only slightly affects growth of the remaining fruit. This small increase in fruit size does not compensate for the loss in yield due to thinning, unless large fruit is much more valuable than small fruit. It is still possible, however, that with a heavy crop load fruit thinning would increase the growth of remaining fruit enough to warrant the extra expense.

Many California growers thin fruit only to remove misshapen "flats" and "fans" and very small fruit. It is doubtful that this type of thinning will increase the growth of remaining fruit. However, it can prove advantageous at harvest, when crews may work more efficiently because they do not have to selectively leave misshapen fruit on the vine. In addition, hauling costs are reduced slightly, and with a lower cullage rate fruit packing can run more smoothly.

TIME OF THINNING

Thinning can be carried out before flower buds open because at that time most fans and flats can be easily identified and removed. However, research has shown that, compared with fruitlet thinning, there is no significant increase in fruit size by flower bud thinning.

Another difficulty in thinning before bloom is that flower buds destined to produce small fruit at harvest cannot be distinguished from those that will produce larger fruit. Accurate differentiation of fruit sizes is not observed until several weeks after bloom. At this time, size differences apparent among fruit will remain basically the same through harvest.

The earlier that fruitlet thinning is performed, the greater the effect on the growth of the remaining fruit will be. Thinning too early, however, can lead to difficulty in distinguishing flats and undersized fruit from desirable fruit. Also, the fruit are more tender at this early stage and can easily be injured by handling. Incidental rubbing or tapping of fruit by thinners can result in injury to—and subsequent scarring of—the surface of fruit, causing them to be offgrade at harvest. In one study, fruit were most susceptible to injury from 1 to 7 weeks after petal fall, with a sharp reduction in susceptibility thereafter. The most severe injury occurred between 1 and 3 weeks after petal fall.

Before making a decision about thinning, consider the crop load, the relative value of large and small fruit, packing shed requirements for cull fruit, and the cost, availability, and skill of labor crews.

CULTURAL CONSIDERATIONS

14

Irrigation Systems

RICHARD P. BUCHNER AND BLAINE R. HANSON

Irrigation management has two goals: to supply water before reduced soil moisture limits vine growth and fruit production, and to minimize losses caused by overwatering. Ideally, with proper management, the irrigation system accomplishes these goals efficiently at reasonable costs for installation and operation.

Unfortunately, there is no single best system for kiwifruit irrigation. Each system is a compromise to most effectively fit a particular vineyard. Choosing a system depends on land slope, soil type, water infiltration rates, water-holding capacity, erosion hazards, leaching requirements, water quality, available flow rate, wind, costs (for water, labor, system installation, and maintenance), cultural practices (for frost protection, chemicals, or fertilizers), and potential diseases, such as Phytophthora root and crown rot.

Tradeoffs are likely. For example, where water costs are high, systems or modifications that enhance irrigation performance can save money. Where water costs are low, high efficiency systems or modifications may not save enough water or power to be cost effective. Where labor costs are high, the choice may go to a more expensive low-labor system.

Cultural considerations play a major role in making a choice. Overhead sprinklers may be the best choice to protect vines from spring frosts or to cool vineyards in midsummer. Sprinkler or drip systems perform well on steep or undulating ground. Drip systems are useful when water supplies are limited or when crowns must be kept dry to reduce *Phytophthora* infection. Surface systems perform well when available water flow rates are relatively high, soils are level to moderately sloping, and water infiltration rates are not excessively high. Low-energy or low-pressure systems are usually used where pumping costs are high. Essentially, careful thought and planning will provide the most satisfactory irrigation system.

IRRIGATION SYSTEMS

There are three basic irrigation systems: low-volume using emitters (drippers or microsprinklers), sprinkler

Fig. 14.1. Microsprinkler emitter at soil surface is placed far enough away to keep trunk dry.

Fig. 14.2. Microsprinkler emitter is suspended above soil.

(moveable or solid set), and surface (basin, furrow, or border).

Drip or microsprinkler systems

The first major type of irrigation system is the localized or low-volume system. Various emitters are available, but drip and microsprinklers are the most commonly used in kiwifruit vineyards.

Drip systems. Drip irrigation is designed to apply small amounts of water frequently to a small area. Because the vines depend on the emission points for water, application must be frequent enough and of adequate duration to meet their daily water requirements. A common misconception is that drip-irrigated vines somehow "use" less water than surface- or sprinkler-irrigated vines. In reality, vine water use or transpiration depends on climate and not on how water is delivered. Water savings are possible, particularly in young vineyards where it is not necessary to wet the entire soil surface, where weed growth is reduced by localized wetting, and where drip systems significantly improve irrigation efficiency compared with other systems.

Drip irrigation systems, widely used in California kiwifruit culture, are a good choice where water, labor, and energy costs are high. They perform well on shallow soils with low water-storage capacity and fine-textured soils with low water-intake rates. They can be used on nonlevel ground. Another advantage: Localized wetting does not interfere with cultural practices in the vineyard and diseases may be reduced because foliage and crowns remain dry. One problem encountered with drip systems: Emitters become clogged because of (1) precipitation of calcium and iron within drip lines, (2) physical plugging by sand, silt, or clay particles, or (3) growth within drip lines of bacteria, slimes, molds, and algae.

Additional drawbacks: animal damage to exposed laterals, lack of frost protection, limited lifespan of exposed plastic parts, expensive components, and moderate to high installation costs. The drip system is not an install-and-your-problems-are-over system; its proper operation requires knowledge, skill, and labor.

Just how many emitters are required per kiwifruit vine has not been well documented. Certainly one emitter, located near the vine, is suitable for a first-year planting. As vines grow, pull back the first emitter to keep soil around the crown dry and add a second emitter to the other side. As vines continue to grow, add more emitters to keep up with the increasing daily water requirement. For the mature vine, experience suggests that four properly selected and managed emitters per vine are necessary and additional emitters may be desirable. Generally, the more soil volume wetted, the better. Place drippers so that soil around the trunk remains dry.

Microsprinklers. Modified for higher flow rates and larger wetted areas per emitter, microsprinkler system designs are similar to drip, except that drip emitters are replaced by one or sometimes two "large" emitters or microsprinklers. One full-turn microsprinkler per vine, located equidistant between vines, is considered adequate in mature vineyards at conventional spacing. Another option: Use two 180-degree sprinklers located on each side of the vine with streams directed away from the trunk. Hoses and emitters can be placed on the ground along the vine row or suspended from the trellis system (Figs. 14.1 and 14.2).

In young vineyards microsprinklers tend to overirrigate because more soil is wetted than necessary. One way to counteract that possibility is to use drip emitters for the first year or two, then switch to microsprinklers as root systems expand. Because microsprinklers wet a relatively large volume of soil, more time can elapse between irrigations because soil moisture storage is greater.

In considering using drip or microsprinklers, remember:

1. Systems perform well on problem sites, including uneven ground, soils with excessively high or low water infiltration rates, and soils with low water-holding capacity. Microsprinklers are better adapted to coarse-textured sands and gravels with high water-intake rates.

2. Irrigations must be frequent and adequate to supply the daily vine water requirement.

3. Filtration and system management are required to avoid plugging of moving parts by chemical precipitation and spider webs.

4. Drip systems perform well where water and energy costs are high.

5. There is excellent control of applied water. High irrigation efficiencies and uniformities are possible.

6. Installation costs are moderate to high. Aboveground components have a limited lifespan.

7. Diseases are reduced, thanks to localized wetting. Irrigations usually do not interfere with cultural operations.

8. Weed control is usually restricted to wetted areas, but control may be difficult because herbicides break down or leach in wet areas.

9. Animals may chew drip laterals.

10. Management and operation require more skill and attention than other methods.

11. Frost control is limited.

Sprinkler systems

Sprinklers and various sprinkler configurations comprise the second major irrigation system available. In kiwifruit vineyards sprinklers can be permanent or solid-set, above or below the leaf canopy, or portable aluminum pipe or hose-pull.

Solid-set. In solid-set systems water is pumped through a network of buried main and lateral pipes to individual risers and sprinklers. Each sprinkler and riser assembly is permanently located and cannot be transported. Solid-set systems are carefully engineered so that pressure, pipe size, sprinkler spacing, flow rates, and sprinkler selection will result in acceptable, efficient water application.

Three possibilities for locating sprinklers exist: above the leaf canopy, below the leaf canopy, or both. Above-canopy or overhead sprinklers modify vineyard climate through frost control in spring or cooling in summer. Potential problems include leaf burn and evaporative deposits on the fruit (depending on water quality), water stains on fruit, and possible introduction of disease because of prolonged foliage wetting. Under-canopy sprinklers tend to avoid these problems, but they reduce frost or heat control and sometimes interfere with cultural operations. Under-vine sprinklers should be located between vines to reduce water stream impact on the trunk and water puddling at the crown. Remember, saturated soil around the crown can aggravate *Phytophthora* infections. Consider using stream sprinklers where trunk wetting is a problem.

Some systems are built to accommodate above- and below-canopy sprinklers (Fig. 14.3). During winter, the lower risers are plugged and the sprinklers are moved to over-vine positions. After frosts end, the upper positions are plugged and the sprinklers are moved to lower positions.

The major drawback to solid-set irrigation: Its components are expensive: pumps, buried pipe, fittings, valves, sprinklers, design, and installation. Energy costs to pressurize water can be expensive. Designs for a low-pressure operation can significantly reduce system and operating costs. Solid-set systems require relatively little labor to operate.

Portable sprinklers. In the second type of sprinkler system, portable aluminum pipe, water is delivered to a series of hydrants via a permanent, buried, main line. Hydrants are located so that each pipe set or line can be conveniently connected to the main line. Sprinklers are attached to 30- or 40-foot sections or joints of aluminum pipe. After an irrigation, or set, pipes are disassembled and moved to a new location where they are reassembled, connected to the main, and charged with water. Pipe moves continue through the vineyard. At the last set, pipes are picked up and moved to the next starting point. Often moveable systems are designed to rotate through the field around the main line. This avoids having to trailer pipes back to the initial set.

The major advantage of portable aluminum pipe: Installation costs are as much as 50 percent less than for solid-set systems. The drawback: Labor is required to move pipes each day, even when the vineyard floor is muddy. As with solid-set systems, care must be taken to reduce water stream impact on the trunk and water ponding at the crown. Some growers have reduced labor costs by buying enough pipe to place a lateral in each location to create a "moveable solid-set system."

Fig. 14.3. Solid-set sprinkler system has the capacity to apply water above and below the leaf canopy. Plugging of emitters is easier to detect with this system.

Hose-pull sprinklers. In the third sprinkler system, hose-pull, water flows through a buried main line to a series of risers located throughout the vineyard. Long, flexible surface hoses connect individual sprinklers to their risers. Each time a hose is pulled, the sprinkler changes location. After a number of pulls are completed, sprinklers are relocated and the pull process resumes. The major advantage of hose-pull, compared with solid-set systems, is initial cost savings. Labor is increased whenever sprinklers are continuously being relocated.

Growers contemplating sprinkler systems should consider:

1. Installation costs are moderate to expensive, depending on the type of system.

2. Low-pressure designs are desirable where energy costs are high.

3. Labor savings are possible.

4. Sprinklers are well suited to nonlevel ground and can be designed to accommodate soil infiltration rates and nonuniform soils. Flow-control nozzles can be used on nonlevel ground to provide uniform water application throughout the field.

5. Sprinklers can be operated at relatively high efficiencies.

6. Sprinklers can be used to modify climate.

7. Solid-set sprinklers allow light, frequent irrigations.

8. Flow rates depend on system efficiency and number of sprinklers.

9. Sprinkler systems should be engineered to operate properly.

10. Water should be of suitable quality to prevent leaf burn and fruit marking by over-the-vine irrigation.

Surface systems

Basins or contours. Formed by two levees or ridges along adjacent contours, with short cross checks at either end, the basin allows all of its surface to be ponded with water. Basins or contours work well on lands that are reasonably flat but not adequately leveled for border check or furrow systems. Relatively large stream sizes are required. System costs are low, but considerable soil movement is required to build and remove levees. Although basin or contour systems are widely used in deciduous fruit and nut production, the required soil movement may make these irrigation systems unsuitable for kiwifruit culture.

Furrow irrigation. In this system, water is delivered to the head end of the vineyard, using gated pipe or siphons drawing from a head ditch. Water is applied into a series of small ditches or furrows. Because the vineyard is graded to a slight slope, water flows down the furrows toward the tail of the vineyard. Water infiltrates into the soil and spreads laterally to wet the entire area. Furrow irrigation, successfully used in annual row crops, vineyards, and orchard sites, may not be a good choice for kiwifruit vineyards because of the tillage required to build, maintain, and smooth furrows.

Border irrigation. In border irrigation, which resembles the furrow technique, water is turned into the upper or head end of a strip check and allowed to move down the slope toward the tail. A sheet of water slowly advances down the check. In kiwifruit vineyards, border widths are usually equal to the between-row plant spacing with vines planted on berms to contain the water stream and keep the crown areas dry to minimize *Phytophthora* infection. Water is delivered to the head end of the check using gated pipe, turnouts, pipes, and valves or head ditches with siphons.

Factors to consider for border irrigation:

1. Low to moderate infiltration rates are required to uniformly wet the entire border strip. Uniform soils are desirable.

2. Moderate surface slopes (.1 to .3 percent) are recommended. Grade before planting.

3. Water flow must be adequate to wet the strip.

4. Soils with high water-holding capacities are preferred because few hours of labor are required to irrigate.

5. Border strip irrigation is not well suited to high infiltration rate soils. In sandy soils stream sizes must be large and runs short to achieve adequate uniformity.

6. Energy use is generally low for efficient systems because water is either gravity fed or delivered at low pressure.

7. Border systems require time and skill to irrigate at high water application efficiencies.

8. System installation is moderately expensive. System maintenance costs are minimal.

9. It is more difficult to estimate applied water for irrigation scheduling.

10. The ability to control frost is limited.

11. Tail water return systems are necessary to achieve high efficiency.

Multiple systems

Frequently more than one type of irrigation system is used to irrigate kiwifruit vineyards. Often, drip or microsprinklers are combined with surface irrigation or solid-set sprinklers. Experience with other California crops shows that one properly designed and operated system is adequate to meet crop water requirements. In many kiwifruit vineyards, multiple systems are valuable for frost control or cooling. When using two irrigation systems, kiwifruit growers need to ascertain that both systems together apply enough water. If 50 percent of the water requirement is achieved with one system, the second should apply the other 50 percent.

IRRIGATION EFFICIENCY/UNIFORMITY

Evaluating performance

Of the many ways to evaluate irrigation systems, some are complex and provide detailed information; others are simple, providing reasonable first approximations. The simple approach is presented here. Those desiring more detailed evaluations should consult *Farm Irrigation System Evaluation: A Guide for Management* by John L. Merriam and Jack Keller (published by Agricultural and Irrigation Engineering Dept., Utah State University, Logan, Utah 84321. 1978). In some areas, Cooperative Extension, Soil Conservation Service, or the Department of Water Resources (mobile lab program) offer assistance with evaluating irrigation systems.

Regardless of the irrigation system used, its performance depends on how it is operated. Even the best system will perform poorly under improper management. Various efficiency measurements have been developed to describe how well a particular system is operating. Different efficiency values are calculated and reported according to how complex the system evaluation is. A particularly useful efficiency value for growers is the application efficiency (Ea). Ea is the amount of water stored in the root zone, divided by the amount of applied water expressed as a percent.

$$Ea = \frac{\text{water stored}}{\text{water applied}} \times 100$$

For example, if a kiwifruit irrigator applies 3.0 inches of water and 2.5 inches are stored in the root zone, the application efficiency would be:

$$Ea = \frac{2.5 \text{ inches}}{3.0 \text{ inches}} \times 100 = 83.33\%$$

In other words, 83 percent of the water is stored for kiwifruit transpiration and roughly 17 percent is lost to evaporation, runoff, or percolation below the root zone. Application efficiency values are very useful for irrigation scheduling. Soil moisture depletion, divided by application efficiency, indicates how much water to apply (see chapter 15, *Irrigation Scheduling*).

Uniformity, another important system characteristic, refers to the evenness of the applied or infiltrated water throughout the field. A uniformity of 100 percent means the same depth of water is applied at all locations. A uniformity of 80 percent means that when 80 percent of the vineyard is properly irrigated, 20 percent is underirrigated. Good uniformity means that high application efficiencies can be achieved with adequate irrigation. Poor uniformity means that substantial water loss due to deep percolation (water that percolates below the root zone) can occur. Table 14.1 lists achievable uniformities and efficiencies for various irrigation systems.

Evaluating drip and microsprinklers

Localized water application systems are relatively easy to evaluate because water applications can be carefully controlled. For a simple evaluation, irriga-

Table 14.1. Attainable potential irrigation uniformities and application efficiencies (assumes adequate irrigation)

System	Distribution uniformity (%)	Application efficiency (%)
Drip/trickle	80–90	75–90
Sprinklers		
Solid-set	90–95	85–90
Periodic move	70–80	65–80
Continuous move	70–90*	75–85
Surface		
Basin	90–95†	75–90
Furrow	80–90†	60–90‡
Border	70–85†	65–80‡

* Higher values for systems using spray nozzles on booms or using impact sprinklers.
† Does not include nonuniformity due to variability of the soil infiltration rate.
‡ Higher values for systems with tail water recovery systems or using cutback irrigation.

tion managers need to measure individual flow rates per vine at selected points throughout the vineyard. Necessary equipment includes a watch that can measure in seconds, a 250-ml graduated cylinder, a 3- to 6-inch diameter funnel, and, perhaps, a large catch can for microsprinklers.

The first step is to identify any problems caused by inadequate maintenance. Watch out for (1) system clogging caused by poor filtration, (2) precipitation of chemicals at emitters, (3) large pressure drops across the filter caused by improper flushing, and (4) possible mixing of emitter types and sizes. Once these problems have been identified and repaired, then an assessment of the system uniformity can be made.

Turn on the water and wait until equilibrium or uniform flows exist throughout the system. Select three laterals for measuring emitter flow rates. The first lateral should be one closest to the pump, the second near the middle of the irrigation system, and the third the most distant from the pump. On each lateral, measure emitter flow rates near the lateral inlet, near the middle of the lateral, and at the end. At each selected vine, place the funnel and graduated cylinder assembly under each emitter and measure how much water flows in 60 seconds. Once you know total water, milliliters per minute can be converted to gallons per hour (gph), using the following relationship:

$$\frac{ml/min}{63} = gph$$

If an individual emitter produces 75 ml of water in 60 seconds, the flow rate will be 1.19 gph (75/63 = 1.19). A microsprinkler may put out 630 ml in 60 seconds, which would be 10.0 gph (630/63 = 10.0).

Another easy way to evaluate drip emitter flow is to use a 35-mm black film container. Most 35-mm film containers hold 34 milliliters (ml). If the container is not 34 ml, this technique will not be accurate. Simply measure how many seconds it takes to fill the container. Then divide 32 by the number of seconds to convert to gallons per hour.

Localized irrigation systems are often evaluated in terms of emission uniformity (Eu). Eu is the average of the lowest 25 percent of vine discharges, divided by the average rate of discharge per vine expressed as a percent. For example, if 16 vines are measured, the average flow for the lowest four vines may be 4.3 gph, while the average flow for all 16 vines may be 5.2 gph. Dividing 4.3 gph by 5.2 gph and multiplying by 100 indicates an Eu of 82.69 percent. Eu values above 90 percent are considered excellent; 80 percent to 90 percent, good; 70 to 80 percent, fair, and below 70 percent, poor. If Eu values are consistently below 70 percent, check systems for plugging or possible design modification.

Evaluating sprinklers

Sprinkler systems are also relatively easy to evaluate. The first step is to determine whether any performance problems are caused by inadequate maintenance. Frequently, problems with uniformity and adequacy of applied water can be corrected by checking and repairing system components. Initially:

1. Observe sprinkler nozzles for wear, using an unused drill bit of the appropriate size. Worn nozzles apply more water compared with other sprinklers and should be replaced.

2. Check sprinkler heads for proper rotation, wear, and leaks. Replace or repair defective heads.

3. Check pipe gaskets for leakage. Replace leaking gaskets.

4. Check that all nozzle sizes and types are the same throughout the system. Replace any incorrect nozzles with the correct size.

5. Visually evaluate sprinkler throw distance. As a field rule of thumb, water streams should throw to the next sprinkler in the pattern. In other words, sprinkler spacing is roughly one-half of the diameter of wetting.

6. Visually evaluate water streams. Poor throw distance with excessive stream breakup (poorly defined nozzle stream or fogging) may indicate operating pressures exceeding design. On the other hand, poor stream breakup (very well defined nozzle stream) suggests lower pressure than the design calls for.

Once maintenance problems have been identified, check nozzle pressures and flow rates throughout the system. More measurements improve understanding of the system. As a minimum, take measurements near the pump and at a location farthest from the pump. Pressure can be measured with a pitot gauge available in most irrigation supply stores. Sprinkler flow rate is measured with a short section of flexible hose, a 1-gallon container, and a watch that measures in seconds.

With the system up and running, place one end of the hose over the sprinkler nozzle so that all of the nozzle flow goes through the hose. Wait several seconds to ensure full flow; then place the hose in the gallon container and note the time. When the gallon container is completely full, again note the time. The difference in the two times is the number of seconds a gallon of water is emitted. Sixty seconds per minute, divided by the time required to fill 1 gallon, is the flow rate in gallons per minute (gpm). Assuming the flow is 25 seconds per gallon, the sprinkler is putting out 2.40 gpm (60/25 = 2.40). Once the flow rate is known, the following relationship is useful to calculate applied water:

$$\text{inches/hour} = \frac{\text{sprinkler flow (gpm)} \times 96.25}{\text{sprinkler spacing}}$$

For example, if sprinkler flow is 2.40 gpm and sprinkler spacing is 30 feet by 36 feet, then

$$\text{inches/hour} = \frac{(2.40 \text{ gpm}) \times (96.25)}{(30 \text{ ft}) \times (36 \text{ ft})} = .21 \text{ inch/hour}$$

The value 96.25 is a conversion factor, so the result is in inches per hour. The applied water is the application rate times the number of hours the system was on. A .21-inch-per-hour system operating for 10 hours would apply 2.10 inches.

Given an appropriate number of sprinkler measurements, how are the numbers evaluated? Sprinkler systems are often designed so that pressure differences throughout the system do not exceed 10 percent. If sprinklers near the pump are operating at 40 pounds per square inch (psi), remaining sprinklers should not differ by more than 4 psi. Where pressures and flow rates are not within 10 percent, system efficiency can be reduced.

For properly engineered sprinkler systems, the evaluation techniques described should provide acceptable system performance. Be careful when modifying an existing system. A change to low-pressure nozzles may affect system uniformity. When modifications are made, it may be wise to do a more detailed system analysis. The text by Merriam and Keller, referred to in the previous section, describes more detailed evaluation techniques.

Evaluating surface systems

When irrigating with surface systems, the amount of water entering the root zone depends on the infiltration rate and the amount of time water stands on the soil surface. The goal is to make sure enough intake opportunity time exists throughout the field to properly wet the root zone.

To estimate the amount of water being applied, first calculate the flow rate onto the field. Average inflow rate per border is calculated by dividing the field flow rate by the number of border strips irrigated per set, assuming valve openings are similar.

The depth of water applied to the strip can be calculated if the flow rate, surface area, and set time are known. For example, if the border strip is 20 feet wide by 600 feet long, inflow rate is 100 gallons per minute (gpm), and the set time is 6 hours, the average depth applied is calculated by:

$$D = \frac{(100 \text{ gpm}) \times (6 \text{ hours}) \times 96.25}{(20 \text{ ft} \times 600 \text{ ft})} = 4.81 \text{ inches}$$

The value 96.25 is a conversion factor, so the answer is in inches. Irrigation managers also need to determine whether approximately the same depth of water infiltrated down the border strip. A rough estimate of the uniformity can be made by measuring the time water was ponded at the head end (inflow) of the strip and at the tail end (outflow). Generally, the time that water stands at the inflow end should be similar to the time it stands at the outflow. If there are big differences in times, uniformity in application will be poor. The solution: Adjust the inflow rates to reduce the differences. For example, if the time at the tail of the field is much larger than the time at the head, reduce the flow rate to decrease the time it takes water to reach the end of the strip. On the other hand, if the head time is much larger than the tail, increase the flow rate so that the water moves faster down the strip. As a rule of thumb, water should reach the end of the vineyard in one-fourth of the total irrigation time.

Another simple, but effective, approach is to use a soil probe or auger to evaluate the depth of wetting at the head and tail and along border strips. Ideally, depth of wetting should be equal throughout the border. Achieving good uniformity usually results in surface runoff at the tail. Cutting back the inflow after water reaches the end of the field and utilizing tail water recovery systems can improve water application efficiency.

No irrigation system is perfect, but by using simple evaluation techniques, irrigation managers can get a very good idea of how their systems are performing and how to manage them to achieve the best possible irrigation.

CULTURAL CONSIDERATIONS

15

Irrigation Scheduling

RICHARD P. BUCHNER, DAVID A. GOLDHAMER, AND DAVID A. SHAW

In California, where growing season temperatures are typically warm, 90° to 105°F (32° to 41°C), and summer rainfall is nonexistent, supplemental irrigation is needed to achieve optimum kiwifruit growth and production. Nonirrigated kiwifruit vineyards are restricted to very deep soils with high water-holding capacities, combined with sufficient winter rainfall to recharge soil reserves, or planting sites with subsurface moisture adequate to meet seasonal water needs. Because these conditions are relatively rare, nearly all California kiwifruit vineyards rely on irrigation.

To achieve adequate irrigation, the grower must determine when and how long to operate a particular system. Good water management requires maintaining an adequate supply of soil moisture at all times. Underapplication of water slows growth; overirrigation wastes water, energy, and money, and often encourages water-related diseases, such as Phytophthora crown and root rot. Also, as technology changes and improves, irrigation systems can also be used to apply fertilizers or pesticides and to heat or cool vineyards. The information that follows offers kiwifruit growers the best information available for making sound decisions about irrigation schedules.

WATER'S ROLE IN KIWIFRUIT VINEYARDS

On a warm summer day, mature, full-canopy kiwifruit vines can transpire 7,000 to 8,000 gallons of water per acre per day. Little of this water remains within the vine. Virtually all of it passes through the vine and is lost to the atmosphere through thousands of microscopic leaf pores called stomates. As the water vapor moves from leaf to atmosphere, carbon dioxide gas diffuses from the atmosphere into the leaf. This inward flow of carbon dioxide supplies the carbon which produces, in photosynthesis, the carbohydrates necessary to support the vine and its crop. Transpiration is a necessary consequence of the leaf having to assimilate carbon during daylight hours.

In photosynthesis, a biochemical process, chlorophyll in plant tissue uses solar energy to convert carbon dioxide and water into simple carbohydrates. The principal products of photosynthesis are the six-carbon sugar, glucose, and oxygen, which is returned to the atmosphere. Biochemically, glucose is transformed into sucrose, fructose, and sorbitol, sugars that build roots, stems, leaves, and fruit. The carbon dioxide for photosynthesis comes from the air surrounding the leaf; the water comes from soil moisture reserves.

The rates of water loss and carbon dioxide uptake are regulated by stomatal function. Although stomatal behavior is complex, plant water status and weather conditions largely influence their response. During the day, when environmental stresses are moderate, stomates are usually open to allow water vapor loss and carbon dioxide uptake. However, when soil moisture is depleted below critical levels, mild plant moisture stress occurs and the leaf stomates close to reduce water loss and avoid dehydration (wilting). Consequently, the inflow of carbon dioxide is reduced. Without carbon dioxide, photosynthesis slows, thereby reducing the carbohydrates available within the vine. Also, with the stomates closed, evaporative cooling is reduced and leaf surfaces begin to heat up. If stress becomes severe, leaf burn, scorching, and decreased vine performance result.

WATER MOVEMENT IN THE VINE

Water transport occurs as a continuum from the soil through the plant and into the atmosphere. From the soil, water moves through the epidermis of roots and into their vascular tissues, up through the trunk's xylem elements into the leaves, and, finally, through the leaf stomates into the atmosphere. As water evaporates from leaf surfaces, it must enter root tissue to maintain the transpiration flow. Essentially, the kiwifruit vine is similar to a water pipe between soil and air.

Water flows, as we all know, downhill—or from high potential (at the top of the hill) to low potential (at the bottom of the hill). Plant water flow occurs similarly. Within a transpiring plant, leaf water potential is usually low compared with soil water potential. As a result, water is "pulled" through the vine. The rate of water flow depends upon the potential gradient between vine and soil.

In the morning, leaf stomates open in response to sunlight, and as the day heats up, water vapor loss from the leaves accelerates, reducing leaf water potential. This reduced potential creates a tension or pull within the kiwifruit vine's water-conducting tissues (xylem), a tension that can be measured by pressure chamber devices.

Because the xylem is a specialized pipe system, tension can be transmitted through it down into root tissue. From root tissue, water is pulled through the xylem elements in the stem, finally evaporating at the leaf surface. The process of water flow through the vine is similar to a wick drawing oil from a lamp. As soils lose moisture or dry out, tensions within the vine must increase to maintain water flow. Unfortunately, the vine pays the price for these increased tensions, and when tensions become excessive, plant cells begin to dehydrate. This results in wilting and stomatal closure. While stomatal closure allows the vine to survive, it affects all growth and crop production. In most plants a direct relationship exists between the severity of water stress and vine performance.

IRRIGATION SCHEDULING

The correct amount of water is supplied to the vine at the right time by irrigating before limited soil moisture reduces plant growth and crop production, while minimizing losses due to deep percolation and runoff. There are numerous techniques for deciding when to irrigate and with how much water. Generally, kiwifruit growers schedule irrigations according to (1) experience, (2) soil moisture measurements, and (3) a water budget.

Experience

With the first technique, experience, accomplished growers carefully watch their vines and often make good irrigation decisions. Less experienced growers irrigate when their neighbors do, follow a calendar schedule, or guess about when to irrigate—methods unlikely to produce the best results.

Observing vines for trouble signs is helpful, but by the time moisture stress symptoms are visible, damage has occurred. Vines under mild to moderate moisture stress have a subtle off-color look, the foliage turning blue-green. Other symptoms clearly visible include poor shoot growth, wilting, small fruit, reduced yield, small leaves, sunburn, and a general lack of vigor. Although other problems can produce these symptoms, water stress is always implicated. Bear in mind that mild to moderate water stress may have little effect on current season production, but there can be carry-over effects in the following years.

Measuring soil moisture

The second technique calls for measuring soil moisture or monitoring plant water status. Soil moisture is measured with shovels, soil tubes, augers, gypsum blocks, tensiometers, and neutron probes. Plant water status is measured with pressure chambers and infrared thermometers, equipment that is used extensively in research but rarely in production agriculture because costs are high, pressure chamber measurements are relatively difficult to take, and little information exists on how to relate the measurements to kiwifruit irrigation decisions.

Measuring soil moisture works well for irrigation scheduling, provided measurement locations are representative, values are accurately related to plant moisture stress, and growers are committed to maintaining, monitoring, recording, and evaluating instrument readings. The major drawbacks are (1) cost, depending on the device, and (2) lack of research information to relate instrument readings to kiwifruit moisture status. Growers need to know what readings signal the need for irrigation (threshold levels). Because research data are limited, many growers evaluate instrument readings based upon vine performance, crop quality, and production. The equipment used to measure soil moisture and plant water status is covered in chapter 16, *Measuring Soil Moisture*.

The water budget

In the third technique, the water budget or water balance method, the concept involves estimating the rate of vineyard water use. When cumulative water use equals a threshold level, irrigation is applied to replace depleted soil moisture. Imagine the soil reservoir as similar to a 12-ounce glass of water—drink 2 ounces of water a day and you will deplete the available water in 6 days.

The major advantage of water budget irrigation scheduling is that it deals with the vineyard as a biological unit. It is a methodology that integrates all factors influencing water use fast and accurately to predict irrigation times and amounts. The drawbacks involve the amount of record keeping (extensive), the effort to obtain water use data (may be difficult), and evaluations of soil type, root depth, and vineyard canopy development (time-consuming).

In reality, irrigation scheduling is most often a combination of the three basic techniques: water budget irrigation scheduling, soil moisture monitoring, and careful observation of vineyard performance to confirm successful irrigation practices.

WATER BALANCE TECHNOLOGY

Using water balance technology to make irrigation decisions requires understanding (1) the rate of vineyard water use and (2) the application efficiency characteristics of the irrigation system. For sprinkler- or surface-irrigated vineyards, growers must also know (3) the available water in the root zone and (4) the yield threshold depletion.

A kiwifruit vineyard uses water as a result of the combination of two processes: direct evaporation from the soil surface (E) and transpiration from kiwifruit leaves (T). The two processes, usually discussed together, are called evapotranspiration (ET). For all practical purposes, kiwifruit ET represents the amount of water required by the vineyard during the growing season.

Remember that plant water loss, primarily an evaporative process, requires energy that comes from the environment. Because the weather largely determines water use, irrigation researchers have developed several methods for evaluating vineyard ET, based upon measuring the weather: solar radiation, air temperature, relative humidity, and wind speed. One relatively simple technique is to measure water loss from a free water surface, such as a U.S. Weather Bureau Class A evaporation pan (E pan)(Fig. 15.1). Most weather stations used for irrigation scheduling are located in a standardized setting, usually surrounded by irrigated grass or pasture. Water depths are measured daily or weekly. The daily evaporation rate is the differences in water level divided by the number of days.

ET based upon Epan measurements

Kiwifruit vines do not evaporate water exactly the same as a free water surface. Biological factors, such as canopy cover and stomatal function, also influence their water use. To account for the physical versus biological differences, a series of pan coefficients (Kp) have been developed. Researchers have calculated these coefficients by measuring kiwifruit water use and then directly comparing them to pan evaporation throughout the season. For example, mature vines at midseason transpire roughly .290 inch of water per day. For the same day, the Epan or free water surface evaporation is .337 inch. By dividing .290 by .337 and multiplying by 100 (.290 ÷ .337× 100 = 86), we can say that kiwifruit water use is 86 percent of the evaporation pan. In other words, K pan or pan coefficient equals .86. The general relationship is:

E pan × K pan = ET kiwifruit

Given this relationship, growers can easily calculate how much water their vines are using by knowing pan evaporation and coefficients. Current pan evaporation values are usually available throughout California and correction coefficients are presented in table 15.1. In areas where current pan evaporation data are not readily available, the average values listed in table 15.1 should provide reasonable estimates for most California locations. To calculate vine water use, multiply the coefficient by the pan values for the desired time period. For example:

where E pan = .34 in/day
K pan = .86
ET kiwifruit = E pan × K pan
ET kiwifruit = (.34 in/day) × (.86) = .29 in/day

Depending on the stage of growth, kiwifruit crop coefficients vary. The most significant plant factor affecting kiwifruit water use is the size of the total leaf area intercepting solar radiation. Thus, the leaf canopy's size, plant density, and stage of leaf development during the season all influence crop water use. Field studies of orchard crops show that ET reaches maximum when 55 to 60 percent of the ground is shaded by canopies at midday. This kind of information is not available for kiwifruit, but assuming that a similar relationship exists, it is safe to say that ET for kiwifruit is about the same at midday with similar shade. In young

Fig. 15.1. U.S. Weather Bureau Class A evaporation pan used to measure evaporation from a free water surface.

Table 15.1. Average daily pan evaporation (Epan), pan coefficients (Kp), and vine evapotranspiration (gallons and inches) for a mature kiwifruit vineyard. Gallons of water per vine per day (GVD) can be determined using the following relationship: GVD=ET(in/day) x vine spacing (ft^2) x .622 (gal/in-ft^2)

Date	Epan (in/day)	Pan coefficient (Kp)	Average vineyard ET (gal/ac/day)	Average vineyard ET (in/day)
May 1–7	.26	.24	1,629	.06
8–14	.27	.34	2,444	.09
15–21	.28	.50	3,802	.14
22–31	.30	.74	5,974	.22
June 1–7	.31	.78	6,517	.24
8–14	.34	.86	7,875	.29
15–21	.34	.86	7,875	.29
22–30	.34	.86	7,875	.29
July 1–7	.34	.86	7,875	.29
8–14	.34	.86	7,875	.29
15–21	.34	.86	7,875	.29
22–31	.32	.86	7,603	.28
Aug 1–7	.30	.86	7,060	.26
8–14	.29	.86	6,789	.25
15–21	.28	.86	6,517	.24
22–31	.26	.86	5,974	.22
Sept 1–7	.24	.86	5,702	.21
8–14	.23	.86	5,431	.20
15–21	.20	.86	4,888	.18
22–30	.18	.86	4,073	.15
Oct 1–7	.15	.86	3,530	.13
8–14	.14	.86	3,258	.12
15–21	.12	.86	2,715	.10
22–31	.09	.86	2,172	.08

Table 15.2. Average daily reference crop evapotranspiration (ET$_0$), crop coefficients (Kc), and vine evapotranspiration (gallons and inches) for a mature kiwifruit vineyard. Gallons of water per vine per day (GVD) can be determined using the following relationship: GVD=ET(in/day) x vine spacing (ft^2) x .622 (gal/in-ft^2)

Date	Average daily ETo (in/day)	Crop coefficient (Kc)	Average vineyard ET (gal/ac/day)	Average vineyard ET (in/day)
May 1–7	.20	.31	1,629	.06
8–14	.21	.44	2,444	.09
15–21	.22	.64	3,802	.14
22–31	.23	.95	5,974	.22
June 1–7	.24	1.00	6,517	.24
8–14	.26	1.10	7,875	.29
15–21	.26	1.10	7,875	.29
22–30	.26	1.10	7,875	.29
July 1–7	.26	1.10	7,875	.29
8–14	.26	1.10	7,875	.29
15–21	.26	1.10	7,875	.29
22–31	.25	1.10	7,603	.28
Aug 1–7	.24	1.10	7,060	.26
8–14	.23	1.10	6,789	.25
15–21	.22	1.10	6,517	.24
22–31	.20	1.10	5,974	.22
Sept 1–7	.19	1.10	5,702	.21
8–14	.18	1.10	5,431	.20
15–21	.16	1.10	4,888	.18
22–30	.14	1.10	4,073	.15
Oct 1–7	.12	1.10	3,530	.13
8–14	.11	1.10	3,258	.12
15–21	.09	1.10	2,715	.10
22–31	.07	1.10	2,172	.08

vineyards, where leaf canopies are expanding, predicting ET using pan data is more difficult because canopy covers vary. Growers with young vineyards should refer to the section on irrigating young vineyards later in this chapter.

ET based upon reference crop water use

To predict crop water requirements, other mathematical formulas have been developed that use temperature, wind, solar radiation, and humidity data to calculate ET (Fig. 15.2). Mathematical predictions are developed in different ways, but they are used the same as pan evaporation data. The major difference is that they predict water use for a reference crop, such as alfalfa or short-growing grass. In California, the trend is toward using short-growing grass reported as ET$_0$. The small zero subscript after ET designates short-growing grass as the reference. Just as Epan values are multiplied by pan (Kp) coefficients to predict vine water use, ET$_0$ values are multiplied by crop (Kc) coefficients to predict vine water use. For example:

Where ET$_0$ = .26
Kc = 1.10
ET kiwifruit = ET$_0$ × Kc
ET kiwifruit = .26 × 1.10 = .29

Notice in the two examples the answers are the same but the values multiplied together differ. The coefficients differ because evaporation from a free water surface is greater than ET from a grass cover crop. To correct for this difference, pan coefficients are smaller than crop coefficients. Research in the southern San Joaquin Valley suggests that pan coefficients can exceed crop coefficients by approximately 24 percent. The important point is that you cannot mix coefficients. Kp values are used for Epan data and Kc values are used for ET$_0$ data. They are not interchangeable. Long-term average ET$_0$ and crop coefficients are shown in table 15.2.

Using evaporation pan data or reference crop data, together with the proper correction coefficients, provides kiwifruit growers with a rapid, accurate, and simple method to predict crop water use.

Soil water storage

Kiwifruit growers using the water budget technique with sprinklers or surface systems need to know how much water is available from the soil moisture reservoir. Determining available water can be difficult due to uncertainties about the depth of vine roots and evaluations of soil textures.

Soil is largely composed of air, water, and solids (organic and mineral). Air and water reside in the pore spaces between soil particles. After a thorough irrigation, the rate of water drainage is rapid as water percolates throughout the soil profile. After several days, the drainage rate declines to a point where the remaining soil moisture is considered stored for root uptake. The point is commonly referred to as field capacity (FC). As soil moisture is removed due to vine transpiration, water content declines and air content increases. Soils with large volumes of pores (fine texture) hold more water than soils with small volumes of pores (coarse texture). The ability of the soil to release water is also a function of pore size. Large pores release water fairly easily, so water held in them is readily available to the vine. As the pore size in soil decreases, water becomes increasingly difficult to extract because more energy is required to move water from small soil pores into the vine.

Eventually, soil moisture levels drop to a point where moisture extraction virtually ceases. There is still water in the soil profile, but it is not available to the kiwifruit vine. This lower limit of soil moisture storage is the permanent wilting point (PWP). The range between FC and PWP is the available water content (AWC).

Because the amount of extractable moisture depends on soil texture, soil scientists have correlated the amount of available soil moisture to soil texture. Estimates of available water per foot of soil for soils of various textures are listed in table 15.3. Notice how clay loams with fine texture and lots of pore space hold more available water compared with sandy soil with limited pore space.

Yield threshold depletion

Although available water represents the amount of moisture that can potentially be extracted by plants, water stress develops before all available water is depleted. The amount of water that can be safely depleted before damage begins is called the yield threshold depletion (YTD). The YTD is the percent of the available water in the root zone that can be extracted without adversely affecting vine growth, productivity, or quality. Specific YTD values are not available for kiwifruit vines; however, experience suggests that YTDs of 50 percent provide an acceptable starting point for scheduling kiwifruit irrigations.

Rooting depth

Given the available water per foot of soil based on soil texture and the safety limits for water extraction (YTD), growers need to determine how much soil the vine is utilizing to calculate how much water can be used safely between irrigations. Vines with deep root systems enjoy more available water and can go longer between irrigations than vines with shallow root systems. For this reason, vines on shallow soils require lighter irrigations more frequently, and deep-rooted vines on deep soils require less frequent, heavier irrigations.

Because plant roots are not readily visible, estimating root depth can be difficult. Researchers in New Zealand have observed rooting depths of 10 feet (3 meters) and moisture extraction at depths exceeding 8 feet (2.4 meters) on deep sand and silt loam soils. In contrast, on shallow soils, roots were restricted to the top 2.3 feet (70 cm) due to unfavorable subsoil conditions. Research on the root depth of California

Fig. 15.2. Typical weather station used to measure weather conditions needed for calculating reference crop evapotranspiration.

Table 15.3. Estimates of available water per foot of soil for soils of various textures

Soil type	Available water (inches depth of water/ foot of soil depth)
Sand	0.5 – 0.7
Fine sand	0.7 – 0.9
Loamy sand	0.7 – 1.1
Sandy loam	0.8 – 1.4
Fine sandy loam	0.9 – 1.6
Loam	1.0 – 1.8
Silt loam	1.2 – 1.8
Clay loam	1.3 – 2.1
Silty clay loam	1.4 – 2.5

kiwifruit vines is limited; however, experience with orchard and vine crops agrees that under favorable subsoil conditions roots will explore deeply. In all likelihood kiwifruit root systems will also be deep if soil conditions are favorable. Experiences with specific vineyard sites usually provide useable estimates of root depth. Where vines have been removed, growers can observe the stumps and get a quick idea of rooting depth. In many cases placing a backhoe pit next to a vine will provide a quick answer. Other growers have used soil moisture measuring devices at sequential depths to evaluate depth of moisture extraction which indicates root activity (see chapter 16, *Measuring Soil Moisture*). Soil physical properties described in soil surveys help evaluate potential rooting depth. Where restrictive layers are present, root depth probably equals the depth to the soil layer or pan. Soil survey descriptions should be verified by on-site observations.

Extractable moisture

The amount of extractable moisture in the root zone can be determined, once you know the texture of the soil, its yield threshold depletion, and its rooting depth. For example, consider a loam soil. According to table 15.3, this soil has an available water content of 1.0 to 1.8 inches. To be on the safe side, assume an average value of 1.4 inches of water per foot of soil. Backhoe pit evaluation indicates a root depth of 3 feet. With a root depth of 3 feet of soil and a requirement of 1.4 inches of water per foot of depth, total available soil moisture is 4.2 inches (1.4 in/ft × 3 ft). Remember, not all of that water can be depleted before moisture stress occurs. Moisture can be safely depleted to the YTD, which is 50 percent or .50. Therefore, the total amount of extractable water is 2.10 inches (4.2 inches × .50).

WHEN AND HOW MUCH TO IRRIGATE

Sprinkler and surface irrigation

Using the information discussed so far, determining when to irrigate involves knowing the amount of extractable soil moisture and how fast it is being depleted. In the previous example, there are 2.10 inches of soil moisture available from soil storage. Daily water use during midsummer, July 1-7 (table 15.2), is .29 inch of water per day. Therefore it will take about 7 days to run out of water (2.10 in/.29 in/day = 7.2 days). On day 7 the soil is dry enough to impair vineyard performance. At this point, the irrigater's goal is to apply the 2.10 inches lost through evapotranspiration. The 2.10 inches is referred to as the net irrigation requirement. It is not, as will become apparent, the actual amount of water that will be applied.

Determining how long to irrigate requires knowledge of how the particular irrigation system performs, its application rate—usually expressed as inches of water per hour—and its known or estimated efficiency. Application rate, the amount of water applied during a given period, depends on the type of system being used and how it is engineered.

When water is applied to a kiwifruit vineyard, water losses cannot be completely eliminated, but they can be minimized with good system design and operation. Water can be lost by runoff, deep percolation, evaporation, and, perhaps, spray drift from sprinklers. In addition, systems with poor uniformity characteristics may overirrigate some areas and underirrigate others. Because not all of the applied water infiltrates the soil, more water is applied to compensate. This is the efficiency consideration. Specific systems, efficiencies, and efficiency measurements are discussed in chapter 14, *Irrigation Systems*.

Well-engineered sprinkler systems usually have application efficiencies in the neighborhood of 70 to 85 percent. That is to say, 70 to 85 percent of the water applied is stored in the root zone. To calculate the gross irrigation requirement, divide the net requirement by the system's efficiency. The previous example's net requirement is 2.10 inches; if the system is 80 percent efficient, then 2.62 inches (2.10/.80 = 2.62 inches) must be applied to refill the soil profile.

The water application rate depends on the system and the location (see chapter 14). If a system delivers two-tenths (.2) of an inch per hour of run time and the gross irrigation requirement is 2.62, the run time can be calculated by dividing the gross irrigation requirement by the application rate. For this example, the system should operate 13 hours (2.62 inches/.20 inches per hour = 13.10 hours) to achieve the necessary soil moisture. Notice that as soil depletions increase, system run times also increase. Long sprinkler sets can encourage disease. If long run times are a problem, readjust yield threshold depletions so that run times are shorter. In essence, irrigate more frequently with less water and less run time.

The same techniques apply to surface systems (flood, furrow, and basin). The drawback is that application rates and efficiencies are more difficult to determine.

Drip irrigation

Scheduling drip irrigations using ET data is similar to scheduling surface systems; soil factors, however, are much less important. Drip irrigation scheduling is essentially independent of soil type or rooting depth. Information about soil moisture is useful for timing irrigation in spring; once irrigations start, however, daily vine water use and system efficiency are the major considerations. Drip systems are usually operated daily to meet individual vine water use. Because virtually all water is supplied directly by the emitter, water from soil storage is not a major factor. Irrigation managers need to know daily vine water use, system application rate, and efficiency. Water use is calculated the same way as for surface systems. For example, if daily water use is 42 gallons per vine per day and efficiency is 90 percent, gross irrigation requirement is more than 46 gallons per vine per day (42 GVD/.90). If the system applies 4 gallons per hour, run time will be 11.5 hours (46 gal/4 gal per hour = 11.5 hours) to supply daily water use.

Microsprinkler irrigation

Because microsprinklers are relatively new, little research exists as to the best way to schedule. One approach: Treat them as large drippers. However, because wetted areas are generally larger with microsprinklers, soil moisture storage is greater; more time, therefore, can elapse between irrigations. Where irrigation is desired every 4 days, daily ET's can be summed up. Given the application rate and the efficiency, the system can run long enough to replace moisture loss due to ET. For example, if for the first 4 days in July vine water use was 42, 44, 43, and 42 gallons per vine per day, accumulated use or net irrigation requirement would be 171 gallons. Assuming a system efficiency of 90 percent, gross irrigation requirement would be 190 gallons (171 gal/.90). If the system's application rate is 10 gallons per hour, run time would be 190 gallons divided by 10 gallons per hour or 19 hours. Take care not to go too many days between irrigations. Such soil moisture measuring devices as tensiometers will insure safety and allow for fine-tuning the system.

IRRIGATING YOUNG VINES

The most significant factor affecting plant water use is the size of the total leaf area intercepting solar radiation. Field studies of orchards show that ET reaches 100 percent when approximately 55 to 60 percent of the ground is shaded by leaf canopy at midday. As a rule of thumb, the percentage of mature orchard ET is approximately twice that of the shaded area. For example, the ET rate of a young orchard shading 30 percent of its floor would be 60 percent of a mature orchard ET. As a first approximation, this relationship may be useful in predicting ET in young kiwifruit vineyards. Using published ET information for young vineyards can be risky because the canopy changes. In a young vineyard, where vines are being trained up the trellis, leaf area is continuously expanding. This expanding leaf area causes a gradual increase in vine water use. Few data exist to document water use of young kiwifruit vines. As a result, water budget techniques tend not to perform well. Perhaps the best solution for young vines is to estimate ET, using the percent ground cover, and then monitor moisture status with tensiometers. Again, data are limited; experience indicates, however, that tensiometers placed in the drip zone in representative locations perform well. Tensiometer depth should accurately represent the root zone. For first-year vineyards, at or near the developing root zone is preferred. Irrigations at soil moisture tensions of 15 to 30 centibars (cb) are appropriate in most cases.

16

Measuring Soil Moisture

HERBERT SCHULBACH

To estimate the amount of moisture in soil, many growers generally "feel" the soil with a shovel, auger, soil tube, or probe. This largely subjective practice has its merits, but often growers overestimate the soil's moisture content. The variety of measuring instruments available can approximate soil moisture conditions, but regardless of the method used, plant response must be correlated.

The shovel, auger, soil tube, and probe (Fig. 16.1) are always useful in evaluating soil moisture, because they allow one to get below the immediate surface. The shovel usually permits one to dig 12 to 15 inches deep. The bucket auger and soil tube, designed to sample soil, are easy to use and allow checking for water tables, winter rainfall storage, and depth of irrigations. The probe, a simple, solid, pointed steel rod with a cross handle, is used to determine depth of water penetration immediately after an irrigation or it is used in gravelly ground that augers and tubes cannot penetrate.

CHOOSING AN INSTRUMENT

Of the numerous instruments developed to measure soil moisture, many have limited effectiveness, reliability, or accuracy. Some are expensive. Two commonly used instruments, acceptable within certain limitations, are the tensiometer and the gypsum electrical resistance block.

To be effective, they require regular servicing and maintenance, in addition to the keeping of good records of readings. They are widely used, particularly where high yields and quality are grower goals and water costs are high. When water is on scheduled delivery, they are less useful because the water must be taken when available.

Tensiometer

A tensiometer is composed of a vacuum gauge connected to a porous ceramic cup by a length of plastic pipe. As the soil in contact with the tube dries, it pulls moisture out of the instrument, causing the suction to be registered on the gauge.

Tensiometers indicate moisture content by measuring soil water tension or suction directly and are best used for irrigation scheduling when moisture is kept in the low suction (high soil moisture—0 to .8 bar or 80 centibars) range; they are not suitable for drier soil moisture levels. Tensiometers are also used to measure excessive moisture and the buildup of a water table. Tensiometers provide continuous readings at the same location, but they require frequent field servicing. In vineyards, they must be protected from freezing and from damage by equipment used, by proper staking or installation of the unit below the surface of the soil, in a box or other enclosure.

Gypsum block

Soil moisture is measured indirectly by the electrical resistance between two electrodes in a small block of gypsum buried in soil. Electrical resistance varies with the amount of water in the gypsum block. In use, gypsum blocks are placed at several soil depths, and wires from them are located at the soil surface so that periodic readings with an electrical-resistance meter

Fig. 16.1. Three tools useful in evaluating soil moisture are the auger (*left*), soil tube (*center*), and probe (*right*).

can be taken. Meter readings can be converted to soil suction values or moisture percent and correlated to plant response. The blocks operate most effectively in the drier soil moisture range (.3 to 10 or 15 bars, depending upon conditions) and can be used to monitor deep soil moisture. They do not give accurate readings in saline-alkaline soil. They deteriorate in 2 to 3 years and have to be replaced, but they require less protection from movement of machinery in the vineyard and from freezing than do tensiometers.

Tensiometers and gypsum blocks have proved useful in scheduling irrigation, solving irrigation problems, and evaluating irrigation practices. Because tensiometers operate in the low suction range, they are more useful in sandy and medium-textured soils. Gypsum blocks may be more useful in heavier-textured soils, which tend to retain more available moisture at the higher suction range. Because of these differences, the two instruments can be used to complement each other for more precise water management.

INSTALLING AN INSTRUMENT

Proper installation of the instrument assures meaningful readings. Correct placement of tensiometers and gypsum blocks depends on soil conditions, size of vine, and the irrigation method used. For each location, install instruments at two depths. Place the upper instrument 12 to 18 inches deep and the lower one 24 to 36 inches deep. It also may be desirable to install a third instrument 48 inches deep to check on deep moisture penetration, water table, or root activity. To make a decision about the site's suitability, depth of placement, and proper interpretation of readings, dig an exploratory hole to observe soil texture and structure, density, compaction, layering, and abrupt changes in physical conditions and water table that may influence water movement and availability.

The number of stations required within the vineyard depends on soil uniformity and how the orchard is managed. At least two stations are needed for areas up to 40 acres. Locations should be in representative areas for determining overall moisture status, with separate stations for problem sites or areas of different soil conditions. Locate instruments within the drip line of the vine.

The instrument's installation should reflect the system being used to deliver water. Placement for one irrigation system may not be suitable for another. Placement for drip irrigation requires locating the instrument near or at a typical emitter. Sprinkler irrigation offers more options for placing the emitter. The same site may not be as accurate for border check systems because opportune times for water to move into the soil are not the same at both ends of the check. Consequently, place installations at two locations, one-third and two-thirds (or one-fourth and three-fourths) of the distance down the check. With the border check, where root distribution is more extensive, gypsum blocks could be installed further out into the drip lines. Placement of instruments on top of the border does not permit monitoring the typical root areas, because the border may reduce soil intake both from sprinkler, rainfall, or gravity irrigation. In placing monitoring equipment to evaluate sprinkler systems, consider the sprinkler's distribution pattern. Locate the monitor where it will receive an average precipitation rate. It should not be in an area of high overlap or in a shadow or missed area. Do not place an instrument next to a vine's trunk, as it is not typical of the root zone. Such placement may offer protection to the instrument, but readings will not be as reliable.

Gypsum blocks. Holes for blocks can be made with augers, soil tubes, or rods; they should be slightly deeper than the desired depth at which the blocks are to rest. A small quantity of a fine mixture of soil and gypsum is added to the bottom of each hole to provide a firm seat for the block.

Before placement, the block is immersed in a container of water and then checked with a meter to see whether a wet reading can be obtained. It then can be pushed to the bottom of the hole with a length of plastic pipe. Wire leads from the block are run through the pipe, with a slight tension on the wire so the block will be held to the end of the pipe. After the block is inserted in the hole, the pipe is carefully removed. The hole is then backfilled, first with a small quantity of soil-gypsum mixture and then with soil; it is packed firmly as it is filled, with care taken not to damage the wire leads.

Adding gypsum to the soil makes the block last longer because gypsum saturates the water with calcium before it moves to and past the block. If the soil is acid, a small quantity of lime may also be mixed into the soil just around the block to prolong its life expectancy. Identify block depths with surface tags or with knots in the wire.

Tensiometers. Tensiometer holes, also made with an auger, soil tube, or rod, should be slightly deeper than the desired depth at which the instruments are to rest; the center of the porous ceramic cup of the tensiometer is the reference point for the desired depth. Place a small quantity of soil at the bottom of the hole; then add just enough water to wet the loose soil and to ensure better contact between soil and cup. (The water also lubricates the hole and reduces potential damage from the soil.) Before installation, add clean water to the instrument and remove air from the porous cup by allowing water to drain through it for several hours with the cap open. An alternative: Use a suction or test pump to pull air from the top of the tensiometer filled with water, while the cup is immersed in water. Tensiometers properly protected from equipment, freezing, or abuse can last many years.

COPING WITH PROBLEMS

Tensiometer soil suction range

The soil suction value selected as the basis for irrigation depends on the type of soil, time of year, vineyard conditions, water supply, and so forth. The same reading on different soils indicates that the suction force holding the water is the same, but it does not mean both soils have the same amount of available water. The amount of water retained or released from the soil at different suctions depends largely upon soil texture.

Although no single soil suction range or values has been widely accepted, suggested ranges or values for irrigating mature kiwifruit vineyards are between 40 and 60 centibars at the 18- to 24-inch depth. Higher values can be used during cool months, and lower readings during hot months, with some allowance made for texture and depth of soil. When a single deep instrument is used, lower values are preferred because soil above the cup tends to be drier. When instruments do not seem to agree with irrigation conditions, check the depth of water penetration to determine whether water has reached the measuring point.

There are several portable, rapid-response tensiometers available which can be used to monitor young plantings. These instruments allow frequent checking of soil moisture over a wide area and in several areas of the root zone. They do not replace the regular tensiometer.

Soil resistance

The interpretation of the resistance readings obtained from gypsum blocks can vary, depending on the source of the blocks and the meters. Blocks are not always similar nor are the scales of different makers of meters similar or equal.

Some precautions

With tensiometers, take several precautions. Low readings on the tensiometer (0 to 10 centibars) may mean that the soil is wet or that the instrument is dry, causing it to break suction. Tensiometers rapidly lose water through the porous cup and become unreliable when soil suction values are above 80 centibars. After irrigation, dry instruments must be serviced by filling them with water and removing air through the top with a suction pump. A zero reading may mean that the instrument is out of water or damaged, or that water did not reach the cup to allow natural refilling of the instrument.

The vine's water requirements, as determined by gypsum blocks or tensiometers, should be compared with estimated or projected water needs based on climatological data. Much information has been developed on seasonal water use of fruit and nut trees. Soil moisture measuring instruments can be used to monitor these seasonal changes to time irrigations properly.

OTHER INSTRUMENTS

The neutron probe, originally a research tool, has gained field acceptance. The probe's unit consists of a radiation source and a meter or recording unit. The radiation source is lowered into an access tube to the desired depth to obtain readings. Because the probe uses a neutron source, the operator is required to be licensed following training. The units are more expensive than other types of instruments. Installation, operation, maintenance, and calibration are more time-consuming and costly.

Other instruments for measuring soil moisture include the penetrometer, which measures resistance to its penetration into the soil; electrical capacitance (sometimes confused with electrical resistance or gypsum blocks); electrothermal methods which measure temperature dissipation in soil; and resistance measuring devices, which use blocks made from ceramic materials, nylon, fiberglass, or materials other than gypsum. Although these units may be suitable under some conditions, there is a lack of experience or research base for these methods.

Instruments developed as an alternative to soil moisture measurement have been only partially successful in scheduling irrigations. These include a pressure bomb that measures the force by which water is held in the leaf; a diffusion porometer that indicates the degree of stomatal opening; and an infrared temperature probe that measures leaf temperature. Basically, these are research instruments or are in a developmental stage.

For more detailed information on instruments or use, refer to UC ANR Publication 21454, *Irrigation Scheduling: A Guide for Efficient On-Farm Water Management*.

CULTURAL CONSIDERATIONS

17

Pollination

ROBBIN W. THORP

Kiwifruit vines are dioecious: Pollen from male (staminate) flowers must be vectored to stigmas of female (pistillate) flowers to produce commercial-sized fruit. Pollen grains are microscopic, light, and can be carried by the wind and thus some pollination can occur without insects. However, in contrast to plants adapted for wind pollination, such as walnut and pistachio, the structure and position of flowers and foliage of kiwifruit vines are ill suited for wind pollination. The inefficiency of wind pollination versus the efficiency of insect pollination in kiwifruit has been substantiated by many observations and experiments in California and New Zealand.

FLOWER BIOLOGY

Flowers of both sexes produce pollen but no nectar; at times, they have a distinct but subtle odor. Pollen is the only reward available to insects visiting kiwifruit flowers. Pollen grains of female flowers are abortive and appear to lack cytoplasm. This raises several questions: Why do insects visit female flowers at all? Are they able to obtain some nutrients from cytoplasmic residues or from lipids on the pollen surface? If not, what attracts them to feed upon this "false reward?" Is the system one of mimicry of male flowers by female flowers relying on mistakes made by pollinators? Research into these questions may provide clues as to whether the system can be manipulated to improve kiwifruit production.

Male flowers have short pedicels, are densely clustered, and are usually open before female flowers (Fig. 17.1). Female flowers are on long pedicels and are often single or with a pair of laterals (Fig. 17.2). Terminal flowers open first. Male flowers are smaller (1 inch in diameter) with about 125 to 185 anthers and about 2 million pollen grains (Fig. 17.3). Female flowers are about 1.5 to 2 inches in diameter and contain about 165 to 200 anthers (Fig. 17.4). Anthers open by

Fig. 17.1. Male flower cluster.   **Fig. 17.2. Female flowers.**   **Fig. 17.3. Closeup of male flower.**   **Fig. 17.4. Closeup of female flower.**

short apical slits. Bumble bees in California and New Zealand vibrate the flowers with an audible buzz, effectively shaking the small, light pollen grains over their hairy body surfaces. This "buzz" pollination by bumble bees and/or carpenter bees is probably the pollination system that originally evolved in *Actinidia* in its native China. The scrabbling behavior of honey bees on the anthers releases sufficient pollen for them to collect.

Female flowers have about 36 styles with long stigmatic grooves apically on the upper surface. The 25 to 40 carpels contain about 2,000 ovules. There is a close relation between fruit size and seed number. About 700 seeds, requiring more than 2,000 pollen grains from male flowers, are needed to produce a fruit of 72 grams. Larger fruit contain about 1,000 to 1,400 seeds. Tiny fruit that have not been adequately pollinated contain 50 to 100 seeds.

ACHIEVING OPTIMUM POLLINATION

Production of a good crop of kiwifruit requires an adequate supply of pollen from male vines to be moved by pollinating insects. There must be sufficient numbers of male vines producing good quality pollen and they must be well spaced through the vineyard. A minimum ratio of male to female vines is 1:8 so that each male vine is surrounded by female vines. Some newer plantings in New Zealand are using ratios of about 1:5 or 1:3 male-to-female vines (see chapter 9, *Vineyard Planning, Design, and Planting*).

Kiwifruit flowers are visited by many insects, especially syrphid flies, small native solitary bees, and bumble bees. None can be relied on to consistently produce commercial crops. Attempts to manage the blue orchard bee, *Osmia lignaria*, in kiwifruit show that the bees visit the flowers effectively and collect pollen for nest provisions, but bee populations have not reproduced well in kiwifruit vineyards.

Honey bees are the only commercially available pollinator for kiwifruit in California. They are rented from beekeepers who provide pollination services and maintain the colonies throughout the year. Although growers usually do not manage or inspect the colonies rented, they should be aware of what a colony is, of the foraging behavior of honey bees, and of the management required for kiwifruit pollination.

HONEY BEE BIOLOGY

Colony organization

The honey bee colony is a perennial social organization having three castes of adults. The queen is the reproductive individual—her prime function is egg laying. The drones (males), of which there may be several hundred, function solely to mate with newly produced queens. The workers (sterile females) perform most of the colony's activities, such as nest construction, maintenance, defense, food gathering and processing, feeding the developing brood, and feeding adult drones and the queen. There are usually 10,000 to 50,000 workers in a colony.

In commercial beekeeping, combs are built in moveable wooden frames and housed in boxes that comprise the bee hive. Brood, honey, and pollen are stored in the combs. The brood consists of eggs and feeding larvae in open cells, postfeeding larvae, pupae, and pre-emerging adults in capped brood cells. The brood is usually located on adjacent frames forming a football-shaped nest. Cells surrounding the brood are usually used to store pollen; honey is stored in cells outside these.

Foraging behavior

Some worker bees collect water to dilute stored honey and to cool the nest; a few collect propolis (a gummy substance used as cement in the hive). Most forage for nectar and pollen, the sole foods for bees. Nectar sugars are concentrated and stored as honey, the principal food of adult bees. Pollen supplies the proteins, fats, vitamins, and other required nutrients, and is converted by nurse bees into brood food. The presence of young brood stimulates foragers to collect pollen.

Bees can forage as far away as 4 miles from their colony, but most foragers tend to stay within a few hundred yards of the colony, if it is in or adjacent to a crop with adequate food rewards. Kiwifruit flowers produce no nectar, so all nectar foraging must occur at other flowers.

Bees foraging for kiwifruit pollen scrabble atop the flowers' anthers and become heavily dusted with pollen. They also have maximum contact with the tips of the stigmas as they work around the anthers of female flowers, and thus transfer pollen effectively (Fig. 17.5).

Fig. 17.5. Honey bee worker forages for pollen on female kiwifruit flower.

Bees exhibit strong tendencies to forage on single vines as long as sufficient pollen is available. Thus, increasing bee density is one way to deplete pollen rapidly. Such depletion may force bees to forage over a larger area and may thus increase cross pollination.

Bees seem to prefer male flowers to female flowers. Pollen loads on hind legs of foragers working male flowers are off-white; those of bees on female flowers are white. Many of the off-white loads contain mixtures of pollen from male and female flowers, demonstrating that the bee had visited both types of flowers during that foraging trip. These can only be distinguished microscopically.

Colony strength (population) is usually measured in terms of numbers of frames covered with worker bees and the total square inches of brood (Figs. 17.6 and 17.7). Flight activity and foraging tend to be related to colony strength. Bees from strong colonies initiate flight at lower temperatures than bees from weak ones, and they exhibit more flight at all temperatures. Queenless colonies usually have no developing brood and therefore little demand for pollen, so foragers from these colonies are usually nectar collectors.

Foraging behavior also is influenced by external factors. Honey bees fly when temperatures are 55°F (13°C) and higher, and they do not fly in rain or in wind stronger than 15 miles per hour. Cloudiness, fog, and mist reduce flight activity, especially near threshold temperatures.

Honey bees visit many plants other than kiwifruit if pollen and nectar rewards are sufficient. Bees placed in a vineyard before kiwifruit bloom may establish foraging areas on earlier-blooming plants. They also shift to other sources as kiwifruit blossoms become less numerous and less rewarding. Bees are highly sensitive to rewards available and may fly to another kiwifruit vineyard or crop where bee density is lower and food is more readily available. Thus, the density of bees and of blooms within a mile or two of a vineyard can greatly influence the number of bees available for pollination.

HANDLING BEE COLONIES

Moving bees into the vineyard

To avoid exposing bees to prebloom pesticides, move colonies into the vineyard during early female bloom, when about 10 percent of the female flowers are in bloom. This will also reduce their visits to competing flowers and to any prebloom pesticides that may have drifted onto them. Bees may need to be moved in earlier if the female bloom seems to be progressing more rapidly than normally, as occurred in the unusually early bloom season of 1992.

Not all colonies need to be moved in at the same time. In fact, there appear to be advantages in moving groups of colonies in at successive intervals. Later introduced colonies seem to have a higher percentage of kiwifruit pollen being brought in by returning foragers than do colonies introduced earlier. This probably is because bees forage only short distances from newly established colonies. Their range increases as the bees become familiar with their surroundings and gain more information about rewards of competing plants in the area. Because the bloom season of kiwifruit is short (3 to 4 weeks), introduce hives at intervals of not more than 4 days apart. It is better to have all hives in early than to miss the bloom in attempting to introduce hives in waves. All hives should be in by 40 percent bloom of female flowers.

Fig. 17.6. One honey bee colony strength measurement is: a frame covered with worker honey bees.

Fig. 17.7. Honey bee colony strength measure: a frame containing about 40 square inches of brood. Y = young brood needing to be fed; C = capped brood; P = pollen stores; H = honey stores.

Colony strength

Strong colonies with developing brood are required for pollination. Flight activity is related to the numbers of bees in a colony and pollen foraging is related to the amount of developing brood. At the time of kiwifruit bloom, beekeepers should be able to provide colonies with eight frames covered by worker bees and four frames with brood.

To ensure that the quantity and quality of rented bees agreed upon are available for pollination, beekeepers should inspect all colonies by the time kiwifruit flowers first appear. As most growers do not feel comfortable inspecting honey bee colonies themselves, they may call in a third party, either a private consultant or a member of the county agricultural commissioner's staff (who handles apiary inspections for bee diseases). This service costs extra, but its availability helps ensure that colonies of the proper quality are being used.

Number of colonies

Recommendations as to the number of colonies per acre are only educated guesses because many variables affect any local situation: colony strength, number of colonies and bees foraging, plant competition within a 2-mile radius (including other kiwifruit vineyards), and weather conditions during bloom. Two to three colonies per acre should supply adequate numbers of bees to kiwifruit blossoms. In seasons when good flight weather is severely limited or there is considerable competing bloom within 2 miles, more hives may be needed. These guidelines are subject to modification with experience under local conditions.

Distribution within the vineyard

Hives should be distributed within the vineyard to provide maximum pollination under the worst weather conditions. However, the extra work required to distribute bees within the vineyard increases the beekeeper's labor costs and usually results in a higher rental fee.

Bees from hives placed around the outside of a vineyard usually cover it adequately, if it is 40 acres or less. Groups of hives can be placed at ¼-mile intervals throughout larger vineyards. Whenever possible, place hives in sunny areas in or around the vineyard to encourage better flight. Avoid placing them where they will be shaded by windbreaks during most of the day.

Protection from pesticides

Bees can be protected from pesticides only by close cooperation among growers, pesticide applicators, and beekeepers. Before choosing a pesticide, see what publications are available from your local farm advisor to help you decide on a pesticide that is least toxic to bees, the formulation to be used, and time of application.

Do not use any pesticides, even those considered nontoxic to adult bees, unless absolutely necessary. Bees foraging in kiwifruit flowers treated with certain pesticides can return with enough chemical to damage the colony. The chemicals may not affect adult bees, but larvae exposed to them may die or develop into malformed adults.

Removing bees

Move bees out of the vineyard as soon as possible after pollination has been completed—usually when 90 percent of the petals have dropped from female flowers and most male flowers are no longer producing viable pollen. By this time, most bees are foraging away from kiwifruit, thus greatly increasing the possibility of becoming exposed to pesticides on other crops.

The written contract

A written contract signed by the beekeeper and grower usually ensures better pollination service. Items to be considered when preparing a contract include dates for moving bees, number of hives and distribution, colony strength, maintenance of bees in good condition for pollination, protection of bees from pesticides, rental fees, and payment schedules.

SUPPLEMENTAL POLLINATION

Various methods of applying supplemental pollen have been tried where weather is not conducive to bee activity for prolonged periods during bloom, where ratios or distribution of male vines are not optimum, or when male vines bloom well ahead of female vines. Most of these involve collecting and processing pollen from male flowers. Male flowers should be collected at the popcorn stage, just before the petals unfold. These are dried at about 80°F (27°C) and 70 percent relative humidity for 12 to 16 hours, then sieved to eliminate other flower parts. A male flower may produce about 9.5 mg of pollen. If not used immediately, pollen can be stored over dry silica gel at 0°F (−18°C) for 1 to 2 weeks without much loss of viability. Quality of pollen is critical to all methods of application.

Hand pollination using male flowers. Use freshly collected, young, newly opened, male flowers. Leave enough of the pedicel to furnish an easy hold and rub in a circular motion against the tips of the styles of female flowers within the first 3 days of opening. One male flower can pollinate five female flowers.

Dusting pollen with atomizers. Pollen collected from male flowers as described above may be applied as a dust with a hand atomizer or similar dusting device. A puff of pollen is aimed at each receptive female flower. This should not be done on rainy days as water quickly destroys pollen.

Spraying liquid suspensions of pollen. Research in New Zealand shows that pollen may be suspended in isotonic liquids for brief periods and still retain viability. Thus, pollen may be applied to female flowers by hand or ground rig sprayers. Pollen collected from male flowers is suspended in the liquid medium immediately before application. Two to three applications at between 30 to 80 percent bloom may be needed. Tests of this method in 1987 in California showed no significant increases in fruit weight or seed number. Weather during kiwifruit bloom in California is usually warmer, drier, and more suitable for pollination by bees than it is in New Zealand. Thus, this method may not be of much benefit in California vineyards.

All of these methods are labor intensive and expensive to apply. Some attempts are being made to mechanize the dust and spray applications to reduce the labor involved.

Entrance pollen inserts on honey bee hives. A device that forces bees to exit the hive through a pollen dust bath coats the bees with male pollen. Those bees visiting female flowers may effectively transfer some of this pollen. This process is less labor intensive, as the bees carry pollen to the female flowers, but someone must keep the inserts filled with pollen during the critical hours of bee foraging.

CULTURAL CONSIDERATIONS

18

Nutrition and Fertilization

JAMES A. BEUTEL, KIYOTO URIU, JOHN POST, AND JAMES PEARSON

In all areas of California, kiwifruit vines require annual applications of nitrogen fertilizer. Other nutrients are generally well supplied to kiwifruit vines by soils whose pH is below 7.2. Where soil pH is higher than 7.2, deficiencies of iron and manganese may occur; these can be corrected by lowering soil pH to below 7.0 with soil sulfur or sulfuric acid, by applying iron chelates in the irrigation water, or by acidifying the irrigation water.

DIAGNOSING NUTRIENT DISORDERS

Poor plant growth, yellow or burned leaves, or nutrient deficiency patterns evident on plants call for a leaf analysis to assess whether nutrient deficiency or excess is the cause. A knowledge of the seasonal pattern of concentration of different elements in the leaves may be helpful in interpreting leaf analysis. In leaves, concentrations of mineral elements change as they emerge, grow to full size, and then senesce in fall. Figure 18.1 shows the generalized shapes of concentration curves of mineral nutrients that can be expected in kiwifruit.

Nitrogen (N), phosphorus (P), zinc (Zn), and potassium (K) start high in concentration, drop rapidly in the first month after emergence of leaves, then remain somewhat steady during summer before dropping rapidly near leaf fall. Magnesium (Mg), manganese (Mn), boron (B), and chloride (Cl) tend to remain constant or only increase slightly during the growing season. However, if boron and chloride are present in the soil in toxic amounts, they will increase greatly during the season and reach their highest levels in the leaves at the end of summer. Calcium (Ca) normally starts low in concentration, accumulates during the season, and reaches its maximum concentration near leaf fall.

Take leaf samples during mid- to late summer when the concentrations of most elements undergo the least change. Critical values for nutrients in kiwifruit leaves (Table 18.1) have been established through experiments and observations based on leaf samples taken during this period. These values show the quantity in percentages (%) or parts per million (ppm) of each element needed in a healthy, productive plant, assuming that the leaves are sampled according to the following directions.

Sample leaves in the July-August-September period; take 25 to 30 leaves from affected plants. Select one mature leaf per shoot that is located just past the fruit on the shoot; on nonbearing vines, choose the fifth or sixth leaf from the base of the shoot. Use the whole leaf blade and petiole (stem of leaf) and take the sample to an analytical laboratory for washing, drying, and analysis. If your leaf analysis results differ from those

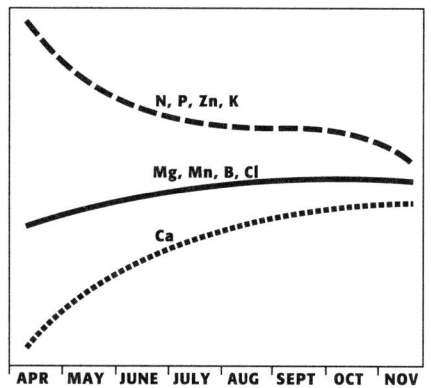

Fig. 18.1. Generalized shapes of concentration curves of mineral nutrients in the leaf during the growing season. Curves show trends, not actual levels.

Table 18.1. Kiwifruit leaf analysis values for California (for July, August, September samples)

Nutrient	Deficient	Low	Adequate	Excess
Nitrogen (N)	<1.6%	1.7–2.1%	2.2–2.8%	>5.0%
Potassium (K)	<1.0%	1.0–1.4%	1.5–2.5%	
Phosphorus (P)	<0.11%		0.13–0.30%	
Calcium (Ca)			2.0–3.6%	
Magnesium (Mg)			0.3–0.8%	
Chloride (Cl)			0.3–1.0%	>1.1%
Manganese (Mn)	<30 ppm		50–200 ppm	
Zinc (Zn)	<13 ppm		15–25 ppm	
Copper (Cu)	<3 ppm		7–14 ppm	
Boron (B)	<25 ppm		25–100 ppm	>200 ppm
Iron (Fe)			not reliable	

shown in table 18.1, correction is advised. How to make these changes is noted here for each critical nutrient.

NITROGEN

Nitrogen, the most important nutrient, tends to be low in California soils and is needed for good cane growth and large fruit crops. Use of nitrogen in California and New Zealand is about 1 pound of actual nitrogen per vine per year or 160 to 180 pounds per acre annually.

Mature vines. Apply about two-thirds of the nitrogen fertilizer needed annually to mature vines in March at budbreak as a broadcast application under the vine canopy. This application gets the kiwifruit vine growing vigorously and provides the nitrogen needed for fruit set in May. A second application of dry nitrogen fertilizer, the remaining one-third needed, is recommended in May to maintain growth of canes and fruit.

Liquid fertilizer applied through the irrigation system can be substituted for dry fertilizer. When applying liquid fertilizer containing nitrogen, use about 10 pounds of actual nitrogen per acre in each application from April through July. Higher rates of approximately 20 pounds of nitrogen per acre per application have injured tender new roots in March and April on sandy soil. Combinations of dry and liquid nitrogen are also satisfactory for kiwifruit.

Leaves and roots of kiwifruit vines seem to be more easily burned by high applications of nitrogen than are other fruit crops growing under similar conditions. When applying dry fertilizer, spread it over the entire root zone, not to a limited area near the trunk, because roots and leaves can be burned when water is applied. Whenever plants are fertilized, they should have good soil moisture. On dry soil irrigate first, then apply fertilizer 1 or 2 days later.

Young vines. Young kiwifruit vines are best fertilized monthly with small amounts of nitrogen fertilizer. In the first year, apply no more than 0.4 ounce of commercial fertilizer (for example, 1 ounce of urea or ammonium nitrate) per plant per month in May, June, and July by spreading the fertilizer in a circle 6 to 12 inches from the trunk. For second-year plants, use 0.8 ounce actual nitrogen once a month in April, May, June, and July. Spread fertilizer in a circular pattern about 12 to 36 inches from the plant. Third- and fourth-year plants may receive 2 to 3 ounces of actual nitrogen every other month from March through July. This is about 30 percent the third year and 50 percent the fourth year of that used annually on fully mature vines. Liquid feeding of nitrogen to young plants on a 2-week to monthly interval can be substituted for dry nitrogen fertilizer. Young plants 1 to 3 years old should not be fertilized with nitrogen after July because nitrogen forces vigorous, late fall growth that is more subject to frost damage than growth on plants not fertilized after midsummer. Once vines bear fruit, the crop tends to suppress late fall growth, causing vines to be less sensitive to fall frost damage.

Late summer and fall fertilization of kiwifruit vines has been a controversial topic between growers and packers. Preharvest kiwifruit fertilization with nitrogen may result in excessive nitrogen uptake followed by poor storage of fruit. Excessive vine growth, resulting in shaded fruit caused by lack of summer pruning and high nitrogen, is a more likely cause of poor fruit storage than late season nitrogen fertilization alone. Postharvest nitrogen fertilization of bearing vines is probably too late in the season to be taken up by the vines and used for the next year's growth. Winter fertilization is not recommend since roots are dormant and the nitrogen can be leached by winter rains.

Experiences with nitrogen fertilization in California and New Zealand have resulted in remarkably similar recommendations, even though the recommendations were developed independently. This similarity would indicate that vine needs for nitrogen are much alike in both regions.

CHLOROTIC VINES

Kiwifruit vines can show yellow leaves with green veins (**plates 2** and **3**). Usually these plants need iron but fail to take up adequate quantities because the soil pH is over 7.2. Correct this problem by lowering soil pH to below 7.0, and then maintain pH in the acid range by applying about 2 to 3 or more tons of sulfur per acre. During the following 12 months the pH in the top soil will be lowered, and often plants will have normal green leaves the next year. This disorder can also be corrected by applying iron chelates to the irrigation water through drip or microsprinklers at rates of 5 to 10 pounds per acre in one or two applications per season. If irrigation water has a pH of 7.8 or higher, due to high bicarbonate content, adding acid to irrigation water lowers the water's pH and helps reduce soil pH, thus making iron more available to the plant. Several acids and acidified products are commercially available. The earlier in the growing season corrective treatments are applied, the sooner the response. Adding chelates to soil around yellow plants (about 1 pound per plant) may work for a year or so, but benefits are short lived.

Sprays of iron generally have not been satisfactory in correcting yellow or chlorotic leaves of kiwifruit. Zinc deficiency in kiwifruit, rare in California, could be corrected by zinc chelate soil treatment through the irrigation system.

POTASSIUM

Potassium deficiency occurs in bearing kiwifruit vineyards in the Sacramento Valley, where soils are low in potassium or high in magnesium. Symptoms include marginal leaf burn and upward rolling of leaves. Small-sized fruit are not usually due to low potassium but to insufficient pruning or poor irrigation practices. Before treating vines, a grower suspecting potassium deficiency should have leaf samples analyzed, following directions given earlier in this chapter.

Treatment may be either adding potassium to the liquid feeding program during the season to give about 350 pounds of K_2O per acre (700 pounds K_2SO_4) or soil applications of potassium sulfate at a rate of 4 to 5 pounds per vine applied in bands on top of the soil after leaf fall. (Caution: A single, concentrated, soil application during spring and summer may injure roots and plants on sandy soils.) Relative effectiveness of potassium treatments on kiwifruit vines deficient in potassium is not well known because experiences in California have been limited. Applying potassium in drip or microsprinkler irrigation or in bands on the soil surface, using potassium sulfate like that used for trees, is likely to give best results.

Do not use potassium chloride (muriate of potash) on kiwifruit because they are sensitive to excessive chloride. Use of potassium fertilizer on normal kiwifruit vineyards may be beneficial, but it is expensive and may have minimal or no value for increasing fruit size or improving storage.

OTHER NUTRIENT DEFICIENCIES

Magnesium deficiency symptoms appear as yellow areas between the veins on leaves as well as yellow edges. They may show on young, fast-growing vines but will disappear the next year. Excessive applications of potassium to the soil may induce magnesium deficiency, but it is not common in California vineyards.

Calcium deficiency could cause fruit and storage disorders, but evidence thus far of calcium-induced storage disorders in kiwifruit has been inconclusive. Sulfur, copper, and phosphorus deficiencies are unknown in California kiwifruit.

Boron deficiency is uncommon in California kiwifruit but would greatly reduce shoot growth and could be corrected with about an ounce of borax per plant on mature vines as a soil treatment or by applying a foliar boron spray. Leaf levels below 25 ppm would indicate a deficiency of boron.

Manganese deficiency, also uncommon in California, occurs when leaf levels fall below 30 ppm and is characterized by yellowing between main lateral veins (**plate 4**).

TOXIC ELEMENTS

Excesses in total salts, chloride, or boron alone will cause leaf burn and defoliation, and may seriously damage plant growth and production. Leaf, soil, and water analysis in summer and fall can confirm which elements are in excess and probably the source of the problem. Leaf analysis will also separate leaf burn due to water or heat stress (**plate 5**), excess nitrogen, potassium deficiency, etc., from that due to excesses of the other elements mentioned.

Chloride in water, soil, or fertilizer causes marginal and interveinal leaf burn and shows at levels of more than 1.1 percent in mature leaves in California (**plate 6**). Correction may be difficult, but it usually involves leaching the soil with low-chloride water. If chloride levels are high in irrigation water, it may be necessary to change the source of water for irrigation. New Zealand researchers claim that some chloride benefits kiwifruit, but limited California observations show that leaf burn caused by excess chloride harms vines. Water with more than 2.5 meq per liter of chloride or 100 ppm chloride injures kiwifruit and causes leaf burn and reduced production.

Boron toxicity causes interveinal and marginal burning of kiwifruit leaves in late summer and fall (**plate 7**). Leaf levels over 130 ppm may suggest boron problems; 200 ppm boron or higher signifies serious trouble. Experience shows that irrigation water with more than 0.5 ppm boron causes boron toxicity. The exact degree of injury to fruit production or keeping-quality of fruit from excess boron has not yet been demonstrated in California. Boron toxicity is usually traced to irrigation water. Where a change of water source is possible, it should be made to reduce boron content.

CULTURAL CONSIDERATIONS

19

Frost Sensitivity and Protection

RICHARD L. SNYDER

Little is known about the frost sensitivity of kiwifruit. Research in New Zealand has shown that dormant shoots are undamaged by temperatures as low as 14°F (–10°C). When spring growth begins, susceptibility to frost damage increases.

In the New Zealand tests, growing shoots were cut and placed in a freezing chamber and the temperature was lowered 1.8°F (1°C) per hour after a 1-hour equilibration at 32°F (0°C). The approximate percentages of flower buds killed during each half hour are given in table 19.1. Longer exposure at damaging temperatures (below 29.3°F [–1.5°C]) increased the percentage of bud kill. Two hours at 28.4°F (–2.0°C) caused nearly 70% bud kill, whereas 30 minutes caused approximately 40 percent bud kill. At 29.3°F (–1.5°C), almost no damage occurred until after 3 hours. The effects of freezing temperatures after small fruit are formed are unknown. For most crops, small fruit are the most sensitive. How sensitive kiwifruit are to autumn frosts before harvest is unknown.

UNDERSTANDING FROST EVENTS

Types of frost events

There are two types of frosts: advection and radiation. An "advection frost" or "freeze" occurs when a cold air mass moves into an area and replaces a warm air mass. Advection frosts are characterized by wind speeds greater than 4 miles per hour, low humidity, and temperatures that often stay below 32°F (0°C), even during daylight hours. Advection frosts are difficult to protect against with any known methods. Fortunately, large-scale advection frosts are rare in California.

"Radiation frost" occurs when skies are clear, winds are calm, and humidity is low. In radiation frosts, cold air does not move in and replace warmer air; rather, the existing air mass cools as energy (heat) is radiated to the sky. Radiation frosts occur frequently in California, but in most cases it is possible to protect kiwifruit from damage.

Table 19.1. Percentage bud kill on cut growing kiwifruit shoots resulting from cooling at 1.8°F per hour after equilibrating for 1 hour at 32°F*

Time	Temperature range		Buds killed
(minutes)	(°F)	(°C)	(%)
0 to 30	32.0 to 31.1	0.0 to –0.5	0
30 to 60	31.1 to 30.2	–0.5 to –1.0	0
60 to 90	30.2 to 29.3	–1.0 to –1.5	0
90 to 120	29.3 to 28.4	–1.5 to –2.0	10
120 to 150	28.4 to 27.5	–2.0 to –2.5	70
150 to 180	27.5 to 26.6	–2.5 to –3.0	95
180 to 210	26.6 to 25.7	–3.0 to –3.5	100

*After Hewett, E. W., and K. Young. 1981. Critical freeze damage temperatures of flower buds of kiwifruit (Actinidia chinensis Planch). N.Z. J. Agric. Res., 24:73–75.

Predicting temperatures

National Weather Service (NWS) fruit-frost meteorologists forecast minimum temperatures using local models, large-scale weather forecast models, upper air data, climatology, and experience. With considerably more information and experience than the average grower, the NWS can forecast minimum temperatures with greater accuracy. Often management practices done before a frost night can reduce the need for protection, so closely monitor NWS 1- to 3-day forecasts during frost season.

In locations where a local NWS forecast is not available or it does not accurately represent a site's microclimate, the following technique can be used to predict nighttime temperature changes.

Minimum temperatures during radiation frosts are predictable using equation 1 from Charles C. Allen, a former NWS fruit-frost meteorologist (Allen, C. C. 1957. A simplified equation for minimum temperature prediction. *Mon. Wea. Rev.* 85:119-120).

$$Tm = Tw - \tfrac{1}{4}(Ta + 16) \qquad (1)$$

where
Tm = forecasted minimum temperature (°F)
Tw = wet-bulb temperature (°F) at 4:45 p.m. PST
Ta = dry-bulb (air) temperature (°F) at 4:45 p.m. PST

Wet-bulb and dry-bulb temperatures are measured with a psychrometer (Fig. 19.1), which is commercially available. Table 19.2 gives sample data and predicted minimum temperatures. Under clear, calm conditions, equation 1 is reasonably accurate, but do not use it during cloudy, foggy, or windy weather. It may also be inaccurate where cold air drains into a vineyard from surrounding mountains and hills.

In addition to forecasting the minimum temperature, it can be used to predict the change in temperature during a radiation frost night. The following equations provide reasonably accurate temperature estimates overnight.

$$T_i = T_o - b\sqrt{i} \qquad (2)$$

where
T_i = temperature at time i after sunset (°F)
T_o = temperature at sunset (°F)
i = time after sunset (hours)
and

$$b = (T_o - T_m) \div \sqrt{h} \qquad (3)$$

where
T_m = the predicted minimum temperature (°F)
h = time from sunset to sunrise (hours)

Using a forecasted minimum temperature from the NWS or equation 1 and equations 2 and 3, one can predict the temperature at any time during a radiation frost night with reasonable accuracy. Equation 1 is used to predict the minimum temperature, only if an NWS forecast is not available or if it does not represent the vineyard microclimate. Equations 2 and 3 are used to predict when the temperature will fall to a specific level. This prediction is useful to estimate when to start sprinklers.

If wind speed increases to more than 4 miles per hour, skies become cloudy, or fog forms, the temperature drop will slow or stop and equations 1, 2, and 3 will give inaccurate results. Also, cold air drainage from upslope into a vineyard will cause the temperature to drop more quickly than predicted. If the wind is blowing faster than 4 miles per hour and the temperature still drops, an advection, rather than radiation, frost is happening. This sometimes occurs on a local scale with severe cold drainage that begins after a shift in wind direction. Thus, to improve future forecasts, note any wind speed and direction changes on severe frost nights.

Energy transfer

The four methods of energy (heat) transfer involved in frost protection are (1) radiation, (2) conduction, (3) convection, and (4) latent heat.

Radiation. The heat or energy you feel when you stand in sunlight or near a fire is radiation. It is the transfer of electromagnetic energy from one point to another. As the temperature of an object or the air increases, the energy radiated increases even more. For example, because it is hotter, the sun radiates considerably more energy than does the earth.

Radiation affects frost protection partly because solar radiation is the source of energy that is stored as heat in the soil, crop, and air during the day. At night, radiation upward from the crop and soil to the sky is the main way that energy is lost. Because the sky has a temperature, there is also downward radiation. A clear sky is colder than the ground, so there is a net loss of energy in the absence of clouds or fog at night. Under cloudy or foggy skies, ground and sky have nearly equal temperatures and the radiation downward equals that upward. Consequently, there is little or no net loss of energy and air temperature does not change much under these conditions.

Conduction. This is a mechanism of heat transfer where energy is transferred from molecule to molecule in contact with one another without movement of the material. An example of conductive heat transfer is the movement of heat through a metal rod when the end

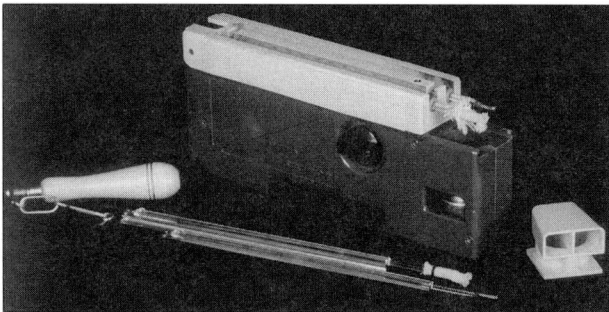

Fig. 19.1. Sling *(lower)* and aspirated *(upper)* psychrometers for measuring wet-bulb and dry-bulb temperatures.

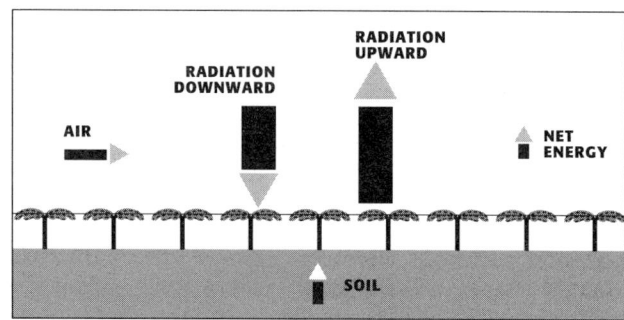

Fig. 19.2. Typical nighttime energy transfers under clear sky, low winds. The volume of each arrow indicates relative amounts of energy from each source.

is placed in a fire. Heat will conduct through the rod and eventually burn your hand. This is the main mechanism in soil heat transfer.

Convection. The energy transfer, where the air moves from one location to another, is called convection. When warm air passes a colder leaf, heat is transferred from the air to the leaf. Similarly, if the air is colder than a leaf, heat is transferred from the leaf to the air. In frost protection, natural convection occurs when warm air, which is less dense (lighter) than cold air, rises, and the cold heavy air settles to the ground. This heat transfer mechanism causes cold air to drain to low spots, just as water flows downhill. Convection also occurs when energy is released by sprinkler irrigation onto a vineyard floor. This warms air near the ground and the warmer air convects upward into the vines.

Latent heat. Air containing water vapor has two kinds of heat: "sensible" and "latent." Sensible heat is heat that you can feel (sense) and it is measured with a thermometer. Latent heat is chemical energy stored in water. When water condenses or freezes, latent heat is released and changes to sensible heat, causing the temperature of the nearby environment to rise. To melt or evaporate water, heat must be applied from the nearby environment. The heat supplied, sensible heat, is converted to latent heat during melting or evaporation. As sensible heat is changed to latent heat, the temperature falls.

The total heat stored in air is the sum of both sensible and latent heat. This is partly why freezing temperatures are less likely to occur on nights with high dewpoint temperatures. When the air temperature nears dewpoint temperature, water begins to condense as dew or freeze as "white" frost on the surface. This changes large amounts of latent heat to sensible heat and slows the temperature drop.

Energy budgets on a radiation frost night

Energy transfers determine how much heat is lost and how low the temperature falls on a frost night (Fig. 19.2). Heat from the soil conducts to the surface where it is radiated to the crop, air, and sky. Heat is also transferred from air to the vines (sensible heat transfer) as it passes through a vineyard. In addition, the sky radiates energy downward to the crop and soil, depending on the sky temperature. Table 19.3 shows a typical energy balance for citrus during a radiation frost night. The energy balance for kiwifruit is similar. Energy transfer values vary depending on site-specific conditions, but generally the net loss is on the order of 18 watts per square meter (4,144 British thermal units [Btu] per minute per acre). This number identifies how much heat is needed for protection.

Table 19.2. Sample data and calculated minimum temperature predictions using Allen's equation (Eq. 1)

Ta (°F)	Tw (°F)	Tm (°F)
50	50	33.5
50	45	28.5
50	40	23.5
50	35	18.5

Table 19.3. Nighttime energy balance in a citrus orchard*

Energy	Watts/sq. meter	(Btu/min)/acre
Energy from soil	+28	+6,446
Energy from air	+39	+8,978
Downward radiation	+230	+52,946
Upward radiation	−315	−72,513
Net energy loss	−18	−4,143

*Unpublished data from Bartholic and Associates reported by Mee, T. R., and J. F. Bartholic. 1979. Man-made fog. Modification of the aerial equipment of crops. B. J. Barfield, and J. F. Gerber, eds. American Soc. of Agric. Eng., St. Joseph, Michigan. pp. 334–352.

PASSIVE FROST PROTECTION

Site selection

Passive frost protection is management performed before a frost event to reduce the potential for damage. The most effective passive protection is choosing a good place to plant. If new property is being planted, first check climate records for the frequency of freezing temperatures during bloom and before harvest. If the frequency of freezing is high, consider as an alternative a crop with later bloom and/or earlier harvest.

Often, climate data are not available where a new planting is planned. In these cases, avoid planting in low-lying areas where cold air can settle (Fig. 19.3). To identify these cold spots, determine whether shallow

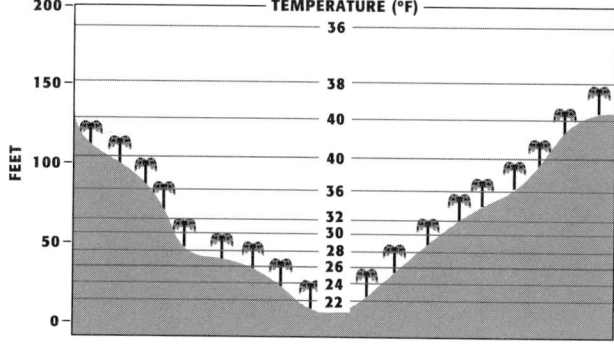

Fig. 19.3. With cold air drainage, cold air flows downslope and settles in the low spots.

ground fogs form there frequently. Ground fogs tend to form first in low-lying areas.

Generally, in a frost-prone area, the best place to plant is on a hill's north-facing slope, because cold air drains to the bottom. On north-facing slopes bloom is slightly delayed. Because the probability of frost drops rapidly in spring, a delay in bloom is beneficial in frost-prone locations. Avoid planting where cold air drainage will be blocked and ponded into the vineyard. Remove brush, trees, and other materials that block the downslope drainage of cold air from a vineyard.

Ground cover management

Ground cover management affects frost protection. Ideally, the ground should be bare, firm, and moist. Never cultivate the ground immediately before or during frost protection periods. Cultivation loosens the soil and increases air spaces that insulate against heat transfer and storage. It also causes more evaporation, which reduces daytime sensible heat storage in the soil.

It is best to have no floor vegetation during frost-sensitive periods. If vegetation is necessary, mow it short, either mechanically or chemically, and remove cuttings if possible. Living or cut vegetation inhibits sunlight penetration to the surface and reduces heat storage in soil. When heat storage is less, minimum surface temperatures will be lower and frost damage more likely.

The exact amount of protection provided by maintaining bare soil or short ground cover is difficult, if not impossible, to predict because of microclimate differences. In some cases, good management can make the difference between saving or losing a crop. There are many examples where a grower let the ground cover grow tall or cultivated and lost a crop to frost damage.

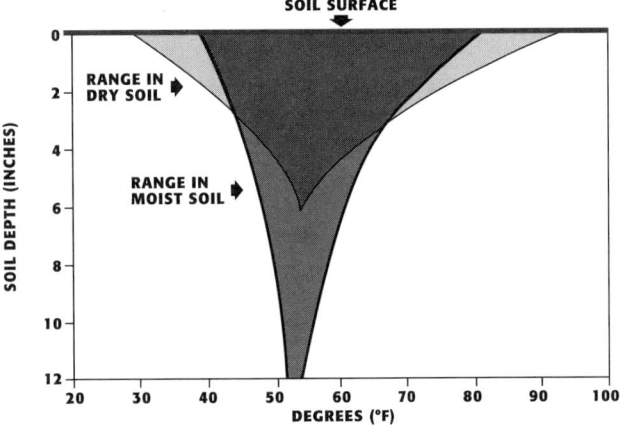

Fig. 19.4. Diurnal temperature ranges with depth for a dry and a wet soil.

Water content in the top foot of soil affects frost protection. Dry soil contains many air spaces and air is a good insulator against heat transfer by conduction. Air also has a low heat capacity, so it cannot store much energy. Water is a good heat conductor and has a high heat capacity, so adding water to fill air spaces in dry soils increases heat transfer and storage.

By adding water and increasing heat transfer and storage, the daily temperature range at the surface is less and the temperature range deep in the soil is greater (Fig. 19.4). A higher minimum soil surface temperature provides more protection because radiation and convection from the soil to the air and crop are greater overnight. The soil surface minimum temperature is higher for a moist soil because more solar heat is transferred and stored during daylight and, thus, more heat is available from below to keep the surface warm at night.

Water content mainly affects heat transfer and storage in the top 1 foot of soil, so deeper irrigation is unnecessary. Maintain the top 1 foot of soil near field capacity during frost-prone periods. For very dry sandy soils, apply no more than 1-inch depth (27,000 gallons per acre). For a very dry heavy clay, 2-inch depth is the maximum needed. Other very dry soils fall between these extremes. Less dry soils require smaller applications.

Note that bare ground can be colder than a vineyard floor with cover following several days of wind that dries the surface layer of soil. In this situation, rewet the soil surface. National Weather Service fruit frost forecasters predict when winds are likely to stop; use their forecasts to time rewetting the surface. Rewet bare soil at least 1 day before a predicted frost night following or during strong winds.

Chemical frost protection

There is evidence that frost damage can be avoided by reducing concentrations of ice-nucleating bacteria on some crops. At this time, use of chemicals to control bacteria concentration for frost protection of kiwifruit is not recommended. More research is needed to confirm if bacterial control is effective.

Use of chemicals to reduce transpiration has been proposed as a method of frost protection. There is no scientific evidence that this method works.

Windbreaks

Windbreaks may or may not help with frost protection, depending on local factors. (See chapter 9, *Vineyard Planning, Design, and Planting*.) If sprinklers are used, windbreaks reduce evaporation and can be beneficial. If no active protection is practiced, windbreaks can trap cold air in a vineyard or they can move cold air around a vineyard, depending on local topography. If a windbreak blocks the flow of cold air drainage out of a vineyard, remove it. If a windbreak causes cold air to move around a vineyard, it is beneficial.

ACTIVE FROST PROTECTION

Using surface water

Flood irrigation has been used for frost protection of some crops where water is available on demand. When using surface water, the objective is to avoid ice formation during the night. As long as the water does not freeze, the vineyard floor temperature will not fall below 32°F (0°C). This increases both radiation and convection from the surface to the crop and protects it. Ice formation blocks the transfer of heat from the liquid water below it, and the ice will cool to below 32°F.

When using surface water for frost protection, run the water across the field as quickly as possible without causing erosion. Remove tail water from the field or the water will cool too long and ice will form.

Concentrate surface water under the kiwifruit when flooding a vineyard. Radiation and convection from surface water are predominantly upward, and the benefit comes from interception of this energy by the plants. Radiation and convection in the middles mainly go up to the sky. Spread the water as widely as possible under the plants. Radiant energy from the water is emitted per unit surface area, so wetting more surface area means gaining more heat for the vines. Start surface water early enough so that the water reaches the end of the field before the critical damage temperature is reached. Stop it after sunrise when the air temperature exceeds 32°F.

Wind machines and heaters

Wind machines and heaters are not used extensively for frost protection of kiwifruit. Spring and fall temperature inversions in California's Central Valley are usually weak, so the two methods are sometimes not effective. In small valleys with cold air drainage, the two methods may provide good protection.

Temperature inversions are needed to effectively use wind machines or heaters. In both methods, the main benefit comes from vertical mixing of air near the vineyard. This prevents the formation of an inversion if the methods are started before the inversion forms (before the temperature near the floor becomes colder than the air above the vineyard). Stop wind machines or heaters when the temperature inversion upwind from the vineyard dissipates after sunrise.

Both heaters and wind-machine fans are effective when located below the top of the temperature inversion. They do not help if located on the sides of hills above the inversion. Also, if heaters are too hot, the rising warm air breaks through the inversion top and reduces effectiveness.

Under-plant sprinklers, foggers, or misters

When using under-plant sprinklers for frost protection, latent heat, radiation, and convection are the heat transfer mechanisms involved. Latent heat is released when water freezes, which increases the sensible heat content of the orchard floor and raises its temperature. If adequate water is supplied so that the heat released by freezing is greater than that lost through evaporation, a liquid-ice mixture will be present and the wet surface temperature will stay at or above 32°F (0°C). This results in greater radiation and convection of heat from the surface to the crop relative to an unprotected orchard.

When using under-vine sprinklers, foggers, or misters for frost protection, evaporation rates determine effectiveness. As sprinkler water cools and freezes, latent heat is released, sensible heat increases, and air temperature rises. At the same time, evaporation removes sensible heat and causes the temperature to fall. Some protection is provided as long as the release of heat from freezing is greater than the loss from evaporation. The amount of protection afforded depends on the evaporation rate, distribution of wetted surfaces, application uniformity, influx of cold air, inversion strength, vine canopy development, and other factors. Assuming calm winds, if the release of heat through cooling and freezing is greater than the evaporative loss plus 18 watts per square meter, the temperature of the wetted surface will not fall.

Under mild radiation frosts, low-application-rate under-plant sprinklers provide protection. A mild radiation frost typically has wind speeds less than 2 miles per hour and dewpoint temperatures above 28°F (−2.2°C). With lower dewpoints or greater wind speeds, evaporation increases and a higher application rate is required. Although the weather conditions are not well defined, there is a point when heat loss from evaporation will be greater than that supplied by freezing. Thus, with some high wind and/or low dewpoints, a low application rate may be detrimental.

Over-vine sprinklers

Many of the principles applied to under-vine sprinklers also apply to over-vine sprinklers. The main difference is that much of the protection comes from direct release of latent heat directly to the vines as water coating the plants freezes. As long as a liquid-ice mixture is maintained on the vines, they are protected. If all the water freezes, vine temperatures can drop below that of unprotected plants.

When the weather is severe, over-vine sprinkler protection is better than that of under-vine sprinklers. However, proper management must be employed to insure protection, including starting and stopping at the proper temperature and using an adequate application and sprinkler rotation rate. A dependable water supply that allows for simultaneous application to all the plants is required.

Table 19.4 gives application rates that are recommended, depending on wind speed and the temperature of an unprotected leaf. A sprinkler-head rotation rate of 30 to 60 seconds provides adequate protection. When the weather is more severe than the system can deliver, do not use over-vine sprinklers. In these situations, the temperature of the ice-covered vines can drop as low as the wet-bulb temperature, which is usually less than the air temperature.

Start and stop sprinklers when the wet-bulb temperature is higher than the critical damage temperature. Otherwise, damage can occur in spite of sprinkler operation all night. To assure no damage to vines, turn the system on or off when the wet-bulb temperature is above 32°F. Measure the wet-bulb temperature with a commercially available psychrometer (Fig. 19.1). Because sprinkler operation affects measurements downwind, take the wet-bulb temperature measurement upwind of your vineyard.

If a psychrometer is not available, a regional dewpoint temperature from the NWS may be used. Although there is some variability in dewpoints within a region, the dewpoint temperature can be used with reasonable accuracy in many cases. Assuming a barometric pressure of 29.52 inches of mercury (1,000 millibar), table 19.5 is used to estimate wet-bulb temperature from dewpoint and air temperature. This method is less accurate than directly measuring wet-bulb temperature, so it may be wise to start and stop at slightly higher values.

Table 19.4. Estimated sprinkler rates (inches per hour) for cold protection for an 0.8-inch diameter leaf with the indicated temperature for an unprotected leaf*

Temp. (°F)	Wind speed (mph)					
	1.1	2.2	3.4	4.5	5.6	6.7
	(inches per hour)					
28.4°	0.06	0.07	0.09	0.11	0.12	0.13
26.6°	0.08	0.11	0.14	0.16	0.17	0.19
24.8°	0.11	0.15	0.19	0.21	0.23	0.25
23.0°	0.14	0.19	0.23	0.26	0.29	0.31
21.2°	0.17	0.23	0.28	0.31	0.35	0.38
19.4°	0.20	0.27	0.32	0.37	0.41	0.44

* These rates assume 100% distribution uniformity of the sprinkler system. For lower values of uniformity (see chapter 14), divide the indicated rates by the percent uniformity.

Adapted from Gerber, J. F., and J. D. Martsolf. 1979. Sprinkling for frost and cold protection. In: Modification of the aerial environment of crops. B. J. Barfield, and J. F. Gerber, eds. American Soc. of Agric. Eng., St. Joseph, Michigan. pp. 327–333.

Table 19.5. Wet-bulb temperatures corresponding to air and dewpoint temperatures for a barometric pressure of 29.53 inches of mercury (1,000 mb)

Dew-point temperature (°F)	Air temperature (°F)									
	32°	33°	34°	35°	36°	37°	38°	39°	40°	41°
	(°F)									
32	32.0	32.6	33.2	33.8	34.3	34.9	35.5	36.1	36.6	37.2
31	31.6	32.2	32.8	33.4	34.0	34.5	35.1	35.7	36.2	36.8
30	31.2	31.8	32.4	33.0	33.6	34.2	34.8	35.3	35.9	36.4
29	30.8	31.4	32.0	32.6	33.2	33.8	34.4	35.0	35.5	36.1
28	30.5	31.1	31.7	32.3	32.9	33.5	34.0	34.6	35.2	35.8
27	30.1	30.7	31.3	32.0	32.5	33.1	33.1	34.3	34.9	35.4
26	29.8	30.4	31.0	31.6	32.2	32.8	33.4	34.0	34.6	35.1
25	29.4	30.1	30.7	31.3	31.9	32.5	33.1	33.7	34.3	34.8
24	29.1	29.8	30.4	31.0	31.6	32.2	32.8	33.4	34.0	34.5
23	28.8	29.4	30.1	30.7	31.3	31.9	32.5	33.1	33.7	34.3
22	28.5	29.1	29.8	30.4	31.0	31.6	32.2	32.8	33.4	34.0
21	28.2	28.9	29.5	30.1	30.7	31.3	31.9	32.5	33.1	33.7
20	28.0	28.6	29.2	29.8	30.5	31.1	31.7	32.3	32.9	33.4
19	27.7	28.3	29.0	29.6	30.2	30.8	31.4	32.0	32.6	33.2
18	27.4	28.1	28.7	29.3	29.9	30.5	31.2	31.8	32.4	33.0
17	27.2	27.8	28.4	29.1	29.7	30.3	30.9	31.5	32.1	32.7
16	26.9	27.6	28.2	28.8	29.5	30.1	30.7	31.3	31.9	32.5
15	26.7	27.3	28.0	28.6	29.2	29.8	30.5	31.1	31.7	32.3
14	20.3	20.6	20.9	21.3	21.6	21.9	22.2	22.5	22.7	23.0
13	19.8	20.2	20.5	20.8	21.1	21.4	21.7	22.0	22.3	22.6
12	19.4	19.7	20.0	20.4	20.7	21.0	21.3	21.6	21.9	22.2
11	19.0	19.3	19.6	19.9	20.2	20.6	20.9	21.2	21.5	21.8
10	18.5	18.9	19.2	19.5	19.8	20.2	20.5	20.8	21.1	21.4

SUMMARY OF RECOMMENDATIONS

1. Avoid planting in low spots. Like water, cold air drains downhill and will fill in a low spot like a lake.

2. The probability of freezing temperatures drops rapidly in spring, so delaying bloom reduces the potential for damage. Planting on north slopes delays bloom.

3. Remove brush, trees, other vegetation, solid fences, and small buildings that block cold air drainage from a vineyard.

4. Clear the vineyard floor of vegetation, and keep it firm and moist. Do not cultivate during frost season. Do not let the soil surface or top foot of soil dry out. The soil water content below the top foot has little impact on frost protection. However, the top foot should be moist. After several days of strong dry winds, rewet the soil surface.

5. Chemicals to reduce bacteria concentration are still being studied as a method of frost protection. Further study is needed before their use is recommended.

6. Chemicals to reduce plant transpiration are not known to be effective for frost protection of kiwifruit.

7. Windbreaks that trap cold air within a vineyard are detrimental. Windbreaks that move cold air around the outside of a vineyard are beneficial.

8. When using surface irrigation for frost protection, keep the water flowing to prevent ice from forming on the surface. Concentrate surface water under the vines where the heat will radiate or convect up into the vines.

9. Under-vine sprinkler rate requirements for frost protection are mainly determined by evaporation rates (higher wind speed and low humidity increase the rate requirements). Design your sprinkler system rates based on weather records. Low application-rate sprinklers provide protection but higher rates are better.

10. Over-vine sprinklers provide more protection than under-vine sprinklers during radiation frosts; however, there is more risk of damage during advection frosts (windy conditions). Rate requirements are given in table 19.4.

11. Start and stop sprinklers when the wet-bulb temperature is above the critical damage temperature. Starting or stopping at lower temperatures can result in damage, even when sprinklers are operated all night.

12. Wind machines provide frost protection if an inversion is present. Start and stop wind machines when the temperature within a vineyard is still higher than that above the vineyard.

13. Use heaters for frost protection, but keep fires small. Locate them in low spots and below the top of the inversion.

PEST MANAGEMENT

20

Weed Control

CLYDE L. ELMORE AND BILL B. FISCHER

Kiwifruit vines are susceptible to competition from weeds at any time, but particularly when newly planted. Weeds compete directly with the vines for water and nutrients. They also hinder harvesting, can attract insects or rodents if allowed to grow around trunks, and may present a fire hazard if allowed to dry.

Kiwifruit vines are most frequently planted on flat ground and trained to a trellis. Sometimes, however, they are planted on berms. Either type of planting prohibits cross discing; thus, controlling weeds is limited to between vine rows with row plows or power-driven tillers with tripping mechanisms. If irrigation water is applied by sprinkler or low-volume emitters, with permanent berms in the vine row, weeds can be mowed or flailed between the rows and chemical weed control used on a narrow band down the vine row. Mulches or organic materials can be used in strips down berms but must be replenished as they break down.

WEED SPECIES

Both annual and perennial weed species are found in kiwifruit vineyards. Annual plants germinate, grow, flower, and produce seeds in one season. Winter annuals germinate in fall, grow during winter, and flower and go to seed in spring before dying in summer. Winter annual weeds commonly occurring in kiwifruit vineyards include annual bluegrass, common chickweed, common groundsel, shepherd's purse, mustard, fiddleneck, and wild oats. Summer annuals germinate in spring or early summer, grow, flower, and produce seed in fall before dying in early winter. Common summer annuals include barnyardgrass, crabgrass, purslane, knotweed, pigweed, flaxleaf fleabane, horseweed, and lambsquarter. In California's mild climate and with frequent irrigation, some annuals may germinate out of season or overwinter and become short-lived perennials.

Summer annuals and perennials cause the greatest harm because they compete with the vines during summer and may interfere with harvesting and other pest management practices. Perennials live 3 years or more and are more difficult to control because their storage organs allow regrowth, even when the plant's foliage is removed by mowing or treated with an herbicide. Common perennials include johnsongrass, dallisgrass, bermudagrass, curly dock, field bindweed, dandelion, and yellow nutsedge.

Cover crops of annual or perennial species have been planted between vine rows to allow better access into the vineyard during winter, and to keep it cooler, improve water penetration, and maintain a solid area to work. Annual cover crops are preferred to perennials because they require less water and nutrients and they are less competitive. Also, annuals are easier to manage than perennials. Weeds down the vine row need control whether a cover crop is used or not.

Allowing vegetation to grow in the vineyard calls for adjusting irrigation and fertilization practices to minimize competition with the vines for water and nutrients. If vegetation is allowed to remain tall in the vineyard during frost season, damage can occur because the vineyard will be cooler than a bare, solid floor. Perennial weeds can become more troublesome because they can better tolerate mowing and compete more effectively for water and nutrients than most annuals.

VEGETATION MANAGEMENT

Prevention and site preparation

Many weeds can be controlled with cultural practices. Repeated shallow cultivations of annual species before their seeds mature reduces most weed populations. Because perennial weed infestations can be spread with cultivations, herbicides may be required for their control. However, it is safer and less costly if perennials are controlled or eradicated from the site before planting. Practicing sanitation in and around the vineyard and preventing weeds from becoming established constitute effective and economical vegetation management.

Control methods

Weeds in the vineyard can be controlled by (1) repeated shallow cultivations using power tillers or weed knives (in the vine rows), (2) strip treating the vine row with herbicides or mulches and mowing between the rows, (3) total mowing, and (4) hand hoeing around vines.

Between the rows, total cultivation is periodically done using a disc or rototiller. Within the rows, a power-driven rotary tiller with a trip mechanism can be used. However, discing or rototilling can cut off the shallow roots of vines; thus, they are unable to utilize the nutrients and water in the upper 4 to 6 inches of soil. Any cultivation done when the soil is wet increases compaction; rototillers are particularly damaging to soil.

Because the vines are trellised and cross cultivation is not feasible to control weeds in the vine row, selective herbicides are commonly used down the row and weeds mowed between rows (strip treatment). (See **plate 8**.) This method uses a minimum amount of herbicide and yet allows maintaining vegetation between rows to prevent erosion or to reduce summer temperatures in the vineyards. The vegetation often needs monthly mowing during spring and summer, except in drip-irrigated vineyards where soil between rows remains dry.

Mowing offers certain advantages. It uses lighter equipment than discing, thus minimizing soil compaction. It also allows access to the vineyard during wet periods, reduces dust, and maintains plant root growth in the surface soil to help water penetration.

USE OF HERBICIDES

The weed spectrum present in kiwifruit vineyards and the vegetation management system desired determine the choice of herbicides and the timing of their application. Herbicides can be used preemergence to prevent growth of weeds, or postemergence to control weeds already growing in the vineyard.

Preemergence herbicides are applied on the surface of the soil, and must be leached into the soil where the weed seeds germinate to obtain control. Frequently application is made in winter to take advantage of rainfall. They can also be applied to clean soil before an irrigation. Selection of herbicides and the rate of application are governed by soil type, weed population and species, and irrigation method, as well as other management factors. The period of control can be governed by the kind of herbicide chosen and the rate of application. Preemergence herbicides degrade faster in moist soil, especially where water is applied frequently with low-volume drip or microspray emitters. Herbicides are generally only used down the vineyard row to remove competition or to ease working on the vines.

Postemergence herbicides are applied to control established weeds. Those that kill only the tissue sprayed are called contact herbicides. Those that move within the plant are called translocated or systemic herbicides. Either type of postemergence herbicide can be used on annual weeds; however, the translocated herbicides are used on perennials to kill below-ground storage organs. Since postemergence herbicides have little or no soil residual activity, repeated applications are required as new plants emerge.

No one herbicide controls all weeds infesting vineyards; therefore, combinations or sequential applications of herbicides are required for best control. These may be mixtures of preemergence materials to control a broad spectrum of weed species. At times, mixtures of a postemergence and preemergence herbicides are applied to control emerged weeds and to prevent establishment of others. All herbicides used in kiwifruit vineyards are selective to some plants; thus, to select the best treatment it is imperative to recognize the weed species present.

The effectiveness and cost of chemical weed control in kiwifruit vineyards are influenced by soil type, method of irrigation, age of vines, and the susceptibility of the weed species present to available herbicides. Few herbicides are registered for use in kiwifruit vineyards. However, with knowledge of the weed infestation, effective control can be maintained with sufficient vine tolerance, when used properly and in accordance with label instructions.

To choose the proper herbicide or combination of materials, keep records of what weeds are present during winter, early summer, and late summer. These three periods can indicate the various weeds to be treated. For more detailed information relating to the susceptibility of weeds to specific herbicides, obtain a copy of the University of California *IPM Pest Management Guidelines* for Kiwifruit from UC Cooperative Extension offices, or read the labels of registered herbicides. Also, make a chart listing herbicides and the weeds they control. Match the weed species present in the vineyard with the chart. For help in identifying weeds consult the *Grower's Weed Identification Handbook* (UC Publication 4030), *Weeds of the West* (UC Publication 3350), farm advisors, or your pest control adviser.

PEST MANAGEMENT

21

Nematodes

MICHAEL V. MCKENRY

Nematodes are microscopic, multicellular, non-segmented roundworms commonly present in soil and adapted by the structure of their mouthparts to derive nutrients from soil microorganisms such as bacteria, or fungi, or other nematodes, or from plant roots.

Communities seldom exist as a single species, and both parasites and nonparasites of kiwifruit occur in soils. Nematode damage and symptomatology are nonspecific compared with most aboveground maladies. Vine damage is eventually manifested as reduced vigor and yield with slight yellowing of leaves. Vine death seldom occurs unless there are other stresses. These symptoms are common for other root-restricting agents as well.

Plant parasitic nematodes reduce root efficiency. Roots of nematode-infected vines are unable to meet aboveground demands for nutrients and water, especially during peak demand periods. Vine stress can be minimized by regulating cropping loads with extensive pruning or with greater attention to irrigation scheduling.

Because aboveground vine symptomology is lacking and nematodes are microscopic in size, laboratory analyses are necessary to determine population levels and to identify species. Good analyses depend on use of proper techniques by the grower, vineyard manager, or consulting laboratory to take soil and plant tissue samples in the field. Sampling methods are outlined at the end of this section.

It must be recognized that methods for controlling nematode populations can upset the equilibrium of soil microbes. For example, use of a sod cover crop may minimize buildup of root knot nematode, but certain species of root lesion nematode are likely to flourish. It is of primary importance, therefore, to get a good analysis of the species present and their population levels. Then, in conjunction with other vineyard factors, such as soil and general plant conditions, one can deal with individual and combined effects on plant growth and crop production.

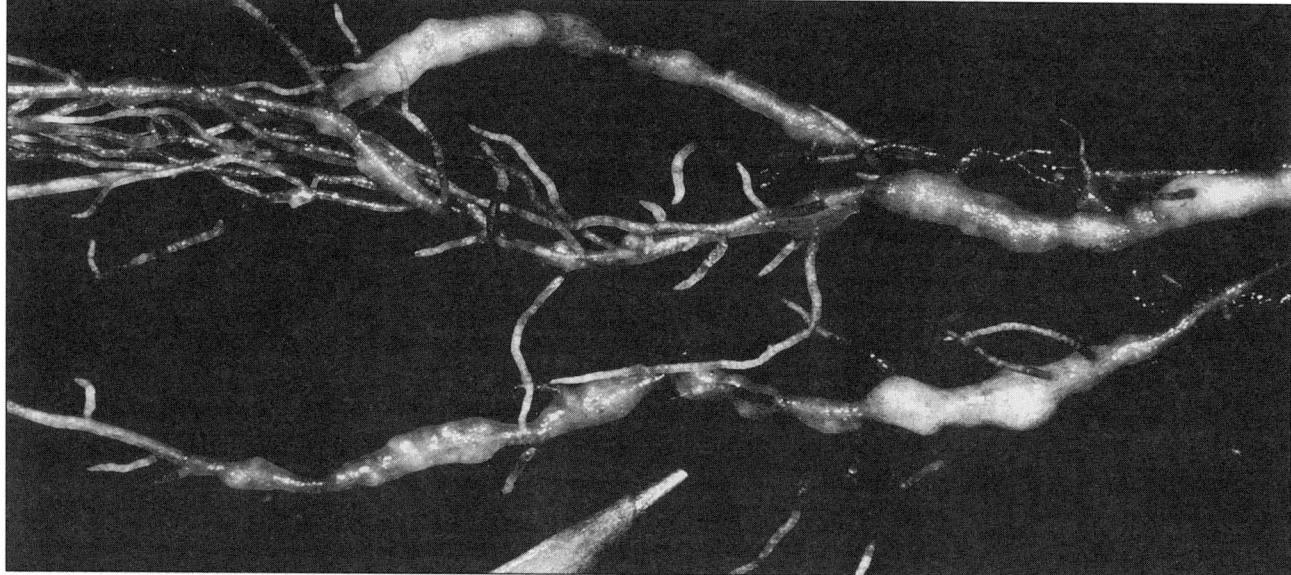

Fig. 21.1. Prevalence of root knot nematode galls in a high-intensity infection.

ROOT KNOT NEMATODES

The plant pathogenic nematode genus most commonly found in California kiwifruit plantings is the root knot nematode (*Meloidogyne* spp.). It is the only genus of economic importance to California growers as kiwifruit are very susceptible to it. Once present in vineyards, population levels soar, often competitively excluding other plant parasitic nematode species. In California, specimens of *Meloidogyne incognita, M. arenaria,* and *M. javanica* have been found to occur in field plantings. In New Zealand, the only major root knot nematode species is *M. hapla.*

From a management standpoint, it is only necessary to determine that root knot nematodes are involved, not the particular species. One can expect to find any or all of these species present in a vineyard. As stated in chapter 4, *The Genus Actinidia,* the rootstock for California kiwifruit consists of seedlings of Hayward or Bruno. These varieties were originally selected in New Zealand soils, and there has never been any selection for resistance or tolerance against the root knot nematodes that commonly occur in California. Root knot nematodes reproduce at a faster rate in warmer climates and, therefore, damage caused by the nematode can be expected to be higher in southern rather than in northern valley soils.

Once a nematode sample has been taken to confirm that root knot is present in a vineyard, the grower can then evaluate its distribution by using a shovel to expose roots and to estimate the intensity of root galling. Figure 21.1 depicts galls within 1 inch of each other on a major portion of the root. This indicates a high intensity of nematode infection. A low intensity of infection is indicated when galls are 4 inches or more apart and are found on few roots.

Life cycle

Second-stage juveniles hatch from eggs and move through moist soil. Vertical distances of 1 foot in sandy loam soil can be traveled in 3 days by those most active. Juveniles are attracted to roots and usually penetrate and enter just behind the root tip. Once inside the root, they establish themselves in the conducting tissues, begin feeding, and after 2 weeks of warm, summer temperatures, the females mature into egg-laying adults. Their development stimulates a cellular change in the plant in the immediate vicinity of the feeding site. This change results in formation of the familiar knot or gall seen on the root surface. Internally, this results in disruption of conducting tissues.

A single gall may be inhabited by one or numerous adult females. The number of females living in a single gall apparently influences its size. The adult female is a sedentary, pearl-colored stage, which, if dissected from the gall, is barely visible to the unaided eye.

The life span of a root knot nematode is not known. It is at least 1 to several months; its greatest longevity but least activity occurs during winter. A single gall can be maintained for many years.

Root knot nematode males, while sometimes present in low numbers, do not feed and are not of direct concern to the grower. The preponderance of the population is expected to be in the root zone, typically 6 to 36 inches deep beneath the vine row, depending on soil conditions and tillage practices. Wheel traffic and its effect on soil compaction and root distribution minimize this nematode's development in the drive row.

Root knot nematode is best adapted to coarse-textured soils including sand, loamy sand, and sandy loam. It exhibits a wide host range, including the roots of many broadleaf weeds and cover crops present in vineyards. Most prevalent in cooler regions north of San Francisco, *M. hapla* has been found in southern California vineyards, perhaps being more active there during winter months. *Meloidogyne incognita, M. javanica,* and *M. arenaria* are most prevalent south of Stockton, in the San Joaquin Valley. Root knot nematodes are less prevalent in California's coastal valleys.

Injury

Root knot nematodes interfere with plant growth and nutrient uptake. They create "sinks" in the root system that channel aboveground photosynthates to them. They further disrupt the orderly uptake of water and nutrients by their physical presence within root tissues. Damage caused by them is increased if plants are stressed.

Small galls or knots, usually present on infected roots, are typically $\frac{1}{8}$ inch in diameter, but can be larger where there has been a multiple attack. They are seldom larger than $\frac{1}{2}$ inch in diameter, even on older roots. Root knot nematode confirmation requires examining the gall to detect adult females.

MONITORING GUIDELINES

Prior to planting

All vineyards should be sampled for nematodes before planting. If a proposed vineyard site has had a perennial crop in the previous 5 years or it has recently lain fallow, take deep soil samples down to the 3-foot level. Sample areas of the field where differences of any kind have been noted in cropping histories, soil textures, soil depths, yields, or management. A single composite sample should include soil from up to 10 subsamples taken from each identifiably different area.

Established vineyards

Plant parasitic nematodes are concentrated where "feeder roots" are most abundant. Therefore, sample for both soil and roots in the berm area 12 to 18 inches from the vine trunk to a depth of 30 inches. Sample around five vines from each identifiable area. These areas might include differences in soil texture, cropping history, vine vigor, or yield. Lump these five subsamples into a single sample representative of the area. The surface 3 inches of vineyard soil may be discarded. Roots should be included in the sample. For each five vines sampled, observe the incidence of root knot galling or other irregularities.

Handling the sample

Two to five pounds of soil for a sample is sufficient. Place soil in a plastic or waterproof bag and label the outside with name, date, and vineyard location. Keep plastic bags away from direct sunlight and store preferably at 40° to 50°F (5° to 10°C). Most importantly, avoid temperatures above 95°F (35°C) or less than 35°F (2°C).

When to sample

Samples can be taken any time of the year. It is best to sample when soil is moist, preferably within a week after rainfall or irrigation. Samples removed during winter usually provide the highest counts of root knot nematode. A typical vine may harbor 0 to 10 million plant parasitic nematodes; thus, expect latitude in sampling results. By standardizing the sampling methods described here, however, there is greater opportunity for correctly interpreting results.

Diagnostic laboratories

Numerous commercial laboratories are available for nematode diagnosis, but the extent of their services varies greatly. Some laboratories send personnel to the vineyard to remove and care for soil samples; others receive samples by mail and return results, leaving all interpretations to the grower. Some laboratory personnel never see the vineyard but make elaborate interpretations of the problem and its control in computer-printout format. To assess the nematological capabilities of a given laboratory, it is helpful to occasionally split a well-mixed sample and send it to different laboratories for comparison.

Number of samples

The number of samples taken may be decided on the basis of cropping history, soil texture differences, geographic location, and the experience of the sampler. There is no set formula. A rule of thumb is to take one sample for at least every 5 to 10 acres, but exceptions are common.

GUIDELINES FOR ESTABLISHING A VINEYARD

Cultural practices

Avoid planting deciduous crops for at least 4 years to minimize damage from root knot nematodes. Minimize damage, also, by preceding the planting with grass crops, including barley and sudangrass, because these crops are poor hosts to most root knot nematode species. Site selection is important, because root knot species are more damaging in coarser-textured soils and kiwifruit is a known host for root knot nematodes. Use cultural practices to reduce population levels preplant because once commercial nematicides are needed in established plantings annual retreatments will probably be required.

Biological agents

There are no biological agents that can be added to soil to effectively reduce nematode populations.

Chemical agents

Soil fumigants are highly effective for nematode control when applied before planting. They are especially useful in controlling endoparasitic nematodes that survive several years in old root systems of previous perennial crops.

The major limitation to effective nematode control involves the movement of the pesticide to the pest. Proper soil preparation and timing are required for successful fumigation. Increasing the rate of pesticide application does not compensate for poor land preparation or conditions. Proper land preparation also benefits the new vineyard. For example, most vineyards are planted in sites previously planted to perennial crops. For good root system development, nematode damage must be minimized for at least 6 months and preferably longer, when a highly susceptible crop such as kiwifruit is planted.

Additionally, most replant situations involve soils that have been subjected in previous planting to considerable vehicular traffic, leading to soil compaction and stratification of the soil profile. These factors limit soil penetration by new roots, generally detract from vineyard development, and hinder good penetration by fumigants. Successful establishment of a vineyard, therefore, depends on eliminating these physical and biological barriers by a complementary schedule of soil profile modification and fumigation, as outlined below.

Site preparation for a new vineyard

Season	Action
Late summer/ early fall, first year:	Remove existing trees or vines and destroy residues by discing, piling, and burning.
	Chisel ground several times to bring roots to surface for removal and destruction.
Fall/winter/ early spring:	Fallow or crop to small grains.
Spring/summer:	Harvest grain if planted. Chisel ground again to maximum depth possible (at least 24 inches).
	If irrigation is required to settle ground after deep chiseling, complete by early summer.
	In coastal climates, plant sudangrass to remove deep soil moisture. Level field.
Late summer/ early fall, second year:	Apply fumigants when soil temperatures are correct. Soil fumigants move optimally and are most effective when soil is dry. These conditions generally dictate that fall fumigations are optimal; October is usually the best month for treatment.
Winter/spring:	Plant vines.

ESTABLISHED VINEYARD GUIDELINES

Soil amendments

Manures are often used to improve vine vigor, even in the presence of nematodes. Manures are complex, with equally complex effects on vineyard soil. Benefits are probably not derived from direct nematode kill, although some control may occur. Any practice that enhances root growth and nutrient uptake serves to reduce the effect of damage from nematodes.

Cover crops

Use of certain cover crops may increase nematode populations; others may decrease damage. Unfortunately, little research information is available, so it is suggested that vineyardists experiencing low or medium population levels of a specific nematode not aggravate the situation by increasing their reproduction potential. For example, planting broadleaf plants or most legumes down a drive row on sandy soil can aggravate an existing root knot nematode problem. Most grasses, on the other hand, are nonhosts for root knot nematode.

Vine stress

Specifically with root knot nematode, it is apparent that cultural practices that enhance nutrient and water uptake reduce plant damage. Alleviating soil compaction, increasing soil penetration by water, improving irrigation methods, or perhaps correcting nutrient deficiencies may help, but these measures do not guarantee reduction of nematode numbers. Further, these cultural practices, especially nutrient application, call for greater management attention than before because of restricted root conditions caused by the presence of root knot nematode.

Biological agents

None is currently available.

Chemical agents

Applying nematicides through low-volume irrigation devices has proved successful. Numbers of fruit, fruit size, and vine vigor are generally improved, when nematodes are problematic, but if they are not at a damaging level, these nematicides are ineffective. Methods and treatments for successful control are under study. Generally, retreatments at low rates are necessary to reduce nematode populations.

Color Plates

4. The Genus *Actinidia*
Fredrick A. Bliss

Plate 1. The grapelike fruits of *A. arguta* (*left*) compared with the standard Hayward variety of *A. deliciosa* (*right*).

18. Nutrition and Fertilization
James A. Beutel, Kiyoto Uriu, John Post, and James Pearson

Plate 2. Iron chlorosis on leaves.

Plate 3. Iron chlorosis causes yellow fruit color (*left*).

Plate 4. Manganese deficiency causes chlorosis between main lateral veins, giving a herringbone appearance.

Plate 5. Heat stress can show up as yellow blotches on exposed leaves. No definite pattern is seen.

Plate 6. Chloride toxicity causes marginal leaf necrosis.

Plate 7. Boron toxicity causes interveinal yellowing, which becomes necrotic as the season progresses.

20. Weed Control
Clyde L. Elmore and Bill B. Fischer

Plate 8. Typical vineyard floor management system. Weeds in the vine row are controlled with herbicides and row middles are mowed.

22. Diseases

W. Douglas Gubler and Kevin E. Conn

Plate 9. (*A*) Healthy kiwifruit vine shows vigorous terminal growth with normal-sized leaves and full canopy. (*B*) *Phytophthora*-infected vine shows poor terminal growth, stunted leaves, and reduced canopy.

Plate 10. Young kiwifruit vine killed by *Phytophthora* spp.

Plate 11. Phytophthora root and crown rot shows sloughing off of cortical tissue. Note complete lack of feeder roots.

Plate 12. Phytophthora crown rot shows reddish-brown tissue of infected crown area, compared with healthy, greenish-colored tissue.

Plate 13. Cream-colored fungal plaques and strands of mycelia between bark and wood indicate presence of *Armillaria mellea*.

Plate 14. Trunk bark wetted with bacterial ooze in bleeding canker disease.

Plate 15. Initial red-orange bleeding of kiwifruit cane newly infected by bleeding canker.

Plate 16. Dry bacterial ooze on cane killed by bleeding canker.

Plate 17. Crown gall on kiwifruit roots.

Plate 18. Bacterial leafspot caused by *Pseudomonas* spp. Note necrotic lesions with yellow halos.

Plate 19. Blossom blight caused by *Pseudomonas* spp. Early infection causes buds to not open.

Plate 20. Blossom blight infected with *Pseudomonas* spp. Note death of petals, stamens, and pistils.

23. Insects and Mites

William H. Olson,
Richard E. Rice,
and Robert H. Beede

Plate 21. Omnivorous leafroller adult at rest.

Plate 22. Nearly mature larva of omnivorous leafroller.

Plate 23. Surface feeding damage of omnivorous leafroller.

Plate 24. Internal fruit damage caused by omnivorous leafroller.

Plate 25. Larva of fruittree leafroller.

Plate 26. Fruittree leafroller adult.

Plate 27. Obliquebanded leafroller larva.

Plate 28. Adult obliquebanded leafroller.

Plate 29. Orange tortrix larva.

Plate 30. Orange tortrix adult female.

Plate 31. Scale on kiwifruit bark.

Plate 32. Closeup of latania scale.

Plate 33. Scale insects on kiwifruit.

Plate 34. Boxelder bug nymphs and adults.

24. Postharvest Physiology and Causes of Deterioration

Mary Lu Arpaia, F. Gordon Mitchell, and Adel A. Kader

Plate 35. Symptoms of pericarp translucency in kiwifruit.

Plate 36. Symptoms of pericarp granulation in kiwifruit.

Plate 37. Symptoms of white-core inclusions.

26. Harvesting and Preparation for Market

F. Gordon Mitchell, Mary Lu Arpaia, and Gene Mayer

Plate 38. Black surface marking, sometimes called "ink staining," can be found when kiwifruit are in contact with bare metal that has been wetted with kiwifruit juice.

27. Cooling, Storage, Transportation, and Distribution

Mary Lu Arpaia, F. Gordon Mitchell, and Gene Mayer

Plate 39. Symptoms of freeze damage as a result of low storage temperature in kiwifruit.

Plate 40. Surface cracking of kiwifruit due to free water contact during low temperature storage.

Plate 41. Symptoms of impact bruising (IB) of kiwifruit at various stages of ripening: *Left*, symptoms of IB in firm fruit; *center*, symptoms of IB in ripe fruit; *right*, control fruit.

Plate 42. Symptoms of transport vibration damage in soft kiwifruit. Fruit, *upper left*, is control.

28. Postharvest Storage Diseases

Noel F. Sommer, J. Emilio Suadi, and Robert J. Fortlage

Plate 43. Kiwifruit skin removed showing advance of the *Botrytis cinerea* lesion.

Plate 44. Typical view of diseased kiwifruit showing external mycelium.

Plate 45. Black bodies (sclerotia) forming in the fungal mycelium serve to maintain the fungus under conditions of desiccation or temperature extremes.

Plate 46. "Nesting" caused by mycelia of rotting fruit growing and penetrating nearby fruit.

Plate 47. Alternaria rot of sunburned fruit.

Plate 48. Alternaria surface mold (*Alternaria alternata*) growing on sepals and stamens in storage.

Plate 49. Juice blotch.

Plate 50. Blue mold rot (*Penicillium expansum*) in kiwifruit.

Plate 51. Dothiorella rot.

Plate 52. Phoma rot.

Plate 53. Phomopsis rot showing juice exudation often associated with the disease.

Plate 54. Buckshot rot caused by *Typhula* spp.

PEST MANAGEMENT

22

Diseases

W. DOUGLAS GUBLER AND KEVIN E. CONN

Although relatively new to California agriculture, kiwifruit has already developed a significant number of diseases, many with a potential to seriously limit production.

Diseases are caused by pathogens, generally microorganisms that invade the host plant and disrupt its normal functions. The pathogens known to cause disease in kiwifruit in California are fungi and bacteria. Infection can occur through leaves, fruit, stems, or roots. Pathogens affecting the aerial plant parts are generally wind-borne or water-splashed. In either case, free water or high humidity is needed for infection to occur. Examples of foliar and fruit pathogens are *Botrytis cinerea*, *Pseudomonas viridiflava*, and *P. syringae*. Pathogens affecting roots are soil-borne fungi, such as *Phytophthora* spp., *Armillaria mellea*, and *Agrobacterium tumefaciens*.

Management of diseases requires understanding the pathogen types and conditions under which infection and disease increase. Strategies aimed at controlling foliar diseases are based primarily on environmental conditions conducive to initiating and increasing disease. Because these diseases require free water for propagule germination and infection, fungicides or bactericides should be used only when conditions favor disease, that is, before rains or sprinkler irrigation.

Disease affecting the roots and crown of kiwifruit can be managed with sanitation and strict water management. In the case of Armillaria root rot, carefully removing old roots from affected sites greatly reduces the inoculum that might cause disease on new plants or replants. Water management can be used to control both Phytophthora root and crown rot as well as Armillaria root rot. Planting on berms increases water drainage from around vine crowns, thus helping to prevent infection by both pathogens.

PHYTOPHTHORA ROOT AND CROWN ROT

Root and crown rot of kiwifruit is caused by several species of *Phytophthora*, a group of water-mold fungi. *Phytophthora* spp. thrive in heavy, cool soils with poor drainage, although they are found in practically all soil types. Optimum temperature for most species of *Phytophthora* is between 75° and 86°F (24° and 30°C); temperatures above 86° to 97°F (30° to 36°C) inhibit growth. When optimum temperature is coupled with saturated or near-saturated soil conditions, the fungus sporulates profusely, producing sporangia from which zoospores emerge. These fungal propagules are capable of swimming through the soil-water matrix, until coming in contact with root tissue, whereupon they encyst and infect the tissue.

Phytophthora spp. are widespread and found in many California orchards, vineyards, vegetable crop fields, and even rivers and irrigation systems. Some species of *Phytophthora* have a wide host range; others have more limited host ranges. Some species attack principally feeder roots of kiwifruit vines; others attack primary roots and/or crowns of vines. Wounds are not required for fungal infection. The pathogen readily penetrates a healthy root when environmental conditions are favorable. Most *Phytophthora* infections occur in fall, winter, or early spring during periods of heavy rainfall and cool soil temperatures.

Symptoms

In the early stages of disease development, vines exhibit delayed budbreak, lack of terminal growth, and small, chlorotic leaves (**plate 9**). As disease development progresses, terminal shoot dieback, sparse foliage, and bronzing of leaves appear. Sparse foliage and wilting of leaves can result in sunburned fruit and vines. A vine heavily infected the previous fall or winter may fail to grow in spring. Also, vines may grow relatively well until stressed by hot weather or a heavy fruit load. These vines usually collapse within the current growing season (**plate 10**).

Vines may gradually or rapidly decline and die within weeks. In addition to vine age and environmental conditions acting upon the vine, it is thought that rapidity of decline is a product of the type of vine infection and the species of *Phytophthora* present. For instance, if the *Phytophthora* species present is less aggressive, the vine will probably decline over several seasons, perhaps never dying, but it may finally have to be pulled for lack of good fruit production. However, if the species present attacks primary roots or the crown, vine death occurs rapidly. Once the crown is rotted and the lower trunk girdled, movement of water from roots to canopy is completely inhibited.

Infected roots are firm, not watery and soft as the name "root rot" implies. Roots, cut open, exhibit a red-brown to dark brown color, depending on the severity and duration of infection (**plate 11**). The advancing margin of infection can be found where discolored, diseased tissue meets white, healthy tissue.

Crown rot symptoms are manifested by decayed bark and cortical tissue at the soil line. When the outer bark is removed, the inner bark is dark brown (**plate 12**). Crowns may become infected independently of roots or primary root infections may advance to the crown. Once the crown is infected at one or more points, either below or at soil level, the rot advances vertically and laterally, eventually girdling the vine's trunk, and the vine collapses and dies.

Phytophthora root and crown rot is usually more common in vineyards subject to periodic and prolonged periods of excessive soil moisture than in vineyards with well-drained, well-managed soils. Root and crown rot also is commonly seen in low areas of vineyards where rain and irrigation water stand for prolonged periods. Free moisture greatly increases the pathogen's production of infective propagules, sporangia, and zoospores. Spread of these propagules in the root zone of a vine, or from vine to vine, is greatly enhanced by saturated soil. In addition, spread of *Phytophthora* from infected areas of the vineyards is aided by surface irrigation and runoff water.

Management

Control is aimed at managing infested soils by using cultural practices known to minimize disease. Eradicating *Phytophthora* is difficult and expensive, and in most instances, rapid recolonization of the treated soil occurs. There are no fungicides registered to control *Phytophthora* on kiwifruit, and no resistant rootstocks are available.

Use great care to prevent introducing *Phytophthora* into noninfested vineyards. Because the fungus is soil-borne, it can readily be introduced into healthy sites on equipment and machinery, on soil from newly planted vines, and with irrigation or runoff water.

When the pathogen is present, disease commonly occurs when vines are planted in heavy soils or when irrigation practices result in free-standing water. Improving surface and below-ground water drainage minimizes *Phytophthora* activity. Plant new plantings and replantings on berms to allow for water drainage in root and crown areas. Remove weeds from the base of vines. Irrigate the vineyard for shorter periods of time but more frequently. Disease also occurs when sprinklers are allowed to spray water directly on the trunk or when drip emitters are placed too close to the vine.

ARMILLARIA ROOT ROT

Armillaria root rot (oak root rot) is caused by the fungus *Armillaria mellea* (Wahl ex Fr.) Kummer. Although this disease is of suspect importance on kiwifruit in California, it has been observed in several plantings in northern California. The pathogen has been consistently recovered from rotting roots and crowns, but inoculation tests show kiwifruit to be somewhat tolerant. Other research indicates that *A. mellea* may be considered a weak pathogen on kiwifruit, infecting its roots and crowns only after vines have been predisposed.

One consistent predisposing agent has been Phytophthora root rot. Regardless of the site, when *Armillaria mellea* was recovered from kiwifruit, *Phytophthora* spp. also were recovered. Thus, the two diseases may act in a synergistic relationship. *Phytophthora* spp. on their own may cause rapid decline and death of kiwifruit plants, but vine death can potentially be more rapid if Phytophthora-weakened plants are also invaded by *A. mellea*. More research is needed to define the extent and severity of this disease.

Symptoms

Kiwifruit vines infected with *A. mellea* decline and die. Removal of the bark from the crown often shows a cream-colored fungal plaque characterized by a strong mushroom odor (**plate 13**).

Management

Armillaria root rot is commonly associated with hillsides or other areas inhabited by oak trees and areas subject to periodic flooding. The pathogen survives in soil or large roots as shoestringlike structures (rhizomorphs) capable of infecting susceptible crops. When clearing land for planting or replanting vines after death, carefully remove and burn roots 1 inch or greater in diameter. Fumigation can reduce soil inoculum.

BLEEDING CANKER

Bleeding canker or Pseudomonas canker of kiwifruit is caused by the bacterial pathogen *Pseudomonas syringae*. The disease has been observed in most areas of the state where kiwifruit are grown. Bleeding canker is more common and symptoms are more severe in years when vines are exposed to winter or early spring temperatures capable of causing chilling or freezing injury.

Symptoms

Symptoms of bleeding canker first appear in early spring, soon after leaf emergence. Young canes exhibit "hooking" at the terminal growing point, leaf wilt, canker blight, and cankers (**plates 14, 15, and 16**). Externally, cane symptoms include dried, shriveled bark. Internally, affected tissue is a discolored red-rusty brown. A pruning wound is often associated with the canker. Cankers may occur on canes, cordons, or trunks. Plants are often killed back past the bud union when trunks are attacked. Less severely affected plants generally resume growth in late spring. When regrowth occurs, profuse rusty red exudate (bleeding) occurs from the canker margins, often to the extent that bark tissue is discolored. Suckering is extensive from rootstock of affected plants.

Pseudomonas syringae has a wide host range and is believed to overwinter on kiwifruit vines as well as on weeds and grasses in vineyards. Kiwifruit vines become predisposed to infection when weakened by freezing or chilling injury.

Management

Control of bleeding canker is currently unresolved, although protecting vines from stresses caused by winter injury should alleviate disease severity. Prune infected vines when symptoms are observed. Make cuts 1 foot below the leading edge of the canker.

CROWN GALL

Crown gall is caused by the bacterial pathogen *Agrobacterium tumefaciens*. The bacterium is found in most agricultural soils and occurs on many species of woody plants. It reportedly occurs on 17 genera of plants in California; it is of dubious importance on kiwifruit.

Symptoms

Galls are the most obvious symptom of crown gall; however, they are not always visible (**plate 17**). Foliar symptoms are typical of a root or crown rot pathogen: lack of vigor, small leaves, poor terminal growth, open canopy, and yield reduction.

Crown gall bacteria infect healthy tissue through wounds, most commonly on roots or the crown. Roots of young vines are often injured during transplanting; older vines are injured by common cultural practices that use machinery, as in weed control. Additionally, vines may be wounded by frost, pruning, and the removal of suckers, or they may develop growth cracks. The bacteria enter wound sites, whereupon plant cells are transformed and begin to divide in a disorganized manner. Tumorlike galls result. Galls range in size from nearly microscopic to 12 inches or more in diameter. Young galls are smooth; the surface of older galls is rougher due to the outer cell layers of the gall sloughing off or breaking off. The exterior and interior of galls are the color of normal kiwifruit tissue but softer; annual growth rings, however, are not present because the tissue is undifferentiated. Central portions of old galls may die and become entry points for secondary infections caused by wood-rotting fungi.

During cultivation, the bacteria may be disseminated in infected plant material or in soil. Local dissemination is due mainly to movement in the soil-water, especially during rains or irrigation. Bacteria are released from galls when they are wet or are old and decaying.

Severity of infection depends on several factors, including number and location of infections, size of galls, secondary infection by decay organisms, and age of the vine. Infections of young vines are most limiting, although the vines are rarely killed.

Management

Control of crown gall is best achieved by avoiding injury to vines. Minimal handling during transplanting and care in using machinery during cultural practices should greatly reduce the risk of wounding. Soil fumigation is not recommended. Fumigants do not kill the bacteria in galls, and in other tree crops the bacterium has been shown to rapidly recolonize fumigated soil.

BACTERIAL LEAFSPOT AND BLOSSOM BLIGHT

Bacterial leafspot and blossom blight is believed caused by *Pseudomonas viridiflava* (Burkholder) Dowson, a fluorescent pseudomonad originally described in 1930 as causing a leaf and pod spot of bean. An opportunistic plant pathogen, it reportedly occurs naturally on 31 species in 14 families of plants. By inoculation, an additional 30 host species, including 5 extra families, have been found susceptible. The pathogen apparently exists as an epiphyte on the leaves of fruit and vegetable crops. *Pseudomonas viridiflava* gains entry through wounds, as a secondary organism, or when the plant has been predisposed to disease by conditions favoring the bacterium.

Symptoms

Leafspot symptoms first appear in late spring as dark angular spots surrounded by yellow halos (**plate 18**). Many spots form near the margins of leaves, but it is not known whether the bacteria enter through plant structures other than stomates. Leafspotting has been observed to occur 2 to 3 weeks after a period of night frosts followed by warm, sunny days. As the season progresses, the leafspot may coalesce to form large irregular patches of necrotic tissue. Leaf infections, it is believed, serve as a source of inoculum for vegetative buds. The bacteria survive within the buds through winter and are dispersed to floral buds and young leaves during spring rains. Buds may show infection by turning brown and failing to open (**plate 19**). Ultimately, they drop. Flower parts, such as petals and stamens, may turn brown and fail to develop fully (**plate 20**). Fruit developing from an infected flower are small and misshapen due to poor pollination.

Isolations from leafspot margins have yielded a variety of bacteria, including many saprophytic fluorescent pseudomonads and *P. syringae*, in addition to *P. viridiflava*.

Management

Research on this disease has not yet developed any chemical or cultural practices.

PEST MANAGEMENT

23

Insects and Mites

WILLIAM H. OLSON, RICHARD E. RICE, AND ROBERT H. BEEDE

Only a few insects have been found to be pests of kiwifruit in California. While insect pests have occasionally caused economic loss, it is likely their full potential as pests of kiwifruit has not yet been realized. At this point, leaf-rolling caterpillars and scale insects are the most significant insect pests.

Because the availability of pesticides constantly changes, no mention is made here of chemical control materials or rates of application. Specific information on control of kiwifruit insect pests can be found in the University of California publication, *UC IPM Pest Management Guidelines* for Kiwifruit, available from UC Cooperative Extension offices.

LEAF-ROLLING CATERPILLARS

The omnivorous leafroller, fruittree leafroller, obliquebanded leafroller, and orange tortrix are four species of tortricid moths found attacking kiwifruit.

Omnivorous leafroller

The omnivorous leafroller (OLR), *Platynota stultana* Walsingham, feeds on a wide range of plants and is the most common leaf-rolling caterpillar found on kiwifruit. At rest, the adult moth's wings are positioned in a bell shape. The snoutlike mouth parts, a blackish-gray, protrude from the head (**plate 21**). Fore wings are dark brown, the outer half a lighter brown; a dark-colored band extends outward from the middle of the wings. Males and females look alike, except that females are larger, about ½ inch long; males are about ⅜ inch long. Also, females possess brown, semicircular plates at the end of the abdomen, in contrast to the tufted hairs at the end of the male abdomen.

Life cycle. Elliptical green eggs are laid in flat clusters and overlap each other like fish scales on such smooth surfaces as the upper leaf surface.

Newly hatched omnivorous leafroller larvae are less than ¹⁄₁₆ inch long; mature larvae are ½ inch long. Larvae usually cast their skins five to six times before pupation. First-stage larvae are cream colored with light brown heads and prothoracic shields. The second and third stages have brownish-black or black heads and shields. The fourth stage may have a blackish brown or black head with brown shield or both head and shield may be brown (**plate 22**). Fifth and sixth stages have brown heads and shields.

The body color of mature larvae may change from creamy to brownish-green or brown; a faint stripe produced by the main blood vessel runs full length in the center and on the upper side of the body. The larvae are distinguished from other caterpillars by the presence of white, slightly convex and oval-shaped tubercles on the upper sides of the abdominal segments (**plate 22**).

The larvae, generally solitary, spin a silken thread and web a protective nest, often webbing a leaf to a fruit. Like most tortricid larvae, when disturbed, they become active and retreat into the nest or wiggle backwards and drop suspended on a silken thread.

Omnivorous leafrollers overwinter as partially mature larvae in plant debris on the ground or on weeds. They continue to develop slowly throughout the dormant period. The overwintering population is decreased by adverse weather, insect predators, and birds. The population is further reduced when pruning, mowing, or cultivation takes place. In spring and early summer, the larval population is low, but it can increase rapidly thereafter.

Females prefer to lay their eggs on smooth plant surfaces, and although egg viability is high, mortality of young larvae is also high because the larvae have difficulty establishing themselves on the plant. Newly hatched larvae may be found on the undersides of leaves where they feed and nest along the midveins. As the larvae develop, some remain on leaves; others feed between fruits that are touching each other or on fruit attached to a leaf by larval webbing.

Mature OLR larvae form brown pupae in their web-spun nest. Moths resulting from these pupae are most active shortly after sunset; if disturbed, however, they may be seen flying during the day. Mating and egg laying take place at night. There are four to six generations of this moth each year.

Damage. OLR and other leaf-rolling caterpillars can directly damage fruit by scarring the surface with their feeding (**plate 23**). On mature fruit, they may tunnel into the fruit (**plate 24**). Early damage, during fruit development, can result in deformed fruit or fruit drop. OLR may feed on flower clusters as well. Later damage is more superficial, but the resulting scars may make the fruit unmarketable.

Management. OLR larvae are able to feed and develop on many different plants; therefore, adjacent orchards, row and field crops, ornamentals, and weeds may be sources of infestation for kiwifruit. Other crops attacked by OLR include grape, alfalfa, apple, apricot, avocado, bushberries, celery, citrus, cotton, lettuce, melons, peach, pepper, plum, prune, sorghum, sugarbeet, strawberry, tomato, and walnut. Susceptible ornamentals include aster, carnation, chrysanthemum, cyclamen, eucalyptus, fuschia, geranium, portulaca, and rose. Susceptible weeds are pigweed, horseweed or mare's tail, panicled willow herb, cheeseweed, California mugwort, and lambsquarter.

Because omnivorous leafrollers infest so many different plants and larval mortality is high, OLR pheromone trap catches from traps placed in a kiwifruit planting are not good indicators of relative infestation levels; they only indicate presence or absence of moths in a field. Studies show no correlation between trap catches using pheromone traps and fruit infestation.

To date, treatment needs for OLR are best determined by monitoring the vineyard, including areas where infestation is suspected or where it has previously occurred. The signs of infestation include presence of larvae, pupae, pupal cases, webbing, and feeding damage produced by OLR larvae. Begin monitoring during the prebloom period and continue through the season. The most important periods are from prebloom to fruit set and for 2 to 3 weeks following large moth catches in pheromone traps.

Base treatment decisions on evidence that larvae or eggs are present in the vineyard, not on high pheromone trap catches. If an examination of the planting indicates an OLR presence, treat immediately.

Fruittree leafroller

The fruittree leafroller, *Archips argyrospilus* (Walker), is a minor pest of kiwifruit, overwintering in egg masses on twigs and emerging in spring as larvae. The larvae are dark green and have black heads (**plate 25**). Adults appear in June or July and deposit overwintering eggs. At rest, the adults appear bell shaped and have dark brown bands running at oblique angles across their wings (**plate 26**). Their wings are mottled with gold and white flecks. There is one generation each year. Sex pheromone traps are available to monitor adult emergence in June and July and to help identify fields that may need insecticide spray treatments during the following dormant season to control eggs or to treat newly hatched larvae in spring. Time insecticide treatments against larvae in spring, based on their presence during field monitoring.

Obliquebanded leafroller

The obliquebanded leafroller, *Choristoneura rosaceana* (Harris), is distributed throughout central and northern California and has been found as an occasional pest of kiwifruit. Overwintering larvae of the obliquebanded leafroller are green to tan in color (**plate 27**). The bell-shaped adults have dark brown bands running at oblique angles across their wings (**plate 28**). There are two generations each year in the Sacramento Valley. Pheromone traps are available to monitor adults' emergence but, like OLR, evidence of larvae in the planting should be the criterion used to determine treatment needs.

Orange tortrix

The orange tortrix, *Argyrotaenia citrana* (Fernald), is typically found in cooler coastal regions. It usually overwinters in the larval stage, but eggs, pupae, and adults are also found. Larvae spend winter within nests constructed of old leaves on twigs, where they feed to a limited extent on bark. They also construct silken shelters on mummified fruit left on vines and do some feeding on fruit. Spring and summer generations overlap considerably because populations overwinter in various developmental stages.

The mature larvae vary in color but are generally yellow-tan to light brown (**plate 29**). The adult female is about ½ inch long (**plate 30**). In contrast to OLR larvae, the tubercles on the orange tortrix's abdominal segments are not prominent and are round, not oval. Furthermore, the head and prothoracic shield remain light brown or tan throughout the developmental stages.

The orange tortrix has a wide host range, and there are two to four generations each year. Adults lay egg masses on smooth bark; the hatching larvae move to the foliage, fasten leaves together with silk, and feed within this protected area. They also may tie leaves to fruit or live in the calyx end of fruit under a net of webbing. They are commonly found between two touching fruit or within clusters of fruit. Upon maturing, larvae pupate in locations where they have been feeding. Monitor the planting for larval presence and use sex pheromone traps to detect adult presence. Base treatment needs on visual detection of larvae.

ARMORED SCALES

Life cycle. Greedy scale, *Hemiberlesia rapax* (Comstock); ivy (oleander) scale, *Aspidiotus nerii* Bouche; and latania scale, *Hemiberlesia lataniae* (Signoret), are all armored scales. Armored scales have a distinct, hard, separable shell or scale over delicate bodies. No honeydew or blackening of plant parts results from armored scale feeding as does occur with feeding by soft scales.

Greedy scale, the most common and widely distributed species of armored scale in California, is thin, light gray, convex, and noticeably pointed on top with a yellow, nipplelike protuberance near one edge. An omnivorous feeder, the scale chiefly infests bark, but it also frequently occurs on leaves and fruit.

Ivy or oleander scale shells resemble greedy scale shells. They are, however, flatter, paler in color, and with a more central nipplelike protuberance. Ivy scale is nearly as abundant as greedy scale.

Latania scale is circular and, although slightly larger, almost indistinguishable from greedy scale. This scale has a wide host range, having been reported on more than 75 cultivated and ornamental crops.

In late spring, female scales lay eggs beneath their cover. Upon hatching, the young crawlers migrate a short distance from the parent scale. There, they settle, insert their mouth parts into the host plant, and begin to feed. These crawlers become adults in early summer and give rise to several generations per year. Scales enter winter as partially mature crawlers which become adults in spring.

Damage. These scales attack the bark, leaves, and fruit of the host plant. Mild infestations are most prominent on 2-year-old wood and older wood near the trunk (**plates 31** and **32**). Moderate and heavy infestations can easily be seen during dormant pruning. Heavy infestations may affect plant vigor and result in scales being present on fruit at harvest, thereby increasing offgrade and premature softening in cold storage (**plate 33**).

Management. Scales have many natural enemies, including lacewings, predaceous mites, and tiny parasitic wasps. When scale populations are not checked by these natural enemies, chemical control is advised. The preferred time for chemical control is during the dormant or delayed dormant period when scales are mostly in the crawler stage. Dormant chemical control is best applied after pruning; spray each row to insure optimum coverage.

Double-sided sticky tape placed on smooth sections of 2-year-old wood in spring and maintained through summer can be used to monitor the scale population and to evaluate treatment results. Large numbers of scale crawlers caught on the tape can indicate poor control or the buildup of a population calling for control measures next dormant season.

SPIDER MITES

Spider mites rarely seriously affect kiwifruit, except occasionally in greenhouses and nurseries. The twospotted spider mite, *Tetranychus urticae* (Koch), is the most commonly found spider mite in kiwifruit in the Sacramento Valley.

Life cycle. Eggs of the twospotted mite are laid singly on the undersurface of the leaf, particularly along the midvein, and are spherical and opaque. Often the eggs are laid within the spider mite webbing; only when population densities are high are they found on the upper leaf surface. Newly hatched larvae have six legs. Large, dark "food" spots form soon after feeding on the backs of twospotted mites. As the mites mature, they become eight-legged with obvious food spots on their backs. Adults are about $2/100$ inch long and are yellowish-green to amber in body color.

As mature females, twospotted mites overwinter under bark and in litter. In spring, as days become longer and temperatures warm, the females move onto the foliage, beginning the production of many generations each year. Foliage injury, short day lengths in fall, and low temperatures can stimulate female twospotted mites to go into their overwintering resting stage.

Damage. Environmental conditions strongly influence spider mite populations. Hot, dry, dusty plantings, the result of neglect or improper irrigation, are more likely to be attacked. Kiwifruit plantings adjoined by neglected or heavily infested almond plantings, a preferred host of spider mites, are particularly vulnerable.

Spider mite feeding results in yellowing of the leaf surface. When mite populations are high, feeding can result in dry, dead leaves followed by defoliation. Sun-exposed fruit, a result of defoliation, can become offgrade. Large amounts of fine webbing characterize their presence.

Management. Natural enemies do a good job of checking spider mite populations, except when they are disrupted by pesticide applications to control other pests or when mite pressure is high from neighboring crops. Check the underneath surface of leaves on vines in the nursery or vineyard during the growing season for the presence of spider mites, their webbing, or their damage; this can be done along with other cultural duties. If spider mites are evident and natural enemies are absent or if leaf damage has begun, undertake the chemical control procedures available for nonbearing nursery stock.

PLANT BUGS

The adult boxelder bug, *Leptocoris trivittatus* (Say), has a dark oval body with many fine red lines on its back (**plate 34**). The red undersides of the wings can easily be seen during flight. Nymphs are small, bright red, crawling insects. These insects invade kiwifruit in early spring (February through March) before their preferred hosts (maple, oak, elderberry, and boxelder) leaf out.

Life cycle. Boxelder bugs overwinter as adults in grassy areas and around buildings. In spring, overwintering adults become active and lay the first-generation eggs. Nymphs from these eggs develop in late spring and give rise to adults in midsummer. These adults produce a second generation that completes development in early fall. Adults then disperse to overwintering sites.

Damage and management. The boxelder bug feeds on floral buds and fruit stems, causing bud and fruit drop. Fruit deformities have been associated with boxelder bug populations, but have not yet been proved to result directly from boxelder feeding. Research is underway to determine their cause.

Direct control measures, if needed, toward the adults in early spring as floral buds are developing.

HARVEST AND POSTHARVEST HANDLING

24

Postharvest Physiology and Causes of Deterioration

MARY LU ARPAIA, F. GORDON MITCHELL, AND ADEL A. KADER

Kiwifruit, a climacteric fruit that can ripen on or off the vine, is extremely sensitive to ethylene action, even at concentrations as low as 20 parts per billion (ppb) and even at low temperatures, such as 32°F (0°C). At harvest, the fruit contains between 5 and 8 percent starch (fresh weight basis), which is hydrolyzed into sugars during ripening, and the soluble solids content nearly doubles. Rapid flesh softening during the first 6 to 8 weeks of storage is paralleled by, and may be related to, the starch hydrolysis.

Kiwifruit growth follows a curve that has three stages (see chapter 6, *Flower and Fruit Development*). Maturity is generally determined on the basis of total solids or soluble solids content. Ripening and senescence follow maturation. The rate of postharvest deterioration depends upon several internal and external factors.

MORPHOLOGICAL CHARACTERISTICS

Botanically, the kiwifruit is a berry with numerous locules filled with many small, soft, black seeds (Fig. 24.1). The green-colored flesh (edible portion) has three regions: the outer pericarp, the inner pericarp, and the columella (core), which is lighter green than the pericarp tissues. The relatively thin brown skin includes a periderm (rather than an epidermis) and hypodermal cells. Cork cells can sometimes be seen covering small wounds. No stomates are observed on the kiwifruit surface, but other openings where trichomes are removed provide adequate gas exchange.

Kiwifruit have large and small hairs on their surface; small hairs may be an arrested early stage of development of large hairs, which are multicelled and sometimes branched (Fig. 24.2a). The large hairs (trichomes) on mature kiwifruit are arranged in fairly regular but discontinuous bands around the fruit; the bands are very close at the stylar end and become progressively further apart towards the stalk end. Most of the small unicellular hairs on the surface of mature kiwifruit are collapsed (Fig. 24.2b) as a result of handling during harvesting and postharvest operations. Brushing kiwifruit removes most of the trichomes ("fuzz"), but this may destroy their basal cells (see broken trichomes in Figure 24.2b) and provide openings for water loss and pathogen attack.

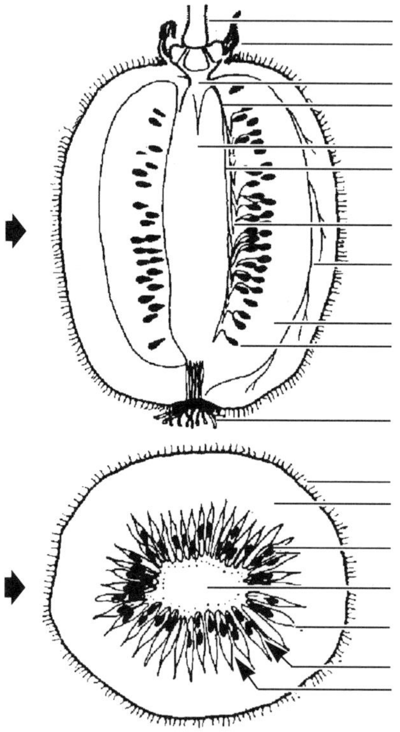

Fig. 24.1. *Top*: Longitudinal midsection of a mature "Hayward" kiwifruit with position of locule shown *left* and vascular system *right*. Arrow ▶ shows position of cross-section.
Bottom: Cross mid-section; *arrow* ▶ shows position of the longitudinal section. (Source: Ferguson, A. R., 1984. Kiwifruit: a botanical review. Hort. Rev. 6:1-64.)

PHYSICAL CHARACTERISTICS

Kiwifruit vary in size when physiologically mature and can be up to 3 inches (76 mm) long and 2 inches (51 mm) in diameter. They have a density of about 1.04 g/cm³ and do not float in water. They reportedly have a packing density of 31.8 lb/ft³ (510 kg/m³), when loose, which would be in the range of the packing density of peaches. Moisture content, near 85 per-

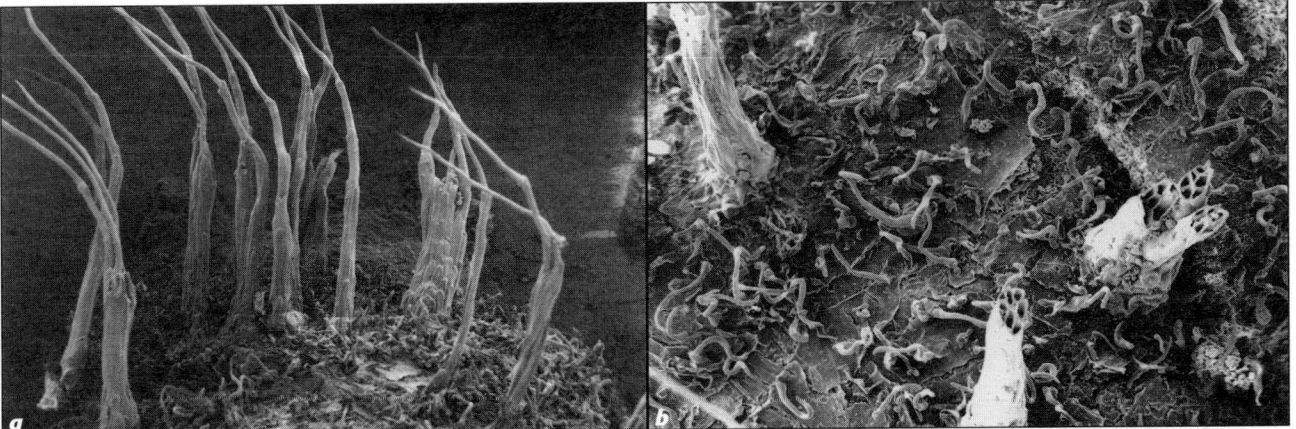

Fig. 24.2. Scanning electron micrographs of kiwifruit surface. (*a*) Trichomes or multicelled hairs are magnified 31.8 X; (*b*) broken trichomes (*lower right*) and small unicellular hairs (mostly collapsed) are magnified 58.4 X.

cent at early harvest, declines to near 80 percent by late harvest, primarily because of carbohydrate accumulation. Specific heat above freezing has been reported 0.87 Btu/lb °F (3,650 J/kg °C); thermal conductivity between 37° and 50°F (3° and 10°C) has been reported at 0.247 Btu/ft °F (0.427 W/m °C). The highest freezing point reported is 29.3°F (–1.5°C), but the soluble solids content (SSC) of the tested fruit was not specified. Based upon freezing point studies with other fruits, this would represent a population averaging 14 percent SSC, which would be typical of kiwifruit after ripening or after prolonged storage.

PHYSIOLOGICAL CHARACTERISTICS

Respiratory pattern and rate

Like all fresh fruits, the kiwifruit continues its life processes until processed or consumed. Through respiration it oxidizes stored food reserves to generate the energy needed to maintain these life processes. The respiratory process also results in changes that lead to ultimate ripening of the fruit—starches are converted to sugars, acid changes occur, flavors and odors develop, and the flesh softens. Energy not needed to maintain life processes is released as heat, a consideration in the temperature management of the fruit.

Respiratory activity of kiwifruit is low, in the same range as that of apples and grapes. Because of this, kiwifruit can be stored for a fairly long time. Although various levels of respiratory activity have been reported, they typically start at 3 to 7 mg CO_2/kg-hr at 32°F (0°C) with a temperature coefficient (Q_{10}) near 3.0, meaning that the rate of respiratory activity increases threefold for each 18°F (10°C) temperature rise. Thus, an estimated rate of respiratory activity of Hayward kiwifruit (in mg CO_2/kg-hr) could average about 3 to 4 at 32°F (0°C), 5 to 7 at 41°F (5°C), 9 to 12 at 50°F (10°C), 16 to 22 at 59°F (15°C), 27 to 36 at 68°F (20°C), and 47 to 60 at 77°F (25°C). A freshly harvested kiwifruit at 77°F (25°C) would therefore respire at 47/3—about 15 times the rate expected following cooling to 32°F (0°C).

The respiratory activity discussed previously is related to kiwifruit held in unripe condition. Kiwifruit belongs to a group of fruits classified as climacteric, those whose rate of physiological processes, including respiration, increases rapidly as ripening approaches. Other fruits in this group include apples, pears, peaches, plums, and avocados. In carefully measuring these changes in kiwifruit, however, we found that the increased rates of respiration and ethylene production do not occur until the fruit are fully ripe (Fig. 24.3).

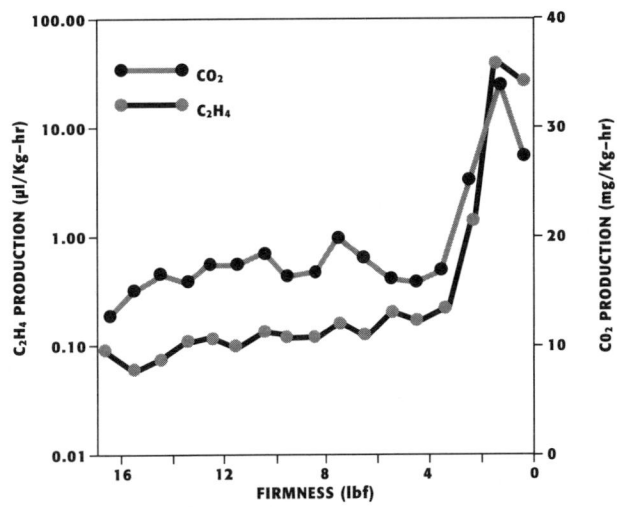

Fig. 24.3. Changes in rates of respiration (CO_2) and ethylene (C_2H_4) production in relation to flesh firmness of kiwifruit.

Thus, maintaining kiwifruit in an unripe condition keeps the rate of respiratory activity low.

Rates of ripening, respiration, and ethylene production vary greatly among individual kiwifruit when placed at 68°F (20°C) immediately after harvest to ripen (Fig. 24.4). The large standard deviations for firmness data indicate large variations among individual fruit in their ripening (softening) rate. Variations in respiration and ethylene production rates are shown among the three replicates, but carbon dioxide and ethylene production patterns are parallel for each replicate (Fig. 24.4).

Ethylene production

Ethylene production rate by mature kiwifruit at harvest is very low (0.1 to 1.0 µl/kg-hr at 68°F [20°C]) and increases markedly with ripening to 50 to 100 µl/kg-hr. The rate of ethylene production can be increased to respond to physical injuries or other stresses, but often such an increase is temporary and the production rate returns to the same level as that of uninjured fruit.

Ethylene production rates vary greatly among individual fruit upon transfer from storage at 32°F (0°C) to ripening conditions at 68°F (20°C). This variation in rates becomes less and the time needed for individual fruit to reach higher ethylene production rates becomes shorter and more uniform with increased storage time at 32°F (0°C). Kiwifruit placed at 68°F (20°C) without cold storage may take about 17±7 days to ripen; those stored for 6 months at 32°F (0°C) ripen in storage.

In all cases, the increased rate of ethylene production is paralleled by an increase in internal ethylene concentration, higher respiration rate, increased SSC (due to starch hydrolysis), and decreased acidity and flesh firmness.

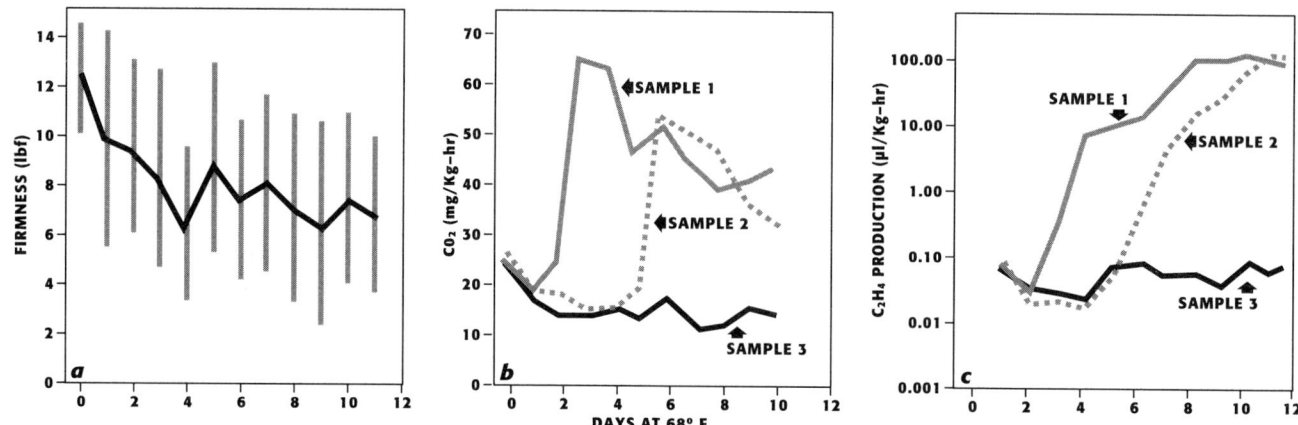

Fig. 24.4. Postharvest behavior of kiwifruit during ripening at 68°F (20°C) immediately after harvest: (*a*) changes in flesh firmness (standard deviation for each data point shown), (*b*) respiratory activity of three replications held under identical conditions, (*c*) ethylene production (log scale) of three replications held under identical conditions (same fruit as in [*b*]).

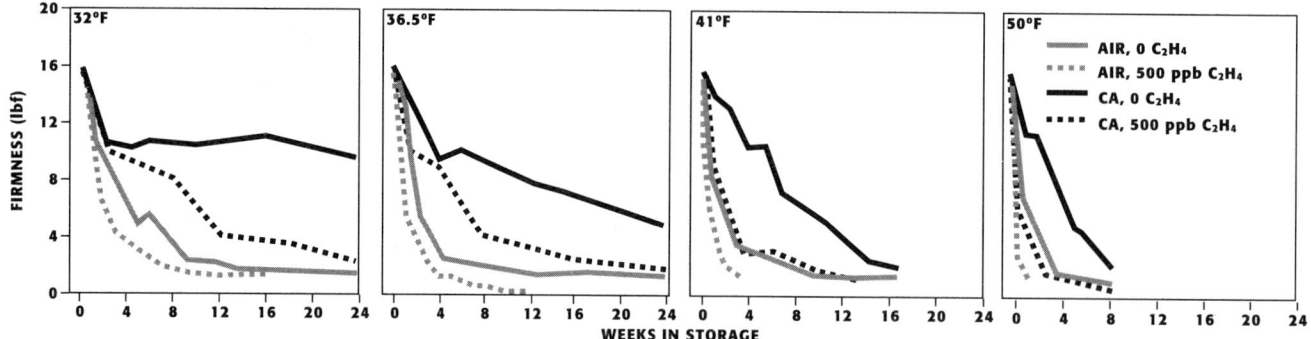

Fig. 24.5. Kiwifruit softening during storage at 32° (0°C), 36.5° (2.5°C), 41° (5°C), or 50°F (10°C) in air or controlled atmosphere (CA) (2 percent O_2 + 5 percent CO_2) with or without the addition of 500 ppb ethylene. LSD values shown were calculated based on a one-way analysis of variance. (Source: Arpaia et al. 1986. Ethylene and temperature effects on softening and white core inclusions of kiwifruit stored in air or controlled atmospheres. J. Amer. Soc. Hort. Sci. 111(1):149-153.)

CAUSES OF DETERIORATION

Flesh softening

Kiwifruit soften rapidly after harvest and ripen completely with time in 32°F (0°C) air storage. Rate of softening is slowed but not stopped at low temperature (Fig. 24.5), increases with increased ethylene in the atmosphere, and can be slowed when placed under controlled atmosphere conditions of elevated carbon dioxide (CO_2) and reduced oxygen (O_2).

Flesh firmness declines sharply during the first 1 to 2 months in storage, coinciding with the conversion of starch to sugars in the fruit. It has been suggested that this firmness decline is, at least partly, a response to the loss in starch. Placing kiwifruit under controlled atmosphere conditions does not stop starch conversion to sugar and does not stop this rapid flesh softening during early storage.

Early harvest of kiwifruit does not help in maintaining flesh firmness during storage. During the normal harvest period, kiwifruit soften at about the same rate in storage at 32°F (0°C) as on the vine. Fruit harvested at an obviously immature stage soften more slowly during subsequent air storage, but the fruit has an unacceptable flavor.

At 32°F (0°C) air storage, flesh firmness declines by an average of about 40 percent of remaining firmness each month during the first 3 months of storage. There are unexplained differences in the rate of softening of kiwifruit from different vineyards, even when the crop is handled and stored under identical conditions. Slowing the rate of flesh softening is a major goal of any long-term kiwifruit storage program.

Responses to ethylene

Ethylene is implicated in much of the flesh softening and ripening that occurs in kiwifruit after harvest. Ethylene at very low concentration in the storage atmosphere has been shown to influence the rate of flesh softening. In past years it has been recommended that ethylene levels be held below 20 ppb to minimize the effect on softening. New research shows, however, that even 10 ppb or below increases the rate of softening, and, therefore, the ethylene level should be held as low as possible, with a goal of staying below 10 ppb.

In the low ethylene range, between 0 and 50 ppb, the higher the ethylene concentration the faster the flesh softening occurs. Even in controlled atmosphere storage, elevated ethylene accelerates softening, and an ethylene-associated, white-core inclusion disorder has been identified that will be discussed later. A 50-ppb ethylene exposure at 32°F (0°C) results in flesh softening equal to fruit exposed to 0 ppb ethylene at 36.5°F (2.5°C).

During any exposure before cooling, the effect of ethylene on flesh softening depends upon exposure time, maturity level of the fruit, and ethylene concentration. Low-maturity fruit show little response to 200-ppb ethylene exposure for as long as 18 hours following harvest; higher-maturity fruit show a substantial response. Low-maturity fruit require about 12 hours exposure to 1,000 ppb ethylene for a firmness effect to show; higher-maturity fruit show substantial effect after 6 hours.

Physical damage

Bruised kiwifruit tissue becomes watersoaked and does not turn brown as does tissue in most other fruits because of the lower content of polyphenols, lower activity of polyphenol oxidase, and higher concentration of ascorbic acid (inhibitor of brown discoloration).

The influence of fruit flesh firmness level on injury susceptibility has been studied, along with an evaluation of fruit response to such injuries. Both impact

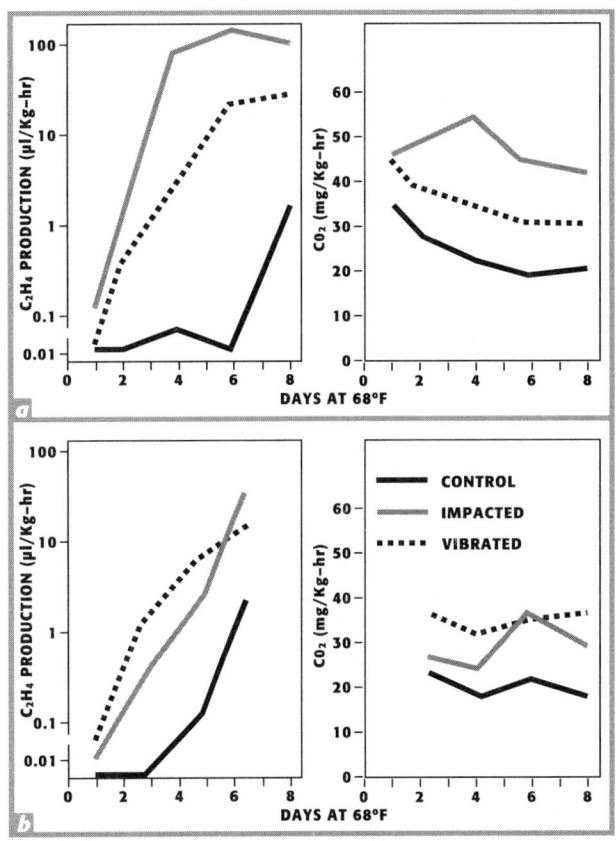

Fig. 24.6. Average respiration (CO_2 production) and ethylene (C_2H_4) production by kiwifruit subjected to mechanical injury after 4 weeks (a) and 8 weeks (b) in storage at 32°F (0°C) and 95 percent RH. Fruits injured at a flesh firmness of 5.3 lbf (a) and 2.5 lbf (b). (Source: Gatti, R. 1984. Susceptibility of kiwifruits to mechanical injury at harvest and during storage. M.S. Thesis, Univ. Calif., Davis.)

bruising (caused by dropping of the fruit) and abrasion or vibration bruising (caused by fruit movement during transport) were evaluated. When firm fruit equal to or greater than 13 pounds-force (lbf) [6 kilograms force (kgf)] were impacted, a light, whitish bruise resulted. The white color resulted from failure of the injured cells to convert starch to sugar, and this could be demonstrated by staining the starch black with an iodine solution. When fruit softened to about 5 or 6 lbf (about 2.5 kgf), a translucent bruise resulted. This injured flesh no longer contained starch. At intermediate firmness between about 13 and 6 lbf (about 6 and 2.5 kgf), no visual bruising symptoms appeared.

Kiwifruit injured at above 13 lbf (6 kgf) flesh firmness did not show any physiological response in either elevated carbon dioxide or ethylene production. However, below 13 lbf (6 kgf), impact bruising and vibration bruising stimulated respiration and ethylene production rates (Fig. 24.6), which may be associated with accelerated deterioration.

Vibration bruising of kiwifruit usually resulted in only minor signs of surface injury, but could cause severe internal flesh injury. Such injury occurred when fruit softened to about 5 lbf (about 2.5 kgf). Concurrent with this injury was a sharp increase in ethylene production that persisted for at least 1 week. Opportunity for such vibration bruising can be expected during transport from packinghouse to distribution market. This provides a compelling reason for attempting to market kiwifruit at firmness above the 5 lbf (or 2.5 kgf) level.

Results of these kiwifruit injury studies suggest that kiwifruit should be picked at or above 13 lbf (6 kgf) flesh firmness (8 mm tip), that fruit drops and abrasion must be avoided throughout handling, and that fruit should be transported to market when at least 5 lbf (or 2.5 kgf) flesh firmness. Other studies show that kiwifruit should be brushed either before cooling or after allowing several days of storage.

Transpiration (water loss)

Kiwifruit are highly susceptible to water loss (leading to shriveling) if kept under relative humidities below 92 to 95 percent. During storage at 32°F (0°C), the lower the relative humidity the greater weight loss. High air velocity in storage increases rate of water loss. Sun-exposed kiwifruit (that have darkened but not burned) may lose water at a rate 25 to 50 percent faster than shaded fruit. Thus, sun-exposed fruit should be packed separately for more immediate marketing. Excessive brushing of kiwifruit can accelerate water loss. Use of polyethylene film liners in shipping containers or packaging kiwifruit in polyethylene film bags reduces water loss during handling and storage.

Physiological disorders

Controlled atmosphere (CA) storage of kiwifruit can delay softening and extend postharvest life. Optimum CA conditions are 2 percent oxygen, 3 to 7 percent carbon dioxide, and no ethylene. Exposure of kiwifruit to ethylene at any level or carbon dioxide levels above 8 percent induces one or more of the following physiological disorders.

Hard-core. The fruit core fails to ripen when the remainder of the fruit is soft and ripe. Hard-core develops in fruit stored for 16 weeks or longer at 32°F (0°C) in 14 to 20 percent carbon dioxide in air. Symptoms of abnormal texture also occur in fruit kept in 8 percent carbon dioxide plus 15 to 20 percent oxygen after 24 weeks at 32°F.

Pericarp translucency. This disorder has been noted in both air- and CA-stored kiwifruit at 32°F. It appears as translucent patches in the outer pericarp tissue at the stylar end which may extend up the sides of the fruit (**plate 35**). Researchers from New Zealand have noted similar internal breakdown in fruit after more than 16 weeks at 32°F in 10 or 14 percent carbon dioxide in air. Pericarp translucency is more severe after prolonged storage, but it can be observed after 12 weeks of storage at 32°F. It is most noticeable following poststorage ripening at 68°F (20°C). The development of translucency is less under CA conditions and is related to both low oxygen and elevated carbon dioxide levels. Levels of carbon dioxide of 3 to 7 percent do not aggravate symptom development. The presence of ethylene at 500 ppb or higher in the storage atmosphere exacerbates symptom development. In the presence of ethylene, symptom development at all carbon dioxide concentrations is greater or equal to development in air storage at 32°F.

Pericarp granulation. The occurrence of granulation is predominantly at the stylar end of the fruit, but as in the case of translucency may extend up the sides of the fruit (**plate 36**). Symptoms of granulation have been reported for both New Zealand and California kiwifruit after 32°F storage. This disorder also is more severe with prolonged storage and after ripening at 68°F (20°C). Unlike translucency, however, fruit stored at varying levels of carbon dioxide (0 to 7 percent CO_2) plus 2 percent oxygen have similar levels of severity as compared to air-stored fruit. Adding ethylene (500 ppb) to the storage atmosphere, however, results in greater numbers of affected fruit.

There is no obvious correlation between pericarp translucency and granulation since symptoms can occur independently. The possible role of storage temperature or seasonal variability has not been described for either.

White-core inclusions. The occurrence of white-core inclusions (WCI) is directly related to the presence of ethylene in the controlled atmosphere (CA) and has not been noted in fruit removed from CA without ethylene or in air storage with or without ethylene. Apparently a result of a synergistic interaction between carbon dioxide and ethylene, this disorder appears to involve disruption of starch metabolism in the fruit core. Symptom development closely parallels the rise in soluble solids content and decline in starch content during the first 6 to 8 weeks of storage. This disorder results in distinct white patches of core tissue that are obvious in ripe fruit (**plate 37**). Symptoms have been observed as early as 3 weeks in storage at 32°F. Factors influencing the incidence and severity include carbon dioxide and ethylene concentration within the storage, timing and duration of ethylene exposure, and storage temperature. Preliminary studies show that low oxygen storage (2 percent O_2) plus ethylene result in no WCI development, whereas 5 percent carbon dioxide in air plus ethylene results in WCI development. When fruit are stored at varying levels of carbon dioxide, 0 to 7 percent CO_2, symptom development is greatest at 5 and 7 percent CO_2. Low levels of WCI incidence may also appear in fruit stored at 3 percent CO_2.

WCI's occurrence and severity also depend on ethylene concentration (50 to 5,000 ppb). There is little difference in the severity or incidence when fruit are exposed to 5,000, 1,000, or 500 ppb ethylene for less than 4 weeks. Symptom development at these three concentrations increases rapidly after the fourth week of 32°F storage and remains at a fairly constant level between 6 and 24 weeks. Fruit exposed to 100 ppb ethylene during CA storage show an intermediate response, whereas the presence of 50 ppb ethylene results in a constant low level of symptom severity. Threshold concentration for WCI development is less than 50 ppb ethylene.

The timing and duration of exposure to 500 ppb ethylene during CA storage (2 percent oxygen plus 5 percent carbon dioxide) may also influence development of WCI. If exposure to continuous ethylene is delayed 2 weeks after the beginning of storage, a corresponding 2-week delay in the appearance and development of WCI occurs. When fruit are exposed to short durations of ethylene at the beginning of storage, occurrence and severity are intermediate, implying that continuous exposure to ethylene is not required for WCI development. If exposure to ethylene is delayed until after the rise in fruit soluble solids content, WCI develops at very low ethylene levels, indicating that any exposure to ethylene during controlled atmosphere storage at 32°F can result in WCI.

Storage temperature does influence WCI development. Symptom severity and incidence are similar when fruit were stored in 2 percent oxygen plus 5 percent carbon dioxide plus 500 ppb ethylene at either 36.5°F (2.5°C) or 32°F (0°C), although symptoms appear earlier at 36.5°F (2.5°C). Greatly reduced levels of WCI occur at 41°F (5°C), indicating a temperature threshold for WCI development between 36.5°F (2.5°C) and 41°F (5°C).

Pathological breakdown

Several pathogens can cause postharvest deterioration of kiwifruit. Botrytis gray mold rot caused by *Botrytis cinerea* is the most important and can directly invade the fruit or enter through wounds. Kiwifruit become much more susceptible to Botrytis (and other fungi) as they soften. Thus, maintaining fruit firmness (by rapid cooling, cold storage, and use of controlled atmospheres) can significantly reduce pathological breakdown. Sunburned fruit and physically damaged fruit are also more susceptible to postharvest diseases. For more details on postharvest pathology of kiwifruit, see chapter 28, *Postharvest Storage Diseases*.

25

Composition, Maturity, and Quality

F. GORDON MITCHELL

Kiwifruit have unusual characteristics that must be understood and properly managed if their full market potential is to be achieved. Many of these characteristics are related to their composition and the pattern of compositional changes, changes associated with maturity and maturity selection and their effect on fruit quality. These factors, composition, maturity, and quality, are discussed here.

COMPOSITION

The major kiwifruit cultivars have several characteristics directly or indirectly related to composition. The fruit retain a bright green flesh color even when ripe; most other fruits normally lose that green color during ripening. The flesh does not brown when cut or injured as do most other fruits. They contain an enzyme able to tenderize meat. Among all fruits of commerce, they provide one of the best sources of vitamin C. To understand these and other characteristics, we need to know the details of fruit composition, and in some cases, how that composition changes with fruit development, maturation, and storage.

Fruit growth

Kiwifruit continue to increase in fresh weight and size until harvested, but the most rapid size increase occurs in the first 100 days following bloom. Dry weight of the fruit increases gradually throughout the growing season and slows somewhat as harvest maturity approaches. As a result of these patterns, the percent total solids slowly increases with continued growth of the fruit and begins to level out with advancing fruit maturity. During prolonged storage there is a slow decline in total solids. The pattern of total-solids change closely parallels the pattern of change in soluble solids content (SSC) in ripened fruit, thus making total-solids content a potential maturity index.

Starch content

Kiwifruit are one of a few fruits that retain a high starch content at maturity. Starch content has been measured at near 50 percent of total dry weight at about 4 months past full bloom. Then begins a decline in starch content that is coupled with an increase in soluble solids content. Starch hydrolysis continues after harvest, even while the fruit are in 32°F (0°C) air storage, and is essentially completed within a few weeks of harvest. Freshly harvested kiwifruit can be cleared of starch within 4 to 6 days if held at 68° to 77°F (20° to 25°C) in an ethylene environment.

Soluble sugars

The increase in soluble sugars that begins as kiwifruit approach maturity continues after harvest and peaks about when starch hydrolysis is complete. Kiwifruit are highest in glucose and fructose content, and have a small amount of sucrose. The soluble sugar content gradually declines as the fruit are held in long-term storage.

Acid content

Kiwifruit are relatively high in acid content, reaching near 2 percent of fresh weight at full maturity and declining slowly following harvest. During early development, the fruit are highest in quinic acid, with a lesser amount of malic acid. By harvest the fruit are highest in citric acid, followed closely by quinic acid and a lesser amount of malic acid. Acid content declines as fruit ripen.

Ascorbic acid (vitamin C)

Ascorbic acid content can be well over 100 mg/100 g fresh weight of kiwifruit tissue. Although this is a small part of the total acid content of kiwifruit, it is extremely valuable to the human diet. Kiwifruit are one of the best available natural sources of vitamin C, with a level at least twice that of the orange. There are conflicting reports of changes that may occur in ascorbic acid content of kiwifruit during storage and marketing. Some reports suggest the ascorbic acid content is stable; others indicate an apparent decline when fruit are stored beyond 4 months.

Soluble solids content (SSC)

Soluble solids content (SSC) of kiwifruit is composed mostly of soluble sugars and acids. The pattern of change, therefore, closely parallels the change in soluble sugars, peaking at the point when starch hydrolysis is complete and declining slowly with time in storage. This decline results from the use of carbohydrates as the source of energy to maintain the respiratory process in the fruit. Although decline is slow, total reduction in soluble solids content over 6 months can be near 2 percent, depending upon fruit condition, storage temperature, and atmosphere.

Chlorophyll/other pigments

Kiwifruit owe their bright green flesh color to the presence of chlorophyll pigment in the tissue. Chlorophyll, present in the tissue of many other fruits when immature, is normally lost during ripening. The standard commercial kiwifruit cultivars, however, retain their chlorophyll content well past normal limits of storage and ripening.

Kiwifruit also have a substantial amount of yellow carotenoid pigments in the tissue. Only when fruit tissue becomes senescent, resulting in chlorophyll loss, is the yellow flesh color seen in Hayward and other standard kiwifruit cultivars. Other species of *Arguta* can have flesh colors ranging from yellow to red to purple.

Browning reactions

A special feature of the kiwifruit is that it does not brown when cut or injured. Flesh browning in fruit tissue is associated with the enzymatic oxidation of phenolics. Kiwifruit have a relatively low tannin content, and thus a limited availability of phenolic substrate, and also have a low polyphenol oxydase enzyme activity level. These, combined with the high level of ascorbic acid (an antioxidant), can account for the lack of tissue browning.

Tenderizing enzyme

Kiwifruit contain a high level of a protein-digesting enzyme, protease, that has been named "actinidin." Meat can be tenderized by applying slices of fresh kiwifruit over the surface. Actinidin is similar to the papain obtained from papaya fruit and is used in prepared meat tenderizers. Because of the presence of this enzyme, fresh kiwifruit cannot be used in gelatin desserts or jellies because the enzyme prevents them from setting.

Fruit composition

The composition of kiwifruit is summarized in table 25.1. This is adapted primarily from information published in a botanical review of kiwifruit. The author notes that the data were drawn from a number of sources, often with the cultivar unspecified, and with variable information as to the status or condition of the fruit under analysis. For that reason, use these data with caution.

MATURITY

Kiwifruit show little visual change as they approach maturity. They are nearly full size well in advance of maturity, and show only small changes in fruit density as they mature. Although there is a large size variation among fruit on the vine, this appears unrelated to fruit maturity. For these reasons, it is unreasonable to attempt multiple harvest from a vine, and any maturity standard must be based upon a single harvest of all fruit.

Maturity indexes

A number of maturity measures are used for various fruits. Common among these are surface color; flesh color; soluble solids content (SSC), which is mostly

Table 25.1. Composition of mature kiwifruit

Fruit component	Fruit content
	(g/100 g fresh weight)
Total solids	16–22
Soluble solids	14–20
Total sugars	7.5–13
Reducing sugars	6–12
Organic acids (as citric)	1.0–1.6
Pectin	0.3–1.1
Proteins	0.5–1.5
Lipids	0.3–0.9
Crude fiber	1.1–2.9
Minerals (ash)	0.7–1.1
	(mg/100 g)
Calcium	25–60
Magnesium	14–27
Nitrogen	140–190
Phosphorous	20–40
Potassium	230–380
Ascorbic acid	80–300

Adapted from: Ferguson, A. R. 1984. Kiwifruit: a botanical review. Hort. Review 6 (1–64); and personal data of authors.

sugars; titratable acidity; SSC/acid ratio; starch disappearance; seed color change; and flesh firmness. All of these have been studied with kiwifruit, and none has been found completely satisfactory. Surface and flesh color change little over long periods of fruit development; acid composition changes somewhat with development, but the level of titratable acids declines only after a period of storage; starch disappearance is not easily measurable until ripening begins. The two measures that have been widely proposed as kiwifruit maturity indexes are SSC and flesh firmness.

Soluble solids content

Soluble solids content (SSC) has been the most widely used maturity measure, and minimum SSC levels of freshly harvested kiwifruit are commonly used as standards. New Zealand uses a 6.2 percent SSC standard and California a 6.5 percent SSC standard. Because much of the starch conversion into sugars occurs after harvest, an initial SSC measure is only valid if taken immediately after harvesting the fruit. Monitoring the SSC of fruit after packing or after any other delay that allows for starch conversion to sugar and will result in higher SSC levels. These provide false information if judged equal to a 6.5 percent SSC standard taken at time of harvest. Such improperly obtained data do not reflect improved eating quality or consumer satisfaction.

The SSC of kiwifruit can be measured with a handheld refractometer. Cut a wedge extending from stem to blossom end from each fruit extract juice into a small vessel, using any small but strong squeezer; a hand-held lime squeezer works well for this purpose. Stir the sample well and place a drop on the stage of the refractometer. Starch in unripe kiwifruit clouds the stage of the refractometer, making readings difficult to discern. Pouring the sample through a few layers of facial tissue can help to clear the solution by retaining some of the starch. If time is not critical, leave the juice in a well-covered vessel to allow the starch to settle; then pour off the cleared juice.

Use the refractometer properly. Temperature-compensated refractometers are best because temperature or reading adjustments are not needed. Follow directions carefully for a noncompensated refractometer. In any case check the refractometer with distilled water to verify a "0 percent" reading before measuring the juice sample. Dry the instrument thoroughly before adding juice. Wipe the instrument dry and clean as necessary between samples.

Any measure of SSC at harvest provides only a part of the information on carbohydrate accumulation in the kiwifruit. As fruit mature on the plant, part of the SSC increase occurs because new carbohydrate is being produced as a result of the plant's continuing photosynthetic activity. With advancing maturity, however, the accumulation of carbohydrates in the fruit slows, yet the SSC steadily increases. This is the point at which the increase in SSC is mostly due to the conversion of stored carbohydrate reserves in the fruit (starch and other insoluble carbohydrates) to sugars and other soluble solids. At the peak of carbohydrate accumulation in the fruit, they have essentially achieved their best potential eating quality, and further harvest delays will not improve their flavor quality.

SSC of ripe fruit

The eating quality of kiwifruit is most closely related to their SSC after complete ripening of the fruit. Under California growing conditions, when all starch is converted to sugars, the SSC of a mature kiwifruit should normally exceed 14 percent, and the fruit will be of good eating quality. The pattern of SSC accumulation in fully ripened kiwifruit usually begins to plateau by midharvest. There is no similar plateau in the SSC level of freshly harvested fruit. Instead, the SSC level gradually increases throughout the harvest season as starch is converted to sugar.

Because of these patterns of change, the measurement of SSC of ripened kiwifruit before and during harvest can be useful in identifying the carbohydrate accumulation plateau, beyond which further fruit quality improvement will be slight. By measuring these patterns over several seasons, a grower or shipper can better predict future performance of fruit from a specific vineyard and therefore improve scheduling of the harvest.

Kiwifruit can be fairly easily ripened to monitor ripe fruit SSC, but the process takes several days to complete. Freshly harvested kiwifruit ripen most quickly when exposed to ethylene, and, for ripening small samples, fresh apples can be used to provide a good source of ethylene. The sample of freshly harvested kiwifruit can be confined with a few apples in a covered, fruit-ripening bowl or a loosely closed plastic bag and held at warm temperature. At 77°F (25°C) complete ripening takes 4 to 5 days; at 68°F (20°C), 5 to 6 days are needed.

SSC monitoring of ripe fruit can be done in the same way as with freshly harvested fruit, but juice extraction from the soft fruit is easier, and starch is not present to cloud the juice, making the refractometer reading more precise. Because of the time required for fruit ripening, this procedure has not been feasible for use as a maturity standard.

Total solids

A procedure for estimating maturity by measuring total solids (dry weight) of fruit is in final stages of development. The procedure uses microwave drying to determine total solids, and measurement can be completed in 1 hour. As noted, the pattern of change in total solids closely parallels the pattern of change of ripe fruit SSC. Cross-sectional slices (⅛ inch or 3 mm thick) or pulp slurry samples of kiwifruit are accurately weighed, dried until they reach constant weight, using an oven power setting that avoids charring, and percent total solids (dry weight) calculated. The total solids level is near 16 percent at very early harvest and reaches at least 18 to 19 percent by late harvest. Because seed content can vary greatly in kiwifruit, it appears desirable to remove seeds in preparing samples for drying.

Based upon a 3-year study in California, this procedure appears to be a good candidate for use as a maturity standard. Its use has already begun in Australia where it was first proposed. A similar procedure is now used to monitor avocado maturity in California. Although the procedure is slower and more expensive than the SSC monitoring procedure in use, its accuracy appears to be greatly improved. A regression line established from preliminary data indicates that about 80 percent of the change in SSC of ripened fruit can be explained by this total solids measure. Based upon that regression line, a total solids reading of 16.2 percent would about equal 14 percent SSC in ripened fruit.

Solids' losses during storage

Kiwifruit in storage are utilizing stored carbohydrates to provide the energy needed to maintain physiological activity (see chapter 24, *Postharvest Physiology and Causes of Deterioration*). During prolonged storage, even at 32°F (0°C), this can result in substantial reductions in both total solids and SSC of the fruit. After 6 months' storage this solids reduction can approach 2 percent of initial weight, and fruit taste acceptability is reduced. To compensate for this, fruit for long-term storage should be picked late in the harvest season when SSC exceeds 16 percent and total solids exceed 18 percent of fresh fruit weight.

Flesh firmness

The level of flesh firmness at harvest is influenced by several factors other than fruit maturity; therefore, this is not a useful measure of minimum maturity. However, although maximum harvest maturity standards are not normally used, it appears that measuring flesh firmness could be useful for kiwifruit. As kiwifruit flesh firmness declines, the variability of flesh firmness becomes greater. The standard deviation (a measure of variability) for flesh firmness measurements begins to increase when average firmness drops to about 13 pounds-force [lbf] (6 kilograms-force [kgf]). Thus, more soft fruit that are subject to bruising injury will occur as the average firmness drops to less than 13 lbf (6 kgf). Furthermore, kiwifruit at about this firmness respond in such a way physiologically to injury (with increased ethylene production) that postharvest life is shortened. For these reasons it appears that kiwifruit harvest should begin by the time flesh firmness drops to about 14 lbf (6.5 kgf), regardless of other maturity measures.

Maturity and storage performance

Storage tests show that late harvested kiwifruit retain their flesh firmness better than earlier harvested fruit. For example, after 6 months in ethylene-free air storage at 32°F (0°C), fruit harvested in late September at about 18 lbf (8.2 kgf) flesh firmness averaged 1.3 lbf (0.6 kgf); fruit harvested in early November at about 15 lbf (6.8 kgf) flesh firmness averaged 3.9 lbf (1.8 kgf). Both lots were stored for a full 6 months following harvest before evaluation. In this test, the flesh firmness improvement was progressive across five harvests taken at about 10-day intervals. This pattern of improved flesh firmness retention with later harvest was consistent over two seasons in samples from six different locations. Thus, kiwifruit destined for long storage should benefit from delayed harvest.

Maturity summary

The present California maturity standard for kiwifruit is 6.5 percent SSC. This initial SSC measurement is only valid when monitored on freshly harvested kiwifruit and would be of greatest value when used as a vineyard harvest guide. A better indicator of flavor quality is SSC of ripened fruit; a minimum of 14 percent has been suggested as a quality guide. Although this is useful as a management tool, the time required to monitor SSC of ripe fruit makes it difficult to use as a legal maturity index. Research suggests that a microwave drying procedure for monitoring total solids may be useful as a maturity standard. A total solids content of 16.2 percent would correspond with about 14 percent SSC of ripe fruit. Late-harvested fruit appear to retain flesh firmness better than earlier harvested fruit during long-term storage. A minimum flesh firmness of about 14 lbf (6.5 kgf) (using an 8-mm tip) might be used to allow harvest of fruit that do not

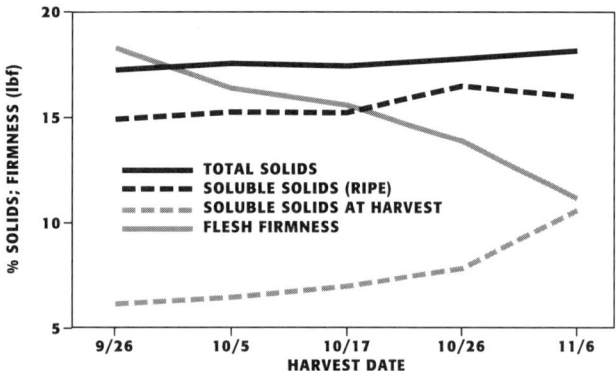

Fig. 25.1. The pattern of changes in flesh firmness, soluble solids of fruit at harvest and after ripening, and total solids of kiwifruit, as monitored at six California locations, 1989 season.

meet other maturity standards. The general pattern of changes in solids and firmness during the harvest season is shown in Figure 25.1.

QUALITY

The quality of kiwifruit is related to production, harvest, and postharvest handling. To be marketed successfully, kiwifruit must be free of defects, such as misshapen fruit, sunburn, insect damage, and mechanical injuries; develop a pleasing flavor, including high SSC and a suitable sugar/acid balance; retain internal characteristics, such as a high level of ascorbic acid (vitamin C); and maintain green flesh color and adequate flesh firmness to allow normal handling, retain suitable flesh texture, and be free of rot.

Many of these qualities are controllable by applying available knowledge to cultural, harvest, and postharvest practices. Training, pruning, thinning, water management, and pest management can all influence many preharvest defects. Proper monitoring of maturity, timing of harvest, and supervision of harvest and packing can control many injury problems, and affect fruit flavor, appearance, and storage softening. Avoidance of ethylene, fast cooling, and good storage management greatly affect storage softening, deterioration, weight loss and shrivel, and development of fruit rot.

Recommendations

Protecting kiwifruit quality requires good management at all stages of crop production and handling.

1. Prune and train to limit crop size. Shade fruit from direct sun exposure, but open the canopy to achieve good photosynthetic efficiency.

2. Thin to remove excessive crop load and to eliminate misshapen and very small fruit.

3. Irrigate to maintain healthy leaf cover; avoid leaf drying that can lead to fruit sunburn.

4. Adopt pest management practices, as needed, to avoid insect or disease infestation of fruit or loss of leaves.

5. Delay harvest until fruit develop a high carbohydrate content; for long-term storage, harvest late to achieve better flesh firmness retention.

6. Harvest before a high incidence of soft fruit begin to appear among fruit on the vine.

7. Supervise harvesting, handling, and packing to protect fruit from mechanical injuries.

8. Avoid exposing fruit to ethylene gas throughout handling and during storage.

9. Rapidly cool fruit to near storage temperature as soon after harvest as possible to delay flesh softening.

10. Maintain a constant low temperature, 32°F (0°C), and high relative humidity during storage to delay flesh softening, fruit shrivel, and development of fruit rot.

11. Continue protection against injuries and ethylene exposure, and maintain low temperature and high relative humidity throughout transportation and market distribution.

26

Harvesting and Preparation for Market

F. GORDON MITCHELL, MARY LU ARPAIA, AND GENE MAYER

Once minimum maturity has been achieved, all kiwifruit from a vineyard can be harvested in a single pick because there are no distinguishing characteristics to help pickers separate immature from mature fruit.

Fruit are harvested by hand, usually into picking bags (Figs. 26.1, 26.2). Because fruit hang in clusters from canes, pickers can usually harvest a large volume in a day, leaving few fruit on the vines. Bottom-dump design picking bags are typically used, and pickers transfer the fruit into field bins (Fig. 26.3).

Pickers normally encounter a few fruit that have softened prematurely, possibly because damage to the stem may have caused them to start ripening as though they had been harvested. If these fruit enter picking bags, bins, or the packing line, they can be crushed and their juice can contaminate healthy fruit. Such contamination can lead to staining of healthy fruit, and the organic matter becomes a medium for growth and spread of surface mold and fruit rots.

To avoid this problem, pickers should remove as many soft fruit as possible. A field check should be made before picking to assess the numbers of soft fruit. If unusual amounts are present, extra labor and supervision should be provided to eliminate such fruit during picking and bin filling.

Carry bins through the field on bin trailers during harvest or distribute them before harvest and load them from the field when full (Fig. 26.4). Most kiwifruit are now handled in standard plywood fruit

Fig. 26.1. Fruit hang in clusters beneath overhead wires, allowing easy access for harvest. Here fruit are being picked into hard-sided, bottom-dump bags.

Fig. 26.2. Pickers grasp individual fruit and pull sideways to snap fruit free from the stem. Pickers often wear soft cotton gloves to reduce fingernail injury to fruit.

Fig. 26.3. To transfer fruit from bags to field bins, full bags are set onto fruit in the bin; with the bag bottom open, the bag is lifted off the fruit. This minimizes chances for fruit injury. Here a soft-sided bag is being used.

Fig. 26.4. In this operation a bin lift trailer is used to distribute empty bins throughout the field, and to pick up full bins and carry them to a packing facility or a transfer point.

bins (47 × 47-inch outside dimension [OD] × 24-inch inside dimension [ID] depth), or in half-bins (12-inch ID). As with other fruits, line the bin with plastic to reduce fruit abrasion against the bin's sides. Bins are normally vented on the bottom; they may also require side venting, depending on the cooling system to be used. Bin side venting calls for using plastic side liners with vents.

PROTECTION IN THE FIELD

Protect kiwifruit from deteriorating during harvest and handling in the field. Deterioration can result from mechanical injuries, delays at warm temperatures (that can lead to softening of fruit, fungal growth, and water loss), extended exposure to direct sun, and exposure to ethylene.

Mechanical injuries

Most mechanical injuries to fruit are associated with rough handling during picking, filling and loading of bins, or transportation. Injuries to kiwifruit are typically from impacts, cuts and punctures, and abrasion. Fit pickers with soft cotton gloves to avoid injuring the fruit surface during harvest. The use of padded, hard-sided picking bags can minimize opportunities for impact bruises as pickers move through the vines. Supervision to assure that fruit are not dropped from the picking bags during bin filling can reduce impacts.

Supervision of bin handling from field to cooler is also needed to avoid excessive injuries. Tractor forklift movement can damage fruit if bins are carried long distances on rough drives before transfer to a truck or trailer. Grading of vineyard drives and limiting the speed and distance of transport by field forklifts can reduce injuries.

During trucking from the vineyard to cooling and/or packing sites, damage can occur because of rough roads, excessive speeds, and long distances. Routing to avoid rough roads and setting speed limits based upon road conditions can reduce injuries.

During transportation, abrasion/vibration injuries are common. Bin side liners can help reduce them, but other modifications may be needed. Air-suspension systems installed on truck and trailer axles have reduced damaging vibrations and injuries in other fruits, and should similarly benefit kiwifruit. For long-distance transportation (more than 50 miles [80 km]), top bin pads may add protection. These pads, used sometimes for pears and stone fruits, consist of a plywood sheet cut to fit inside the bin and lined with a thick foam plastic sheet. The pads are placed over the fruit and held in place with short rubber trucker straps secured several inches down in the corner of the bins and then hooked to the pad corners. The slight tension of the straps helps the pad immobilize top fruit and reduce abrasion.

Protection from heat

While they are held in the field, protect harvested fruit from excessive exposure to sun. Even though kiwifruit are usually harvested during mild weather, the dark fruit can absorb considerable heat from exposure to direct midday sun. Any fruit awaiting transport should be held in shade. Although the effect of warm temperatures on kiwifruit has not been monitored, other dark fruits have been shown to heat to at least 10°F (6°C) above air temperature as a result of exposure to direct sun.

Prompt transportation from the field minimizes deterioration in kiwifruit. If they are to be cooled before packing, they should be placed in the cooler always within a few hours of harvest. If they are to be packed before cooling, immediately transfer them to the packinghouse and complete packing within 6 hours of harvest. Besides minimizing deterioration, minimizing the time fruit are held at warm temperatures can reduce cooling costs by limiting the amount of heat they can gain following picking.

Ethylene exposure

Throughout handling, avoid exposing kiwifruit to ethylene gas. Measurements have indicated fairly low ethylene levels (typically below 10 parts per billion) in vineyards and along highways in rural areas of California where kiwifruit are grown. Because petroleum-fueled truck, tractor, and forklift engines can produce large amounts of ethylene, do not hold kiwifruit in closed-in areas where they are operating. Similarly, in delivering to a cooler or packinghouse, hold the fruit in an open area free of possible ethylene contamination from equipment, smoke, or other produce that are actively generating ethylene, and where only electrically powered forklifts are used.

PACKING PREPARATIONS

Whether kiwifruit are packed before or after cooling depends on the desirability of achieving rapid, thorough cooling, balanced by the effect of that cooling on fruit handling during packing.

Kiwifruit cool more quickly with forced-air cooling in field bins than in packed flats (see chapter 27, *Cooling, Storage, Transportation, and Distribution*). When the cold fruit are subsequently packed, however, some fruit warming occurs from exposure to warm temperatures, and the high-moisture environment of the cooler can soften the dead floral parts on fruit and make removing them more difficult (Fig. 26.5). One small test of kiwifruit brushing (to remove dead floral parts) suggested that brushing injuries could be greater on recently cooled fruit than on warm fruit or on fruit held for a few days in cold storage.

If freshly harvested fruit are packed, their cleaning (by brushing) is easier and potentially more thorough than if the fruit were first cooled, and there are possibly fewer injuries from brushing. Also, refrigeration is not lost as a result of rewarming cooled fruit or of discarding previously cooled cull fruit. This procedure, however, delays movement from vine to cooler, and fruit packed in flats are more difficult to cool than fruit in field bins. Because flesh softening is associated with delays in harvesting and exposure to heat and ethylene, precautions must be taken during packing delays to avoid ethylene contamination of the fruit.

An alternative to cooling before or after packing is to partially cool the fruit before packing and to complete cooling after packing. This is commonly done with some fruits, but has not been critically studied for kiwifruit. Cooling fruit to near the air's dewpoint temperature and packing within 1 day following harvest reduces deterioration. For kiwifruit, avoidance of ethylene exposure during the delays remains critical. Whether partial cooling before packing eases problems associated with cleaning cold fruit is not known. The moderate temperature of the packed fruit entering the cooler could ease cooling packed fruit.

Avoiding ethylene

To avoid exposure to ethylene during kiwifruit packing, enclosed fruit storage and packing areas require good air ventilation. That means forbidding the operation of internal-combustion engines, which can quickly generate unacceptably high ethylene levels in the atmosphere, preventing delivery trucks from idling during unloading, and using only electric forklifts. It also means not exposing kiwifruit to smoke or exhaust fumes from other sources and forbidding cigarette smoking where kiwifruit are being accumulated or handled. Allow no other ethylene-producing commodities in the vicinity of kiwifruit, and remove soft or decaying kiwifruit from the area.

In tests, only a few hours exposure of kiwifruit to ethylene before cooling initiated rapid flesh softening that continued during subsequent cold storage (Fig. 26.6). Kiwifruit tolerate only a small fraction of the ethylene concentration acceptable for most other commodities; thus, any potential source of ethylene must be eliminated.

Cleaning and presizing

Kiwifruit normally pass through several steps for cleaning, elimination of undersized and substandard fruit, and segregation of fruit by size before packing.

Kiwifruit can be dumped with standard inversion-type dry bin dumps (Figs. 26.7 and 26.8) that are equipped with padded lids to protect the fruit from injury during inversion. As the dumped fruit are metered onto distribution rolls, sorting may be needed to eliminate obviously soft fruit before they are crushed and their juice contaminates sound fruit. The distribution rolls should not be of bare metal because kiwifruit juice can solubilize metal ions and cause dark "ink spots" on otherwise sound fruit that contact those rolls. We have caused such "ink spots" by lightly rubbing kiwifruit over a steel plate wetted with kiwifruit juice, and have seen similar symptoms in commercial packs (**plate 38**).

Kiwifruit juice on any roll or belt can contaminate sound fruit, and the juice becomes colonized by

Fig. 26.5. Mature kiwifruit retain many of the dead floral parts at both the stem and blossom ends, and these can become sources of inoculum for fungal infections. Brushing is intended to remove, as thoroughly as possible, these and any other organic debris on the kiwifruit surface.

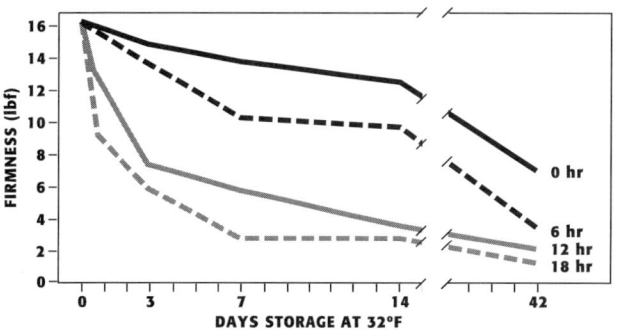

Fig. 26.6. Short exposures of freshly harvested kiwifruit to ethylene can result in excessive flesh softening that will extend well into the storage period. Here, kiwifruit exposed to 1 ppm (1,000 ppb) ethylene for 6 to 18 hours immediately following harvest and then stored at 32°F (0°C) for 7 weeks were 4 to 6 pounds softer than fruit not exposed to ethylene.

microorganisms. During storage, surface fungal growth on contaminated fruit can cause dark spots, necessitating resorting before shipment.

Frequent cleaning of all packing line equipment is desirable to minimize contamination and to maintain clean fruit. In critical locations, such as roll and belt beds, it may be desirable to provide continuous cleaning to eliminate most contamination. Cleaning equipment can often be installed underneath return sections of rolls and belts, where they are easily serviced but not intrusive.

Because of their shape, kiwifruit can be injured by presizers that are used for other fruits. Most notably, drop roll presizers can crush flat or oval kiwifruit and spread juice to contaminate otherwise sound fruit. Because Hayward kiwifruit tend not to be round, this type of presizer should not be used. Other nonrolling, fixed-opening presizers can be used without damage to kiwifruit, but their level of accuracy is low. Thus, some undersized fruit will remain on the line for elimination later.

Trash eliminators remove loose dirt, leaves, and other debris from the line. Typically, fans placed under an open roll bed blow trash for capture in a vacuum line and removal.

Brushing fruit

Kiwifruit are brushed to remove dead floral parts as well as small trash that has become entangled in the surface trichomes ("hairs"). Under normal, dry field conditions, the floral parts that remain attached to the kiwifruit are brittle and easily removed by brushing. Under moist field conditions, or following cold storage, those floral parts absorb moisture and become soft and flexible, making removal difficult.

Brushing is not intended to remove the trichomes from the fruit, but some removal will occur. The brushes' speed can be slowed so that minimal trichome removal will occur. The soft bristles in the brushes should be long enough to reach the floral parts at each end of the kiwifruit.

Many brush beds utilize the flow of incoming fruit to push the forward fruit over the brush rolls. With a constant supply of fruit entering the line, dwell time can be fairly standard. However, any delays or slowing of delivery can result in some fruit spending excessive dwell time on the brushes. Kiwifruit brush beds, therefore, should be equipped for automatic cleanout.

The potential for fruit injury during brushing has been noted previously. Kiwifruit coming directly from the field and fruit that have remained several days in cold storage appear less prone to injury than those brushed soon after initial cooling. This increased susceptibility to injury may be associated with increased fruit turgidity following cooling, a condition that decreases as fruit lose water during storage. Because such injury can result in an initial increase in ethylene production by the kiwifruit, it can potentially accelerate fruit deterioration during storage.

Fig. 26.7. At the packing line, bins are placed on the dump line for processing.

Fig. 26.8. Bin dumping is by a dry inversion dump. As the bin enters the dump it is covered by a padded lid; after inversion, the lower section of the lid becomes a gate through which the fruit can flow onto the delivery belt. Here, a soft rubber wheel is used to monitor the depth of fruit on the delivery belt and to control the speed of movement of the belt accordingly. Some other units use sonar monitors to accomplish this.

SORTING

Quality control requires adequate numbers of well trained and supervised sorters viewing the fruit (Fig. 26.9). The sorting facility should have sufficient space to accommodate peak volumes. Sorting space needs should be determined based on the most difficult conditions to be routinely encountered: smallest fruit size (greatest number of decisions per unit volume), highest percentage of defects, greatest number of separations to be achieved, and maximum volume of fruit to be sorted.

Sorting for defects is normally done by hand. Presently in early stages of development are electronic optical sorters that can separate fruit by size, color, shape, and presence of defects. These provide hope that future sorting may be more accurately accomplished and the volume of hand sorting reduced.

Supervisors of sorting operations must monitor the quality of both incoming and outgoing fruit. To achieve efficient, high-quality sorting, supervisors must be able to slow or speed delivery of fruit to sorting tables as fruit size and quality change. Supervisors should train workers so that they are familiar with sorting requirements and their responsibilities.

Fig. 26.9. Fruit reaching the sorting tables are divided into two narrow roller conveyors, and a removal belt is placed between these. The roller conveyors turn the fruit for better sorter visibility, and second-grade fruit are placed on the removal belt. Cull chutes are beside each worker to receive unmarketable fruit.

Space requirements

The amount of space required for sorting depends on the relative fruit size being sorted, because many more small than large fruit are sorted per package or per ton. Sorting space also depends upon the percentage of fruit rejected or diverted, because accurate separation of defective or alternate grade fruit slows sorting. Thus, the sorting line must accommodate the number of workers needed to efficiently sort small-size lots containing a high level of defects.

The amount of sorting space required also depends on the number of decisions that must be made in fruit separation. This includes removing all fruit with unmarketable defects and may also include separating more and less round fruit and/or lighter and darker colored fruit.

Worker training/supervision

Sorters must be trained to recognize fruit defects and to know where to draw the line on market acceptability. The supervisor is responsible for knowing the grade level to be packed and should be constantly updated on inspection results. The supervisor must then be able to retrain workers, as needed, to meet changing packing requirements.

The sorting line supervisor greatly influences the quality of the pack being produced. Although there are legal minimum quality standards, many shippers base the reputation of their labels on packing to a level above the minimum. Thus, the sorting line supervisor must be kept aware of management policy regarding the quality level desired for packed fruit.

The sorting line

To sort efficiently, workers must be able to view all parts of each fruit and to remove or divert with ease defective or lower grade fruit. Reasonable worker comfort is also needed to maintain efficiency over long working hours. Because the sorting line must handle fruit without causing injury, attention must be given to all aspects of designing and lighting the line.

The sorting line must be sufficiently narrow to avoid the need for excessive worker reach, and fruit removal from the line should be either to a convenient cull fruit chute at the edge of the line or to a center diversion belt just beyond the line. Often, unmarketable fruit goes to the cull chute next to the worker. Second-grade fruit is transferred to the center diversion belt which, ideally, should be at or near the same level as the sorting line to avoid excessive reaching or throwing of fruit.

These needs can be met by dividing incoming fruit flow from the delivery belt onto two narrow sorting lines and leaving space between these for a middle removal belt to accept second-grade fruit. Workers along each narrow sorting line then have a defined area of responsibility, and fruit segregated from both lines are placed on the center diversion line. Where substantial sorting is required, there is an advantage in having the first workers that view the fruit assigned to sort cull fruit with following workers segregating them to the removal belt.

Lights should be placed to illuminate all fruit on the sorting line without glaring into the workers' eyes. They should be located so fruit illumination is not impeded either by equipment or by workers.

To avoid injury to fruit, delivery belts, sorting belts, and the elimination system must be designed to prevent excessive drops, rolling, shearing, or throwing of any marketable fruit as they are sorted.

In regard to worker comfort, each worker must have access to cushioned pads, platforms, and stools that place them at comfortable working height. These, along with good lighting and carefully designed sorting tables that prevent unnecessary reaching, assist worker efficiency.

Fruit sizing

In California, some kiwifruit are "eye sized" by packers who select fruit, often from a return-flow belt, to pack into a specific size plastic tray (Fig. 26.10). Most kiwifruit, however, are sized mechanically.

Because Hayward kiwifruit tend to be long and slightly flat in shape, they can be damaged by some dimension sizers, as discussed in the section on presizers. Drop-roll sizers that actively rotate the fruit can crush flat kiwifruit, injuring fruit and potentially contaminating equipment and other kiwifruit with juice from damaged tissue. The juice can provide a substrate for growth of microorganisms, aggravating surface mold growth on contaminated fruit during storage and distribution. Dimension sizers that do not roll the fruit are normally less precise in size separation.

For these reasons, many kiwifruit packing lines in California are equipped with weight sizers (Fig. 26.11) that are often electronically controlled to provide greatest versatility in size adjustment and distribution. These weight sizers are designed with "singulators," intended to deliver a single fruit into each cup of the sizer. The

Fig. 26.10. Here, packers select kiwifruit for packing by size from a return-flow belt. Fruit should be thoroughly sorted for quality and defects before entering the packing belt.

Fig. 26.11. Fruit from the sorting table are delivered to a sizer, and are "singulated" onto sizer lanes and dropped into cups of a weight sizer. The sizer cups are adjusted to drop the weighed fruit onto a cross belt for delivery to a packing belt.

fruit weight is then monitored and the fruit dropped at the designated point on the distribution belt.

Under commercial development are optical sizers that utilize data from camera images to estimate fruit size. Here, singulated fruit pass under a camera or cameras which monitor multiple images of the fruit. A computer calculates the volume of the fruit and signals for the proper point of discharge to the distribution belts. Development of both mechanical and electronic components of these sizers shows promise for accurately sizing a range of commodities, including kiwifruit.

A possible future incentive for use of optical sizers is their potential for performing additional tasks such as separation by shape or color and identifying at least some defects on the fruit surface. For kiwifruit, the separation of flat and round fruit could be simplified as these developments progress.

The sizer selected for kiwifruit should be capable of (1) operating without injuring fruit, (2) sizing fruit to the accuracy required, and (3) delivering the volume of fruit needed for efficient operation of the packing line. Estimate volume potential of a sizer under commercial packing conditions at about two-thirds of the machine's rated capacity. The sizer should be easy to clean and maintain and easy to adjust as sizes of incoming fruit change.

PACKING OPERATIONS

Kiwifruit are packed into small shipping containers to protect them during storage and handling and to facilitate their movement throughout marketing. Many kiwifruit in California are packed into single-layer flats holding approximately 7 pounds (3 kg) (Fig. 26.12). Some sized fruit are bagged into small consumer bags holding 1 to 2 pounds (or ½ to 1 kg), with the bags in turn placed into packages holding about 22 pounds (10 kg). There is increasing use of three-layer tray packs and volume-fill packs (Fig. 26.13) holding about 20 to 23 pounds (9 to 11 kg).

Fruit in single-layer flats are held in storage for up to 6 months without becoming misshapen (flattened) or injured. Lower fruit in multi-layer or bulk packs can be flattened or damaged from the weight of fruit above

Fig. 26.12. Kiwifruit flats (here, wood flats are being used) are assembled with plastic liners and plastic trays. For automatic tray packing, these travel on a belt beneath the fruit delivery belt.

Fig. 26.13. Graded and sized kiwifruit are volume-filled directly into plastic-lined lugs for distribution to markets that use bulk displays for consumer packaging.

them, if they have softened excessively in long-term air storage or during handling and distribution. With good temperature management and avoidance of ethylene exposure, especially with controlled-atmosphere storage, fruit softening may be delayed so that such packs are successful in long-term storage.

Avoiding injuries

Like other fruits, kiwifruit must be protected from injuries during packing. The package, packing materials, packing procedures, and specifications should be designed to minimize injury. This involves (1) immobilizing the fruit, (2) cushioning the fruit against impacts, and (3) protecting the fruit from compression.

Immobilizing fruit prevents loose fruit from being damaged by rolling, rubbing, and vibrating during transportation. Kiwifruit are immobilized when uniformly and tightly packed into plastic trays. Top cushion pads placed over the tray in the package hold fruit in place to prevent movement. Tight filling and closure of consumer bags, and tight packing and top padding of volume-fill or bagged fruit in larger containers also immobilize fruit.

Cushioning to avoid impacts when fruit are put into packages can also reduce impact bruising. Most tray packing and bagging can be achieved with little fruit drop, but bottom cushion pads may be useful in volume filling and for reducing impact injuries when individual packages or groups of packages are dropped during handling and palletizing.

Compression bruising can occur with overfilling of packages or with packages breaking during storage and distribution. In either case, the fruit are forced to support the weight of packages stacked above. As fruit become older and softer with long-term storage, compression bruising increases.

The entire packing line should be constructed and operated to minimize fruit injury. The line can be designed to avoid shearing fruit (changing their direction); moving belts or air jets can be used to assist such movement. Minimizing the height from which fruit must drop can reduce injuries, and filling chutes can be equipped with curtains and padding to break falls of fruit. Supervisors should control the flow of fruit into the system to avoid excessive accumulation of fruit on equipment.

Because little sorting for fruit quality can be done by packers, it may be desirable to add space where sized fruit can be sorted just before packing. This usually requires few sorters, depending upon the volume of fruit flow and the quality of incoming fruit.

Packing options

Plastic trays are either hand packed from return flow belts (where packers also size the fruit by eye) or from tubs of sized fruit, or the fruit are semi-automatically filled into trays as they are delivered from the sizer. The single-layer flats, assembled before packing, usually consist of the package ("flat"), a plastic liner, and a plastic tray. Packed trays are placed on a conveyor belt

Fig. 26.14. Sized fruit are filled into assembled flats through a delivery chute. Worker controls the speed of the belt holding the flats to match the flow of fruit delivery.

Fig. 26.15. More workers may be needed to adjust, fill, and orient fruit into trays.

Fig. 26.16. After fruit are properly packed, the plastic liner is folded over the flat and a simple corrugated lid (above the packing line) is used to close the flat.

Fig. 26.17. Completed trays are palletized by fruit size, usually onto soft wood pallets that will be shipped with the fruit.

for final quality check, folding the liner closed, padding, and lidding. Hand packers need easy access to empty containers and packaging materials and to removal belts for the packed containers.

For the semi-automatic tray pack, assembled flats move on a conveyor beneath the chute that is delivering sized fruit (Figs. 26.14 and 26.15). An operator controls the speed of the conveyor belt to synchronize the speed of package movement to the rate of fruit delivery. That operator and other workers then position the fruit in the trays, filling voids and removing excess fruit. For multi-layer tray packs, only the trays move on the belt under the delivery chute, and filled trays are hand placed into shipping packages. In the final step, the plastic liner is folded over the fruit and the package is lidded (Fig. 26.16).

Bagging of kiwifruit in California is usually done by using small, hand-assisted baggers, with the worker hand filling and closing the bags which are then placed into master containers. Volume-fill packing of kiwifruit in California has been limited in scope, with hand-assisted filling into packages to a specified weight. Should this packing method expand, equipment for automatic operation that is widely used for other fruits is well developed and readily available through equipment manufacturers.

The package

Packages used for kiwifruit in California include both wooden and corrugated single-layer flats, and corrugated lugs that hold multi-layer tray packs, bags, and volume-fill packs. Wood flats normally have no bottom cleats and are usually lidded with either a cleated wood veneer lid or a flat (noncleated) corrugated lid. Corrugated packages are generally of tray-form design with full-closure side flaps that serve to cover the filled package.

Flats, either wood or corrugated, are sometimes strapped in sets of three to make approximately 20- to 22-pound (9- to 10-kg) units for easy handling. Corrugated master packages that hold three corrugated flats have been used, but they have become less popular.

The wood flats have sufficient stacking strength to support the weight of one or two pallets of product without collapsing. Corrugated containers need to have this same ability for short periods; for long storage, individual pallet loads of kiwifruit should be in stacking racks or frames so that no package must stand more than the weight of one-pallet-high stacking. Corrugated packages are usually designed with stacking tabs that assist in aligning packages within a stack to achieve maximum stacking strength.

Wood flats typically have narrow side slats that allow space near the top and bottom of the flat for air movement. Corrugated flats or lugs need side-ventilation openings to facilitate air circulation. Despite the restricted airflow created by the plastic liners inside the flats, these openings assist temperature management.

Palletizing

Packages are segregated by size and stacked on pallets after they have been closed or lidded (Figs. 26.17 and 26.18). Care must be taken to align the stacks to provide for greatest stacking strength of individual packages and for the security of the pallet load. Palletizing corner frames are sometimes used to aid alignment. Stacking tabs on corrugated lugs and flats can facilitate alignment. Pallet squeezes can be used to square up a pallet after stacking. Most kiwifruit are palletized and shipped on soft wood "disposable" pallets designed for a single use. Palletizing glue may also be used to bond packages within the pallet.

Packages on the pallet are usually stabilized by either strapping or netting the loaded pallet before shipment. Sometimes corrugated tie sheets (the size of the pallet) are placed between the layers of packages in the pallet to stabilize the load (one or two sheets near the top to center of the pallet stack). Horizontal straps used with fiber corner angles may help immobilize glue-bonded pallet loads for short transport; vertical straps can be added for longer transport. Alternatively, the entire pallet can be wrapped in plastic netting to provide stability.

Fig. 26.18. Completed pallet loads of kiwifruit are transferred from the packing area to a forced-air cooler to assure rapid cooling of packed fruit. Only electric forklifts are used in kiwifruit handling to avoid ethylene contamination of the fruit.

27

Cooling, Storage, Transportation, and Distribution

MARY LU ARPAIA, F. GORDON MITCHELL, AND GENE MAYER

As with other fresh fruits, efficient temperature management is essential to successful marketing of kiwifruit. This means rapid cooling within a few hours of harvest and storage at 32°F (0°C). Because kiwifruit are extremely sensitive to very low levels of ethylene, care must be taken to avoid ethylene exposure in all phases of handling. Fruit exposed to ethylene exhibits accelerated flesh softening even at 32°F (0°C). Where prolonged storage is desired, controlled atmosphere (CA) offers the only effective means of avoiding excessive flesh softening. When transporting soft kiwifruit, extra care must be taken to immobilize the fruit within the package so that transit injury is reduced.

COOLING

Field heat must be removed quickly from kiwifruit after harvest because the fruit can lose water rapidly. After 3 to 4 percent water loss, the fruit may exhibit noticeable shriveling, predominantly at the stem end. As with all fresh fruit, the rate of water loss is directly related to the vapor pressure difference between the fruit and its environment. Temperature and relative humidity control this vapor pressure difference. At warm field temperatures and low relative humidities common during harvest, the rate of water loss can be 25 to 50 times greater than at the recommended 32°F (0°C) and 95 percent relative humidity in a kiwifruit storage. Thus, 1 hour in the field after harvest may result in as much water loss as 1 or 2 days in storage.

Another reason to rapidly cool kiwifruit after harvest is based on the kiwifruit's propensity to rapidly soften after harvest. The softening process in kiwifruit is temperature dependent. For example, fruit softens three times faster at 41°F (5°C) than at 32°F (0°C). Rapid heat removal helps minimize flesh softening during subsequent 32°F (0°C) storage if the fruit is not exposed to ethylene during cooling. This is discussed in detail in the next section.

Hydrocooling of kiwifruit is not recommended as prolonged wetting of the fruit reportedly worsens the occurrence of decay. Forced-air cooling, widely used on other fruits, is also preferred for rapidly cooling kiwifruit. It involves creating a slight pressure difference on opposite sides of bins or pallets to cause cold air to flow through side ventilation openings in the containers to rapidly cool the fruit. The intimate contact between cold air and warm fruit results in rapid heat removal. For efficiency, about 5 percent side area ventilation is needed, although a modified system, serpentine forced-air cooling, can be used to cool fruit in bins that have about 5 percent bottom ventilation.

Unless kiwifruit are packed immediately upon arrival at the packinghouse, they should be cooled and held cold in bins to await packing. The airflow requirement for cooling kiwifruit in bins has not been measured, but they should cool similarly to plums. For that fruit the following data have been developed for $7/8$ cooling in 5 percent side-vented bins ($7/8$ cooling time is the time required to cool the fruit $7/8$ of the distance from its initial temperature to the temperature of the cooling air):

	Hours to $7/8$ cool		
Type of container	6	9	12
Field bins, 5% venting			
Airflow-ft^3/min/lb fruit	0.8	0.5	0.3
Static pressure - inch H$_2$O	0.7	0.28	0.12

Metric conversion: ft^3/min/lb × 3.75 = m^3/hr/kg fruit
inch H$_2$O × 25.4 = mm H$_2$O

Because the fruit is at least partially warmed during packing, recooling will be needed after packing. Thus, all packed containers need partial or complete cooling in a forced-air cooler. Most kiwifruit are tray packed into a one-layer flat with the trays enclosed in a plastic film wrap or liner. It is not possible, therefore, to cool by passing air directly around the fruit as with non-plastic-wrapped packs. Airflow requirements for the containers used in California have been measured with these results:

Type of container	Hours to ⅞ cool		
	12	18	24
(all plastic wrapped and top padded)			
Wood flat, ¼-inch (6 mm) cleats on lid			
Air flow - ft³/min/lb fruit	1.0	0.5	0.3
Static pressure - inch H₂O	1.3	0.5	0.23
Wood flat, no cleats on lid			
Air flow - ft³/min/lb fruit	1.0	0.6	0.4
Static pressure - inch H₂O	1.4	0.7	0.4
Corrugated flat, 5% side vents			
Air flow - ft³/min/lb fruit	0.9	0.4	0.26
Static pressure - inch H₂O	2.1	1.0	0.6

Metric conversion: ft³/min/lb × 3.75 = m³/hr/kg fruit
                    inch H₂O × 25.4 = mm H₂O

For short-term holding with reasonable storage relative humidity (90 percent), a modified corrugated flat has been tested as effective. The flat is wax-coated and has about 2.5 percent side area venting, all located near the bottom of the sides. With the plastic tray in position, all air flows through the containers under the trays but still does not directly contact the fruit. A plastic bubble top pad is placed over the fruit before closing the lid. The plastic pad is cut slightly oversize so that it seals well around the edges of the container. Weight loss is greater than in the plastic wrap pack, but visible shrivel has not been observed after 3 to 4 months' storage at 32°F (0°C) and 90 to 95 percent relative humidity. Forced-air cooling requirements for this container are greatly reduced so rapid cooling can be achieved.

Type of container	Hours to ⅞ cool			
	3	4	6	12
Corrugated flat, no wrap, plastic top pad				
Air flow - ft³/min/lb fruit	1.1	0.7	0.4	0.14
Static pressure - inch H₂O	1.3	0.7	0.23	0.04

Metric conversion: ft³/min/lb × 3.75 = m³/hr/kg fruit
                    inch H₂O × 25.4 = mm H₂O

Summary

Kiwifruit should be promptly cooled to 32°F (0°C) after harvest to minimize fruit shrivel and flesh softening. Care should be taken to avoid any exposure to ethylene contamination. Forced-air cooling is the preferred method for rapidly cooling the fruit in either bins or packed containers. With forced-air cooling it is possible to design the cooling and packaging systems to achieve the best overall results, depending on the storage life and environmental conditions encountered.

STORAGE

Minimizing flesh softening after harvest is the cornerstone of successful kiwifruit postharvest handling. Flesh softening occurs rapidly during the first few weeks of air storage. The drop in flesh firmness roughly corresponds to the conversion of starch to soluble sugars as discussed in chapter 24. Even when fruit are held at 32°F (0°C), approximately one-third to one-half of the remaining flesh firmness may be lost per month.

Kiwifruit should be stored as near to 32°F (0°C) as possible and under 90 to 95 percent relative humidity. Care should be taken to assure that the storage temperature is no lower than 32°F (0°C). The freezing point of kiwifruit is difficult to predict. A freshly harvested fruit at 6.5 percent soluble solids content (SSC) may have a freezing point near 31°F (–0.5°C), especially in the stem end of the fruit where the lowest SSC is found. Freeze damage is characterized by a water-soaked appearance on both the fruit flesh and core (**plate 39**). After time in storage, when starch has hydrolyzed and SSC levels reach at least 14 percent, the freezing point declines considerably, although even at this point a lower storage temperature is not recommended.

Because kiwifruit are subject to shrivel, a high relative humidity is essential in the storage room. This can be achieved most easily with a large refrigeration coil surface to minimize the temperature difference between the coils and the room air. Supplemental humidification can be used, but this requires more frequent defrosting of the refrigeration coils. When water is added in such a system, care must be taken to avoid free water contact with the fruit; the result can be surface cracking (**plate 40**). An airflow rate just sufficient to maintain uniform temperature throughout the mass of the product should be used (normally about 50 to 65 feet [15 to 20 m] per minute). All potential sources of ethylene contamination should be eliminated in the storage and handling area (ideally less than 10 ppb [0.01 ppm]). If these general guidelines are followed, flesh softening and fruit shrivel are minimized. For long-term storage, use of controlled atmospheres (CA) has been shown to be effective, provided that both 32°F (0°C) and ethylene-free atmospheres are maintained.

Temperature and ethylene management

The two postharvest environmental factors that have the greatest effect on softening are temperature, which influences the rate of flesh softening, and the presence in storage of ethylene, which can hasten the softening process at a given temperature by approximately 50 percent.

It has been demonstrated that symptoms of mechanical injury in kiwifruit are accentuated once flesh firmness drops below 5.0 lbf (2.27 kgf). Using this guideline and allowing for softening that may occur during distribution, a 6.0 lbf (2.72 kgf) cut-off point for maximum storage duration can be used when comparing treatments in terms of the time required for fruit to soften:

Weeks to a flesh firmness less than 6.0 lbf (2.72 kgf)

Temperature		Ethylene (ppb)	
°F	°C	0	500
32.0	0	4.3	2.0
36.5	2.5	2.0	1.0
41.0	5.0	1.3	0.8
50.0	10.0	1.2	0.3

Fruit held at 36.5°F (2.5°C) softens substantially faster than fruit stored at 32°F (0°C). Fruit held at 41°F (5°C) in turn softens substantially faster than fruit stored at 36.5°F (2.5°C). At the recommended storage temperature of 32°F (0°C), the presence of 500 ppb (0.5 ppm) ethylene results in a similar softening pattern as fruit held at 36.5°F (2.5°C) with no ethylene. In other words, exposure to ethylene may negate the positive effects of good temperature management. Care must be taken, therefore, to achieve both ethylene-free air and near 32°F (0°C) storage.

Cooling delays after harvest, even of short duration, can influence subsequent softening at 32°F (0°C). Ethylene exposure during these delays further hastens softening. As little as 200 ppb (0.2 ppm) ethylene exposure during an 18-hour cooling delay at 68°F (20°C) results in substantially accelerating the rate of flesh softening during subsequent 32°F (0°C) air storage. Fruit harvested later in the season are generally more adversely affected by cooling delays and ethylene exposure. The rate of fruit softening can be decreased by cooling the fruit to an intermediate temperature of 41° to 50°F (5° to 10°C) for 12 to 48 hours, but it is still not as effective as immediate cooling.

It is best to keep the ethylene level as low as possible. One study evaluated the rate of flesh softening when fruit were stored at 32°F (0°C), while exposed to varying ethylene levels ranging from 0 to 50 ppb (0.05 ppm). Flesh softening was substantially slowed when the ethylene atmosphere was held below 10 ppb (0.01 ppm) (Fig. 27.1). Thus, although storage of kiwifruit with less than 20 ppb (0.02 ppm) ethylene has been recommended, these results indicate that less than 10 ppb (0.01 ppm) ethylene is preferable.

During long-term storage, some fruit may decay due to Botrytis rot (see chapter 28, *Postharvest Storage Diseases*). It is known that infected fruit have a higher rate of ethylene production and therefore influence the softening rate of surrounding fruit. The closer a fruit is to an infected fruit, the faster it softens (Fig. 27.2). Even fruit in tray corners furthest from an infected fruit soften more rapidly than fruit from matched trays that contain no infected fruit.

Kiwifruit show increased respiratory activity and ethylene production when fully ripe at 68°F (20°C), but fruit that have softened to eating firmness at 32°F (0°C) do not exhibit this behavior; rather, there is a general decline in respiration and a very low rate of ethylene production (Fig. 27.3). If soft kiwifruit, however, are warmed to 41° to 68°F (5° to 20°C), as would possibly occur during some postharvest procedures, the fruit's ethylene-producing ability is expressed even after they are returned to 32°F (0°C) storage. This elevated level of ethylene production by the fruit itself may well influence the softening rate of surrounding unwarmed fruit at 32°F (0°C).

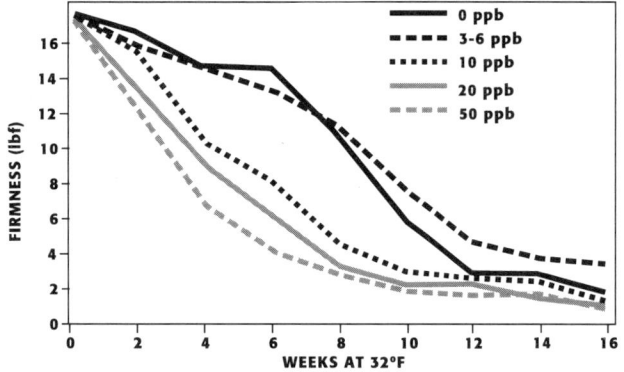

Fig. 27.1. Softening of kiwifruit in cold storage at 32°F (0°C) with different levels of ethylene ranging from 0 to 50 parts per billion (ppb).

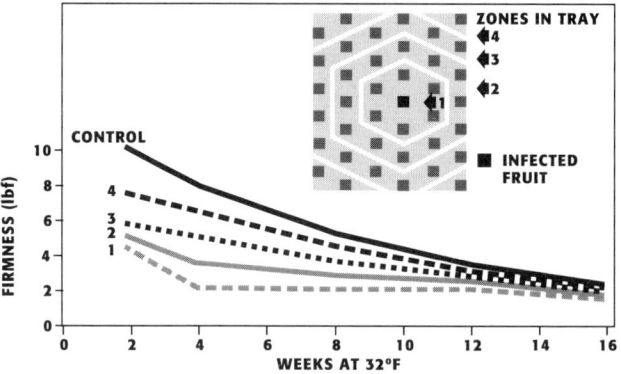

Fig. 27.2. Softening of kiwifruit surrounding a single *Botrytis* infected fruit in cold storage. Larger numbers indicate fruit further from the infected fruit, but still in the same tray.

CONTROLLED-ATMOSPHERE (CA) STORAGE

Extensive studies have been conducted in California and elsewhere to evaluate the usefulness of controlled atmospheres (CA) for long-term storage of kiwifruit. CA storage involves the use of reduced oxygen (O_2) and elevated carbon dioxide (CO_2) concentrations to lengthen the storage potential of a given commodity. Worldwide consensus recommends that storage atmosphere for CA of kiwifruit be a combination of 2 percent oxygen and 5 percent carbon dioxide (2% O_2/5% CO_2). Gastight refrigerated chambers may be constructed or polyethylene tents within large refrigerated storage rooms may be used for CA storage. Although it is possible to successfully store kiwifruit in polyethylene CA tents, extra care is needed to insure proper temperature control and to avoid any gas leakage in the system.

The major benefits of CA are the retention of flesh firmness as compared to air storage (Fig. 27.4) and a reduction in the development of Botrytis rot (see chapter 28, *Postharvest Storage Diseases*). A certain amount of flesh softening still occurs in CA storage, predominantly during the first 6 to 8 weeks of storage. This loss in firmness parallels the disappearance of starch in the fruit. It has been hypothesized that the two phenomena are linked and that kiwifruit softening in either CA or air storage is due to both starch degradation and cell wall breakdown. CA storage does not influence the increase in soluble solids content (SSC) or the decrease in titratable acidity as compared to air storage.

In several years of observations, fruit stored under 2% O_2/5% CO_2 at 32°F (0°C) has ripened to good quality at 68°F (20°C) even after 24 weeks of storage. Another indication that CA-stored kiwifruit can ripen normally is reflected in the patterns of respiration and ethylene production observed at 68°F (20°C) following storage. Even after 24 weeks of storage, fruit exhibit the characteristic increase in both respiration and ethylene as described previously. Absolute production values are comparable to those after no storage at all.

It has also been observed that CA storage does not greatly affect the subsequent performance of kiwifruit in air storage at 32°F (0°C), as the rate of flesh softening (as measured by the slope of the softening curve) in air seems relatively unaffected by previous CA storage (Fig. 27.5). CA conditions, therefore, should be maintained until just before marketing to optimize the fruit's market life. Air-stored kiwifruit should perform equally as well as CA-stored kiwifruit of the same firmness during subsequent market handling.

Successful CA management

The success or failure of CA storage for kiwifruit depends on the speed of atmosphere establishment, ethylene contamination, temperature, and O_2/CO_2 composition. CA should be established immediately after harvest and cooling. Establishment of CA within 1 day of harvest or after 1-week delay in 32°F (0°C) air exhibits less flesh softening compared with a 2-week delay. This indicates the benefit of CA in retarding flesh softening can be achieved only if CA conditions are established within a few days of harvest. If delays exceed 1 week, the softening process has already been initiated and the benefits of CA are reduced severely. This consequence must be considered when designing and operating commercial kiwifruit CA facilities. The size of each CA room should be related to the anticipated daily volume of fruit so that room loading and atmosphere modification can be completed within 1 week from fruit harvest.

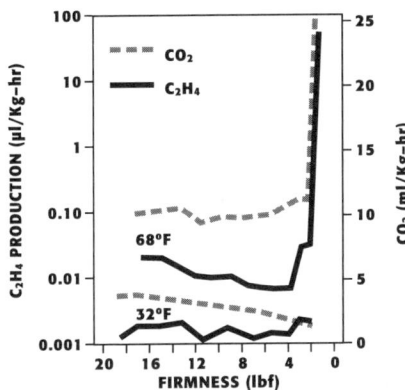

Fig. 27.3. Ethylene (C_2H_4) production and respiratory activity (CO_2) of kiwifruit at room temperature (68°F [20°C]) and in cold storage (32°F [0°C]).

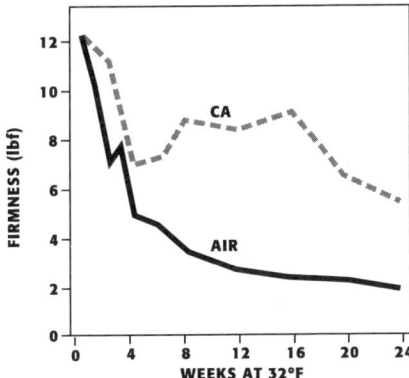

Fig. 27.4. Pattern of fruit softening at 32°F (0°C) in ambient air and controlled atmosphere (2% O_2 + 5% CO_2) storage.

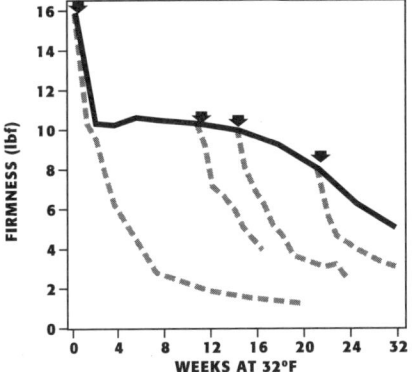

Fig. 27.5. Pattern of fruit softening at 32°F (0°C) in controlled atmosphere (2% O_2 + 5% CO_2) storage (—) and after moving to ambient air (— —) at the times indicated by the arrows.

Ethylene. As with air storage, the presence of ethylene in CA can have a substantial detrimental effect on storage potential. The effect of ethylene contamination during CA storage is twofold. First, the positive benefit of CA in terms of reducing flesh softening is negated. The second effect of ethylene contamination is the increased development of physiological disorders: flesh translucency, flesh graininess, and white-core inclusions. (These physiological disorders are discussed in depth in chapter 24, *Postharvest Physiology and Causes of Deterioration*.) White-core inclusions have been found in California kiwifruit only when the CA atmosphere has been contaminated. It has not been reported in kiwifruit stored under similar conditions in New Zealand.

Ethylene's influence on flesh softening and the development of white-core inclusions in CA depends on the same factors that govern the overall success of CA: ethylene concentration, the timing of exposure to ethylene, temperature, and CO_2 concentration. Ethylene accelerates softening of kiwifruit in CA in proportion to its concentration similar to the effect in air storage. The occurrence and severity of white-core inclusions also depend on ethylene concentration.

Weeks at 32°F to flesh firmness less than 6.0 lbf (2.72 kgf)

Storage condition		
Atmosphere	Ethylene concentration (ppb)	Weeks
Air	0	3
2%O_2/5%CO_2	5,000	8
2%O_2/5%CO_2	1,000	12
2%O_2/5%CO_2	500	12
2%O_2/5%CO_2	100	16
2%O_2/5%CO_2	50	24
2%O_2/5%CO_2	0	>24

The timing of ethylene exposure during CA has been found to impact the rate of softening and development of white-core inclusions. Studies where stored fruit have been exposed to ethylene during different periods indicate that continuous exposure to ethylene in CA is not required for development of white-core inclusion. Generally, the disorder can be induced by ethylene exposure in combination with CA at any time during storage at 32°F (0°C). The severity of the disorder, however, is usually greater when exposure occurs during the first few weeks. In general, the longer the duration of exposure to ethylene, the greater the incidence and severity of white-core inclusions and the greater the rate of softening during CA storage.

Temperature. As discussed previously, storage temperature influences the rate of flesh softening in air storage. The addition of ethylene to the storage atmosphere accelerates the rate of softening especially at higher temperatures. For fruit kept in CA with or without ethylene, there is a similar response to temperature (Fig. 27.6).

Weeks to a flesh firmness less than 6.0 lbf (2.72 kgf) in CA

Temperature		Ethylene (ppb)	
°F	°C	0	500
32.0	0	>24.0	10.3
36.5	2.5	20.0	6.8
41.0	5.0	6.2	1.6
50.0	10.0	4.5	1.0

The incidence and severity of white-core inclusions in CA plus ethylene is also temperature dependent. Although the disorder has been observed at 41° to 50°F (5° to 10°C), it is much less severe than at colder temperatures.

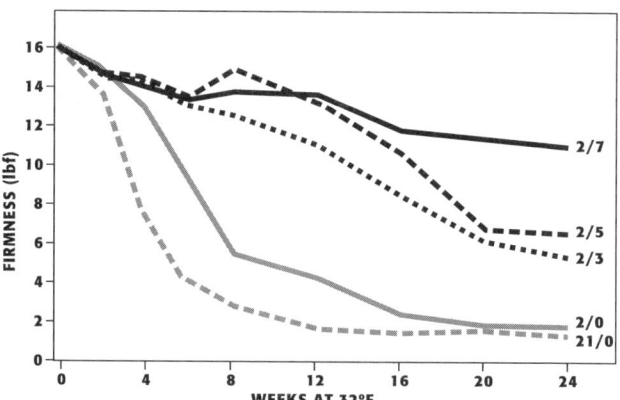

Fig. 27.6. Pattern of fruit softening in controlled atmosphere storage (2% O_2 + 5% CO_2) with no ethylene and under temperatures ranging from 32°F (0°C) to 50°F (10°C).

Fig. 27.7. Pattern of fruit softening in controlled atmosphere storage using different mixes of oxygen and carbon dioxide. Numbers indicate percent O_2 followed by percent CO_2.

CO₂ concentration. Observations from both California and elsewhere indicate that CO_2 concentration has a greater influence than O_2 concentration in retarding flesh softening of kiwifruit during CA storage (Fig. 27.7). Although flesh softening may be slowed in the presence of only elevated carbon dioxide, best results are attained when the oxygen concentration is also reduced to 2 percent. Care must be taken when exposing fruit to elevated levels of CO_2, however, as fruit injury may occur at concentrations greater than 8 percent CO_2. Fruit injury is expressed by both the development of off-flavors and abnormal ripening behavior following storage (hard-core, flesh translucency and graininess; see chapter 24, *Postharvest Physiology and Causes of Deterioration*).

Summary

Controlled atmosphere storage using a combination of 2% O_2/5% CO_2 has been shown to slow fruit softening and development of decay. Successful CA storage depends on rapid establishment (less than 1 week following harvest), careful temperature maintenance (32°F [0°C]), exclusion of ethylene at all times during storage, and close attention to O_2 and CO_2 concentrations.

TRANSPORTATION AND DISTRIBUTION

Kiwifruit protection during transportation and distribution is similar to that during handling and storage. With advancing postharvest age the fruit may become more severely affected by abuses that occur during this period. Thus, attention must be given to ethylene avoidance, temperature management, protection against water loss, and avoidance of various mechanical injuries.

Only sound fruit should enter the marketing system. Fruit coming from storage should be carefully inspected for flesh firmness, incidence of mechanical injuries, and decay. Pulp temperatures should be measured and fruit should be protected against warming during loading.

If kiwifruit are impacted during loading or unloading they can be bruised (**plate 41**). Impact bruising of firm kiwifruit, in which starch has not been fully hydrolyzed, appears white because the starch in the injured tissue has not been converted to soluble sugars. Soft kiwifruit, in which starch hydrolysis is largely complete, develop a dark, watersoaked bruise as a result of cell rupturing.

Fruit that softens to under 5 lbf (2.27 kgf) becomes especially susceptible to injury from transport vibration; the less firm the fruit, the greater its susceptibility to injury (**plate 42**). Although it would be desirable to restrict marketing to more firm fruit, this would limit the potential air storage life of Hayward kiwifruit to about 4 months, and only CA-stored fruit would be sufficiently firm to be marketed beyond this time.

Injuries to soft fruit during transport and distribution not only lower fruit value because of visual damage, but injured fruit immediately respond with elevated respiration and ethylene production (see chapter 24, *Postharvest Physiology and Causes of Deterioration*). These in turn stimulate elevated respiration of surrounding nondamaged fruit, so that all fruit show accelerated physiological and physical deterioration. In addition, injuries become avenues for the spread and development of fruit-rotting organisms.

If fruit rotting is noted in fruit being prepared for transport, then all fruit should be thoroughly reconditioned. Any infected fruit should be removed and soiled fruit trays discarded. Fruit should not be out of refrigeration any longer than necessary to minimize warming during reconditioning, and reconditioned fruit should be promptly and thoroughly recooled before loading.

Removal of any fruit that has rot protects the subsequent health of fruit. When the fruit-rotting organism, especially *Botrytis cinerea*, becomes well established in one fruit, it then spreads to surrounding fruit, and incidence of rotted fruit quickly escalates. Further, these infected fruit respond to infection by elevating their level of physiological activity, more ethylene is produced, and surrounding healthy fruit soften more rapidly. See chapter 28, *Postharvest Storage Diseases* for details.

Temperature management

The need to maintain low pulp temperatures during kiwifruit storage is well documented. Transport and distribution simply extend the storage period, and fruit respond to temperature management similarly. If pulp temperatures are not near 32°F (0°C) when loading, then fruit should be returned for further cooling. Before loading, the transport vehicle should be thoroughly cooled and any other produce in the load should be cold. Loading should occur in a refrigerated loading dock, unless outside air temperatures are close to ideal transport temperatures.

The transport vehicle's temperature setting should be as low as possible without freezing the fruit. A 32°F (0°C) pulp temperature during transport is ideal. However, temperature fluctuations in the refrigeration systems of transport equipment usually require a somewhat higher thermostat setting.

Unfortunately, the thermostatic temperature setting of the transport vehicle is lower than the transport temperature of most of the mass of fruit in a load. With tightly stacked pallets and limited air circulation, fruit can warm several degrees because the heat of respiration of the kiwifruit is not adequately removed. These higher pulp temperatures accelerate the rate of deterioration of the fruit. During prolonged transport, as often occurs in export handling, this can help lower the delivered quality of the fruit.

Some believe that there is no advantage in cooling fruit to below the expected transport temperature. This overlooks a substantial "flywheel" effect that can be gained by loading colder fruit. Just as it is difficult to cool fruit in the center of the load, so it can take several days for that fruit to warm significantly. This is due to the slowed respiration rate (and lower heat production) of fruit and the insulation provided by the tightly stacked load.

Water loss

Fruit shrivels in response to the total cumulative water loss that has occurred since harvest. Water loss can be severe during transport and distribution, depending upon the temperature, relative humidity, and air velocity encountered. It is difficult to predict the relative humidity that will be encountered within transport vehicles or distribution warehouses. It is normal, however, to find significantly lower relative humidities in such facilities than in fruit storage facilities, and thus accelerated water loss may be expected. Higher fruit temperatures during transport also accelerate water loss from fruit. Any protection against water loss that is included in the packages (plastic trays and wraps) can be important in minimizing further water loss during transport and distribution.

Ethylene contamination

The need to avoid ethylene exposure continues throughout transportation and distribution. Even fruit that have softened substantially in long-term storage continue softening in the presence of ethylene; the magnitude of flesh softening depends largely on the ethylene concentration of the atmosphere. The possible role of fruit injuries and decay in accelerating ethylene production has been discussed. Because fruit are probably warmer during transport and distribution than in storage, the ethylene production rate is higher. Most important, if cold fruit from storage are allowed to warm significantly during loading, the ethylene production rate rises, and even when the fruit are recooled to the earlier storage temperature, that ethylene production rate never returns to the previous low level.

Other sources of ethylene contamination must be avoided. Just as kiwifruit cannot be stored with or near other ethylene-producing products, so they also cannot be transported with them. Ethylene-producing equipment (such as propane forklifts) must not be used in loading or unloading, and kiwifruit loading and unloading areas must be free of ethylene-contaminated truck exhaust fumes.

One concern in long-distance transport of kiwifruit is whether to provide fresh-air ventilation to remove accumulating ethylene from the cargo atmosphere. This is a difficult decision that depends on the ethylene levels in the cargo atmosphere and in the outside air used for ventilation. Ethylene levels in the cargo atmosphere depend on accumulated ethylene from respiration of the kiwifruit, contamination during loading, contamination from other sources, and any ethylene leakage that may occur into the cargo atmosphere. Ethylene levels of outside air that may be used in ventilation depend on the source of the air and may be elevated from such causes as exhaust fumes from petroleum-powered vehicles, contamination from other ethylene-producing produce, or higher ethylene atmospheres in industrial centers.

Ripening kiwifruit for early market

Although much effort is devoted to avoiding ethylene exposure of kiwifruit in prolonged storage, ethylene treatment may be desirable during harvest and early storage to accelerate kiwifruit ripening in order to capitalize on marketing opportunities. At harvest, and for about 6 weeks of storage, kiwifruit benefit from ripening if they are destined for immediate marketing or consumption.

Ripening can be achieved by applying ethylene gas at concentrations between about 10 and 100 ppm for at least 24 hours to fruit that are warmed to between 68° and 77°F (20° and 25°C). At these temperatures, ripening of freshly harvested kiwifruit takes 5 or 6 days to complete, and that time decreases as fruit remain in cold storage before treatment. Facilities and procedures are similar to those used for banana ripening.

For best ripening, the fruit must be warm and ethylene gas concentration around the fruit should be at least 10 ppm. Kiwifruit flats and lugs may need to be spaced on the pallets and exposed to good air circulation so that the warm air and ethylene contact the fruit. Some modern banana rooms use a forced-air warming system similar to forced-air fruit coolers, and these should be useful for kiwifruit ripening. Because of the plastic wraps commonly used for kiwifruit, it may be desirable to apply about 100 ppm ethylene and/or extend the ethylene treatment time to about 48 hours to assure adequate fruit exposure. Fruit in large bulk shipping containers must also be warmed and exposed to ethylene for efficient ripening, and this may require that lids be opened, plastic liners opened, and fruit warmed in circulating warm air. In this case, a 10-ppm ethylene exposure should assure good ripening, provided the fruit are warm when treated.

Pretreating of kiwifruit for later ripening has not been tested, but may be worthy of trial. With Bartlett pears, freshly harvested fruit that are treated with ethylene for 24 hours at 68° to 77°F (20° to 25°C) and then rapidly cooled and loaded for transport remain firm during marketing, but ripen quickly when warmed by the distributor or consumer. From past observations we can expect similar results with kiwifruit.

These ripening procedures are only for fruit that will be marketed immediately after harvest or within the first few weeks of storage.

All of the steps described to secure ethylene exclusion from kiwifruit destined for storage remain essential. Any ethylene treatment and ripening of kiwifruit for immediate marketing must be done in complete isolation from other fruit destined for storage, and treated fruit must not go into storage with other kiwifruit.

Summary

Good kiwifruit management during transportation and distribution includes monitoring and selection of sound fruit and providing an environment that protects the fruit from unnecessary deterioration. Fruit should be as free of injuries and disease as possible and should have reasonable flesh firmness. Fruit should be held as near 32°F (0°C) as possible, and should be protected from warming. All steps possible should be taken during transport and distribution to assure that kiwifruit are maintained in an essentially ethylene-free atmosphere. Fruit should be handled so as to avoid impact and compression bruising, and when possible transport vehicles should be equipped with air-ride suspension systems to minimize vibration (roller) bruising of the fruit.

28

Postharvest Storage Diseases

NOEL F. SOMMER, J. EMILIO SUADI, AND ROBERT J. FORTLAGE

The most threatening disease of kiwifruit in refrigerated storage has been gray mold, caused by the fungus *Botrytis cinerea* Pers. ex Fr. This fungus causes no rot in California kiwifruit vineyards or in refrigerated storage at 32°F (0°C) until the fruit become susceptible late in storage. Unfortunately, kiwifruit ripen rapidly in storage and may be ripe and susceptible to fungus colonization within about 15 weeks, even when they have been handled well. With poor handling, the disease may appear much earlier.

This chapter describes how Botrytis rot affects kiwifruit and points out differences between the disease in California and in New Zealand. Emphasized are (1) the natural resistance possessed by kiwifruit until they ripen, (2) factors affecting their ripening in storage, and (3) possibilities and problems in using fungicides. Finally, several diseases in addition to Botrytis rot are discussed briefly; although they have been observed rotting kiwifruit in storage, they are not expected to rival Botrytis rot as major threats.

The information provided here is based upon our original research and observations.

BOTRYTIS ROT

Botrytis cinerea is familiar to many as the cause of summer bunch rot and storage rot of grapes. It is commonly found in many commodities stored or transported at low temperatures, including apples, pears, stone fruits, feijoas, strawberries, raspberries, and boysenberries, as well as grapes. Cabbages and carrots placed in low-temperature storage for several months are often attacked by *B. cinerea*, often in concert with *Sclerotinia sclerotiorum* (Lib.) de Bary, causing serious losses. Botrytis rot is an ever-present threat to cut flowers in refrigerated storage and transit.

Description

The first indication of *B. cinerea* in kiwifruit storage is extreme softness localized at the fruit's stylar or stem end (**plate 43**). Alternatively, the soft area may involve a wound, usually on the side of the fruit. Generally, the fungus is first visible on the fruit surface as small white tufts of the fungus mycelium (threadlike structures). In time, the enlarging diseased area becomes covered with the white mycelium of the fungus (**plate 44**). At that time, one commonly observes a slight color change to gray, often near the center of the lesion surface. That change indicates that the fungus is producing conidia, which are vegetative reproductive spores (Fig. 28.1). Black lumps frequently develop in the mycelium-covered lesion surface. These are dark masses of mycelia called sclerotia, which ordinarily serve no function in storage rot but are important in the field (**plate 45**). They serve to overwinter the fungus in cold climates.

Conidia production on rotted fruit in packed containers in storage is limited because the germinating spores normally cannot penetrate the skin of sound kiwifruit. On the other hand, infection caused by aerial mycelia is a common threat. In the high humidity of storage rooms, mycelia from rotted fruit develop abundantly and may extend out an inch or more from disease lesions. Mycelia touching a nearby sound fruit readily penetrate the skin to

Fig. 28.1. Conidiophore of *Botrytis cinerea* with nearly mature spores barely visible to the naked eye.

establish infection. Newly diseased fruit develop aerial mycelia that, in turn, infect other fruit. The result is a constantly enlarging "nest" of diseased fruit (**plate 46**).

Temperature effects

Botrytis cinerea grows optimally at 74° to 77°F (23° to 25°C). It is incapable of growth at temperatures above 92° to 96°F (33° to 35°C). The success of the fungus in refrigerated storage is primarily the consequence of its ability to grow, albeit slowly, at about 28°F (−3°C) or below. Consequently, refrigeration cannot completely prevent Botrytis rot. Nevertheless, the fungal growth rate at 32°F (0°C) is minuscule compared with that at higher temperatures. It is therefore necessary to promptly remove field heat from fruit and to maintain the temperature at 32°F (0°C).

Loci of infection

The time and method of primary or initial infection (not nesting) are related to control. *Botrytis cinerea* commonly colonizes old or senescent tissues, often blossom parts, of many species; from that tissue the fungus spreads to fruit. New Zealand researchers developed a field spray schedule with the fungicide Vinclozolin to control Botrytis storage rot. However, it was concluded that in New Zealand infections invariably start at the stem end and that all infections are the result of contamination of the stem scar at or following harvest. In Italy, all *B. cinerea* infections of kiwifruit are at the stem end. Italian workers attributed infections to colonization of stamens at or following bloom and the formation of quiescent infections beneath the calyx. The infections become active only after a time in storage.

In California, infection and fruit storage rot originate from stylar and stamen infections, stem scar infections, and wounds.

Stylar and stamen infections. In California, most Botrytis rot develops at the stem end. Frequently, 5 percent or more of the rot is initiated at the stylar end without any indication of a wound. Therefore, stylar-end rots surely are the result of colonization of at least one style by *B. cinerea*. When the fungus reaches the body of the fruit, a quiescent infection is evidently established. The flesh appears highly resistant to infection until fruit has softened in storage, at which time Botrytis rot develops. Stamens are also colonized at bloom, and it is likely that similar quiescent infections are at the stem end beneath the calyx. Because stamens are more numerous than styles, it is reasonable to expect that most of the quiescent infections would be at the stem end.

Table 28.1. Percentage of fruits with one or more fungus-colonized styles or stamens as related to incidence of rot in storage (%)*

Plot	Fruits with infected styles or stamens	\multicolumn{5}{c}{Days in storage (32°F)}
		91	122	150	181	204
		\multicolumn{5}{c}{Rotted fruit in storage}
	(%)	\multicolumn{5}{c}{(%)}
B	56	0.9	1.4	1.9	1.9	1.9
C	56	0.0	0.9	0.9	0.9	0.9
D	72	1.4	2.3	3.7	3.7	3.7
E	20	0.0	0.0	0.0	0.0	0.0
F	3	0.0	0.0	0.0	0.0	0.0
G	28	0.0	0.0	0.0	0.0	0.0
Correlation coefficients (r)		0.76	0.92	0.90	0.87	0.85

*Ethylene exposure was avoided. No fungicides were applied.

In studying Botrytis infection of stamens and styles after blossoming and before stamens are shed, styles and stamens from each immature fruit were collected and placed in coin envelopes. The styles and stamens were surface-sterilized with hypochlorite (laundry bleach diluted in water 1 part to 10 parts) and placed in Petri dishes. Dishes were placed at 68°F (20°C) for 24 hours, followed by several days at 32°F to kill weedy fungi that do not tolerate low temperatures. Fungi were permitted to grow by incubating the dishes at a temperature permitting fungal growth. Data from these experiments show (Table 28.1) that the fraction of fruit having one or more *B. cinerea*-colonized stamens or styles was roughly related to disease incidence. Fruit from the plot in which 72 percent of the fruit had one or more infected floral parts exhibited the highest rate of rotting (3.7 percent). On the other hand, in fruit in which the incidence was 28 percent or less, no disease developed.

Stem scar infections. The stem scar is an obvious possible locus for infection, particularly when the fruit is separated from the stem. However, fruit tissues beneath the stem scar contain several substances, separable by thin-layer chromatography, that are highly inhibitory to *B. cinerea*. Disappearance of this fungal inhibition appears to coincide with fruit softening in storage.

In our tests involving inoculation of the stem scar at or soon after harvest, kiwifruit did not appear to be readily infected. In one test, for example, fruit were picked by two methods. Half of the fruit were picked with the stems in place; the stems were not removed until 1 week later. The other half were harvested normally by separating the fruit from the stem. No significant differences were observed in the amount of rot that developed in storage.

Fungal spores in the large, open stem scar would seemingly be vulnerable to postharvest-applied fungicides. The absence of disease suppression by fungicides applied after harvest suggests that the stem scar is not a major locus. On the other hand, in another test, approximately 50 conidia were placed in a drop of water in each stem scar immediately after the fruit was separated from the stem in the vineyard. Upon fruit softening in storage, the number of inoculated fruit that rotted was significantly higher than the number of rotted uninoculated fruit. It is obvious, from experiments of the latter type, that fresh stem scars are a locus of infection under certain circumstances.

Wounds. Fruit handled immediately after harvest, while still firm, suffer remarkably few wounds that rupture the skin. However, many wounds can be expected if fruit are handled after they have partially softened. In addition to providing a locus for infection, wounds cause fruit to hasten ripening, thereby favoring disease development.

Geographic differences

Differences evidently exist between the behavior of Botrytis rot in kiwifruit in California and in New Zealand. In California, blossom blight and young fruit rot in the field are rare. In New Zealand, by contrast, blossom blight by *B. cinerea* and *S. sclerotiorum* is evidently common. Presumably, New Zealand's moist climate favors blossom blight, whereas California's usually dry weather during blossoming does not.a

In New Zealand, Botrytis rot of kiwifruit appears as early as the fourth week of storage. In our experience, visible rot is highly unusual so early in California kiwifruit in storage at 32°F (0°C). Even in fruit seriously exposed to ethylene, rot has been rare before late December or January. Reasons for the difference are not known. An obvious possibility is that strains of *B. cinerea* in New Zealand differ significantly from California strains in their ability to rot firm fruit soon after harvest. If so, the almost certain eventual introduction into California of New Zealand strains of *B. cinerea* capable of rotting kiwifruit after only 4 weeks storage is a dismal prospect.

FRUIT CONDITION, HANDLING, AND STORAGE

The condition of fruit at harvest, methods of handling, and storage environments may dramatically influence the time and, possibly, the amount of disease in storage. Conversely, attention to certain aspects of production and handling can dramatically improve market quality of stored fruit, as discussed below.

Fruit firmness at harvest

Considerable variation in fruit firmness at harvest has been noted. Not only do fruit in the same field vary greatly, but considerable differences in firmness are believed to exist among vineyards.

With everything else equal, it appears likely that the softer the fruit at harvest, the earlier disease will appear. A rule of thumb has been applied that fruit become diseased only after they have softened to less than 2 pounds force (lbf) as measured with a penetrometer with an 8-mm diameter tip and with the fruit skin removed at the point of penetration.

In another in our series of experiments, the average firmness at harvest of fruit obtained from widely separated vineyards in California appeared to be related to time of first appearance of rot in storage (Table 28.2). However, it is not the average firmness at harvest that is paramount; it is the fraction of softest fruit. The softest 30 percent of the fruit were found to be highly correlated with disease.

The reasons for varying fruit firmness between vineyards are not well understood. Fertilizers, particularly those high in nitrogen, may be a factor. Fruit on densely shaded canes have been observed to soften early. Some shaded fruit soften and drop to the ground before harvest. Thus, in densely shaded vineyards, a fraction of the fruit are abnormally soft as a consequence of shading. Many of the softest fruit harvested are detected by sorters and packers and are eliminated. However, fruit abnormally soft but with a firmness of about 4 or 5 pounds force (1bf) or more are not detected by sorters and are not eliminated. Such fruit are likely to become susceptible to rot much earlier than other harvested fruit. Further, soft fruit can be expected to become ripe in storage and produce

Table 28.2. Firmness and Botrytis rot in fruit from different plots after indicated days in storage (32°F)

Plot	Days in storage (32°F)							
	0	48	88	103	120	138	161	190
	Firmness*							
	(lbf)							
A	14.4	4.5	3.1	(2.5)	1.8	1.8	1.6	1.5
B	14.0	5.6	3.8	2.3	(2.3)	2.0	1.8	1.4
C	14.6	8.8	5.1	3.4	(2.3)	2.3	1.8	1.7
D	15.6	8.9	3.5	(2.9)	2.2	1.7	1.3	1.2
E	15.0	9.4	6.3	4.4	3.1	2.4	2.0	2.0
F	17.0	8.2	5.7	4.7	2.8	2.4	2.0	1.8
G	17.3	6.8	4.9	3.6	2.3	2.0	(1.4)	1.2
Avg.	15.4	7.5	4.6	3.4	2.4	2.1	1.7	1.6

*Firmness in pounds force (lbf) was determined using a penetrometer with an 8-mm diameter tip and with the fruit skin removed at point of penetration. Numbers in parentheses indicate the time of appearance of first rot.

ethylene in sufficient amounts to hasten softening in nearby fruit.

Use of trellises to minimize dense shading and summer pruning to permit better light penetration into vines may significantly reduce the amounts of soft fruit at harvest and fruit rot in late storage.

Although an obvious relationship exists between fruit softening and disease susceptibility, it is not believed to be a direct cause-effect relationship. When freshly harvested fruit were artificially softened by exposure to ethylene at 2 to 3 ppm for 3 days at 68°F (20°C) before storage at 32°F (0°C), appearance of the first fruit rot was advanced by less than a month, not as early as anticipated. Some stored fruit lots, with or without exposure to ethylene, did not have rotten fruit, suggesting that these vineyards may have been largely free of *B. cinerea*.

Thus, the short time (about 4 weeks) that ethylene exposure apparently advances the appearance of rot in storage suggests that softness in itself does not cause fruit to become susceptible to *B. cinerea*. Instead, other factors may be involved which parallel softening during natural ripening but do not closely parallel rapid softening caused by ethylene exposure.

Temperature management

Cooling fruit promptly after harvest is necessary. Delays in cooling can significantly shorten their storage life. Because fruit do not show the adverse effects of this delay until after long storage, the adverse effects of cooling delays may not be recognized. Fruit in the center of bins, for example, may require a long time to cool, particularly if air movement is limited.

It is generally assumed that, because kiwifruit are lower in soluble solids at time of harvest than fruits of many species, they cannot safely be stored at temperatures below 32°F (0°C). Failure to refrigerate harvested fruit for a time can lead to their warming and, if the period is long, the time at which they ripen may seriously advance, making them susceptible to rot.

Atmosphere modifications

Modified atmospheres are widely used to slow ripening, delay senescence, and suppress fruit rots in storage or transit of a number of fruit species. In California, elevated levels of carbon dioxide gas (10 to 15 percent) have long been used to suppress Botrytis rot in strawberries and brown rot, *Monilinia fructicola* (Wint.) Honey, in sweet cherries. The rots are suppressed to some extent because carbon dioxide slows the metabolism of the causal fungi. In part, the rot is suppressed because ripening and senescence of fruit are delayed and the fruit remains in better physiological condition. Possibilities for using elevated carbon dioxide atmospheres in kiwifruit storage are limited because kiwifruit quality is adversely affected in storage atmospheres exceeding 7 percent.

Carbon dioxide levels vary in a controlled atmosphere (CA) according to species or variety of fruit, but they often are about 5 percent. Tests indicate that kiwifruit storage life could be improved and the length of the rot-free period extended by using CA. In relation to disease, the major benefit is likely to be a lengthening of storage time before fruit become susceptible to Botrytis rot. Direct suppression of the fungus by CA is likely to be modest. Premature softening of fruit by ethylene can lead to excessive levels of rot. Serious rot losses occurred in the years before the extreme sensitivity of kiwifruit to ethylene was fully appreciated.

Handling fruit of low firmness

Kiwifruit in tests lost about half of their initial firmness during the first 6 weeks of storage at 32°F (0°C) (Fig. 28.2). Firmness was further reduced by about half

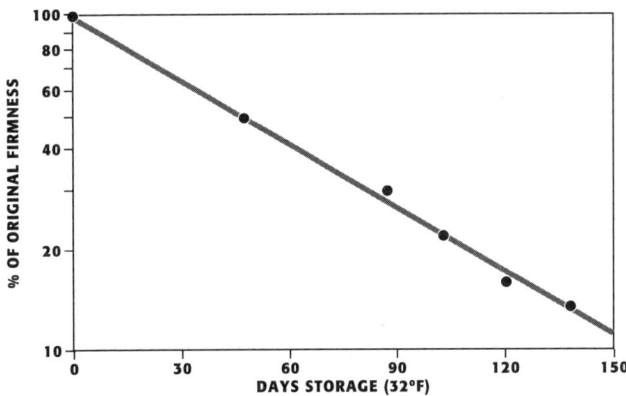

Fig. 28.2. Semilogarithmic plot of kiwifruit softening during storage at 32°F (0°C). Fruit from seven plots averaged a firmness of 15.2 pounds at harvest.

after a second 6-week period and again by half after a third 6-week period. By then, the fruit were very soft, fragile, and susceptible to damage by handling. Injuries involving a wound in fruit skin are likely to be contaminated by spores of *B. cinerea* and other fungi. Furthermore, injured fruit respire more rapidly than uninjured fruit and ripen early. Injured fruit produce significant amounts of ethylene that hasten ripening. Therefore, the onset of disease may be advanced, and there is often an increase in total rot as a consequence of the handling of partially softened fruit.

CHEMICAL CONTROL

Fungicides have been much less useful in controlling postharvest diseases in kiwifruit than have been efforts to improve storage and handling. Avoidance of ethylene contamination and improved temperature management have been particularly effective in reducing disease.

Preharvest sprays

Seemingly, fungicides might be beneficial applied either in the vineyard or as a postharvest treatment. In the vineyard, fungicide applications might reduce infection of styles and stamens and otherwise reduce inoculum present. With good coverage of blossoms and fruit, the colonization of styles and stamens by *B. cinerea* could be materially reduced. Fungicides applied soon after harvest might be expected to reduce the incidence of mycelial infection and nesting of fruit in containers.

Tests were conducted in San Diego County, the Central Coast, and the San Joaquin and Sacramento valleys using fungicides in the vineyard to reduce the incidence of rot in storage. Results indicate that rot was significantly reduced if sprays were applied at full bloom, about 11 days later, and about 21 and 7 days before harvest. Good coverage was achieved with all four applications in the test. One or two applications provided little benefit. We have concluded that benefits of field spraying would seldom warrant the costs of application in California. (Recent work suggests one or two sprays may provide some benefit: See the *UC IPM Pest Management Guidelines* for Kiwifruit, available at Farm Advisors' offices, for current recommendations.)

Postharvest fungicides

In a series of tests, fungicides applied after harvest showed little or no promise as a preventative of Botrytis rot in storage. The most effective fungicide tested limited mycelial contact infection from rotting fruit to nearby sound fruit in containers. There was little benefit in reducing primary infections. Many other fungicides had little effect when applied after harvest, except on nesting.

No fungicide tested has been used commercially for postharvest application, and treatments are often not acceptable in some foreign markets. Thus, postharvest applications of fungicides to reduce nesting appear highly questionable.

Sulfur dioxide (SO_2) as a storage fumigant suppressed *B. cinerea* but resulted in noticeable fruit injury one or more months after fumigation. The typical "bumpy" appearance of the fruit is believed to result from localized chemical injury (Fig. 28.3). Where injury was most severe, greater moisture loss resulted in depressions on the fruit surface.

Tests with pads containing sodium metabisulfite slowly released SO_2. Although used in grape storage, use of the SO_2 fumigation and sodium metabisulfite pads often injured kiwifruit. Some tests were promising, but the differences between effectiveness and fruit injury were considered too unpredictable to provide a safe treatment for kiwifruit.

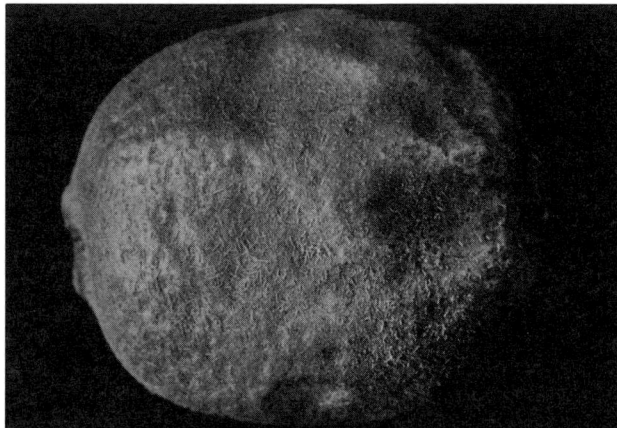

Fig. 28.3. "Lumpiness" of kiwifruit surface as a result of previous treatment with sulfur dioxide gas.

MINOR STORAGE DISEASES AND PROBLEMS

Alternaria rot

Alternaria alternata (Fr.) Keissler invades and produces a dry rot in sunburned fruit (**plate 47**). The rot is of little significance because it only involves damaged fruit that should be eliminated in sorting.

Surface mold. *Alternaria alternata* and certain other fungi colonize styles, stamens and, to some extent, calyces in the vineyard. Under highly humid storage conditions, *A. alternata*, which can grow at temperatures as low as 26° to 28°F (–3.5° to –2°C), grows over the sepals, stamen fragments, and styles (**plate 48**). If the fruit are placed at low humidity, the mycelia shrivel and become barely noticeable. Nevertheless, when transit vehicles are first opened, receivers may become alarmed, believing the mycelia, which are then highly visible, presage serious rot problems. Improved fruit brushing in packing houses has largely eliminated surface mold by removing the calyces, stamens, and styles utilized by the fungus as substrate for growth.

Juice blotch. On occasion, fruit lots handled in packing houses may contain some fruit so soft that they are crushed. The resulting juice may contaminate surfaces over which sound fruit pass. Juice on sound fruit placed in highly humid storage rooms may support the growth of *A. alternata* or other fungi that have adapted to the low temperatures of storage rooms. The dark blotches, which defy cleaning, adversely affect the fruit's appearance but have not resulted in fruit rot (**plate 49**). In one instance, the blotches were white because of the presence of an unidentified chalk-colored fungus.

A somewhat different discoloration occurs when fruit contact juice that is on unprotected metal (see chapter 26, *Harvesting and Preparation for Market*).

Blue mold

Penicillium expansum (Lk.) Thom, a common pathogen of fruits in refrigerated storage, is particularly common in apples and pears. It produces a very soft, wet rot in the commodities it attacks. Its occurrence in kiwifruit storage has been mostly limited to overripe fruit and, therefore, it is not a threat (**plate 50**).

Penicillium expansum is believed to infect fruit only through injuries to the fruit skin or by acting as a secondary invader of lesions made by another fungus, such as *B. cinerea*. As expected of a wound pathogen, it typically occurs as a side rot in kiwifruit. Although initially white, the fungus colony turns blue as the colony starts to produce conidia. The fungus grows at temperatures below 32°F (0°C).

Dothiorella rot

A *Dothiorella* species has occasionally been observed in overripe kiwifruit. It is possibly the same fungus, *Dothiorella gregaria* Sacc., which attacks citrus and avocado fruit in California. It attacks peach fruit and causes a "white rot" of apples in eastern states. In addition to fruit rotting, the fungus causes cankers in peach and other trees.

To date there has been little to indicate that this fungus will affect California-grown kiwifruit as either a fruit rot or as a disease in the vineyard, as the fungus has been observed only in overripe fruit (**plate 51**). In New Zealand, a fungus that is possibly the same has reportedly developed during ripening.

Phoma rot

Occasionally a rot of kiwifruit, especially near the end of the storage season, has been observed; from it has been isolated a species of *Phoma*. Rots have been on the sides of fruit and have been associated with wounds. The fruit surface has characteristically become depressed, often craterlike, without superficial mycelium. The flesh in the area beneath the crater-shaped depression is frequently pink or purple in color (**plate 52**).

Although at times frequent in ripe kiwifruit, its occurrence has been sporadic. There is little to suggest that Phoma rot is likely to cause losses.

Phomopsis rot

Phomopsis rot was first reported in 1968 in New Zealand-grown kiwifruit on the Chicago market. In 1971, the same rot was observed at Davis, California in local supermarkets. Activity of vinegar flies suggested the presence of yeasts as secondary organisms. In Chicago, 45 isolates from diseased fruit developed only the asexual Phomopsis state. Of 17 similar isolates made at Davis, 12 produced only the asexual state but five produced the sexual state, which was described and named *Diaporthe actinidiae* Som. & Ber.

Subsequently, Phomopsis rot has occasionally been observed in both California-grown and New Zealand-grown kiwifruit (**plate 53**). It appears to be found mostly in overripe fruit and does not appear likely to become a threatening postharvest disease. Some leaf spots, wilted canes, and trunk cankers in the vineyard have yielded a *Phomopsis* species.

Sclerotinia rot

Sclerotinia sclerotiorum (Lib.) de Bary, along with *B. cinerea*, causes a blossom blighting of kiwifruit in New Zealand. This disease has not been observed in California.

Sclerotinia sclerotiorum, like *B. cinerea*, grows at temperatures below 32°F (0°C) and seriously damages stored vegetables, such as carrots and cabbage. This fungus and its close relative, *S. minor* Jagger, have been isolated from California kiwifruit in storage. However, there is little to suggest that the disease will endanger stored kiwifruit.

Mucor rot

Mucor piriformis Fischer has caused losses of strawberries in California fields and storage. It has been found in stone fruit shipments from Chile to the United States, and it has caused losses in winter pears stored in the Pacific Northwest. It is capable of growing at temperatures below 32°F (0°C) and could affect kiwifruit in storage, but so far it has been observed only occasionally.

Buckshot rot

Buckshot rot, caused by *Typhula* spp., is believed to have only recently appeared in California kiwifruit storage (**plate 54**). The fungus is particularly well adapted to low temperatures. Most members of this genus are snow mold fungi, some of which attack overwintering crops in northern regions at about the time snow melts. It has been a relatively minor problem in vegetable storage, particularly in carrots and celery.

SUMMARY

Maximum disease-free storage life of kiwifruit can be expected if fruit are very firm at harvest, if fruit injury has been avoided in handling, if cooling has been prompt and the temperature maintained at 32°F (0°C), and if ethylene exposure has been avoided. Kiwifruit in California have been resistant to pathogens until they ripen in storage. Unfortunately, kiwifruit ripen within about 15 weeks at 32°F. Controlled-atmosphere storage appears to be required to ensure a longer rot-free storage period. Controlling Botrytis rot by fungicides may be beneficial where rot is serious but generally the previously mentioned handling provisions have yielded the most benefits. Diseases other than Botrytis rot have usually been found only in ripe fruit.

Index

A

Abbott variety, 9
abrasion bruising, 91–92, 100
abscission
    flowers, 16
    leaves, 13
accelerating ripening, with ethylene, 114–115
acids
    distribution in vine, 12
    in fruit, 16–17, 90, 94, 95, 111
acreage
    worldwide, 1, 2, 3
    yield per acre, 31
Actinidia, 1, 9
Actinidia arguta, 9, 74, 75
Actinidia chinensis Planch. See *Actinidia deliciosa*
Actinidia deliciosa
    commercial development, 1–2, 9
    history, 1–2
    illustrated, 74, 75, 76
    worldwide acreage in, 1, 2, 3
    worldwide production, 3–5
    See also specific varieties
Actinidia eriantha, 9
Actinidia kolomikta, 9
Actinidia polygama, 9
actinidin, in fruit, 95
advection frosts, 61, 62, 67
    See also frost
air movement, summer pruning and, 33
Allison, Alexander, 1
Allison variety, 9
Alternaria rot, 78, 79, 120–121
amino acids
    distribution in vine, 12
    synthesis, 13
anaerobic conditions, sensitivity to, 13
Archips argyrospilus (Walker), 85
Argyrotaenia citrana (Fernald), 77, 85–86
Armillaria root rot (oak root rot), 19, 76, 80, 81–82
    See also crown rots; root rots
armored scales, 77, 86
ascorbic acid, in fruit, 16, 94–95
Asia, 1, 9, 10
    See also China
Aspidiotus nerii Bouche, 86
augers, for measuring soil moisture, 50, 51
Australia, 3, 5
available water content, 47–48

B

backhoeing, 18–19
bacteria, ice-nucleating, controlling, 64
bacterial diseases
    bactericides and, 80
    bleeding canker, 76, 82
    blossom blight, 76, 83, 118, 121
    leafspot, 76, 83
bags
    packing fruit in, 92, 105, 106, 107
    picking bags, 99, 100
bare root plants, 19–20, 24
bark
    Armillaria root rot (oak root rot) and, 76, 82
    bleeding canker and, 76, 82
    mineral storage in, 13
    orange tortrix and, 85
    phytophthora root and crown rot and, 76, 81
    scale and, 77, 86
    starch storage in, 12
barley grass, nematodes reduced by, 72
basins, 39, 42, 48–49
bees, 53, 54–56, 57
bermudagrass, 19, 68–69
bilateral cordon development, 28–29
bins
    bulk, 3, 105–106
    harvesting, 99–100
black surface marking (ink staining), 78, 79, 101–102
    See also juice blotch
Blake variety, chilling requirements, 9
bleeding canker, 76, 82
bloom. See flowers, bloom
blossom blight, 76, 83, 118, 121
blotch, juice, 78, 79, 121
    See also ink staining
blue mold, 78, 79, 121
blue orchard bees, 54
border irrigation, 39–40, 42, 48–49
borers, protecting trunk from, 19
boron
    accumulation in leaves, 58
    deficiency, 60
    requirements, 18, 58
    toxicity, 74, 75, 58, 60
Botrytis rot (gray mold), 116–118
    chemical controls, 117–118, 120
    controlled-atmosphere storage and, 111, 119
    described, 116–117
    ethylene production increased by, 110
    geographic differences, 118
    handling fruit of low firmness and, 93, 119
    illustrated, 78, 79
    loci of infection, 93, 117–118, 119
    softness of fruit and, 93, 110, 116, 118–119
    temperature and, 117, 119
boxelder bugs, 77, 87
bronzing, phytophthora root and crown rot and, 80
browning reaction, 91, 95
bruising
    abrasion, 91–92, 100
    impact, 78, 79, 91–92, 106, 113
    vibration, 78, 79, 91–92, 100, 113
Bruno variety
    chilling requirements, 9
    rootstocks, 9, 21
brushing fruit, 88, 92, 101, 102, 120
bucket augers, for measuring soil moisture, 50, 51
buckshot rot, 78, 79, 122
budbreak, 10, 14, 15, 80
budding (propagation method), 21
bud drop, boxelder bugs and, 87

buds
  brown, blossom blight and, 76, 83
  budbreak, 10, 14, 15, 80
  defined, 30
  formation, 14–15
bugs
  boxelder bugs, 77, 87
  See also insects
buildings
  costs, 7, 8
  in Sacramento Valley, 8
  See also equipment
bulk bins, 3, 105–106
bumble bees, 54

C

Calchico, Inc., 2
Cal Chico No. 3 variety, 9
calcium
  accumulation in leaves, 58
  deficiency, 60
  in fruit, 95
  requirements, 58
  stability of leaf concentrations, 12
California
  acreage, 1, 2, 3, 4
  blossom blight, 118, 121
  Botrytis rot (gray mold), 118
  budbreak, 10
  commercial development of kiwifruit, 1–2
  diseases, 80–83
  insects, 84–86, 87
  male cultivars used, 9
  marketing California kiwifruit, 5
  mites, 86–87
  packing containers, 5
  postharvest diseases, 118, 120–122
  preharvest sprays, 120
  primary source of cultivars, 9
  production and trade, 3, 4
  soluble solids content (SSC) standard, 96
  white-core inclusions, 112
  See also Sacramento Valley; San Diego; San Joaquin Valley; Southern California; United States
California Kiwifruit Commission, 5
callus formation, xylem sap and, 13
cambium, frost injury and, 12
canes
  defined, 30, 31
  growth, 10
  taping, tying, or clipping, 32
canker, bleeding (Pseudomonas), 76, 82
canopy. See leaves
Caplan, Frieda, 2

carbohydrates
  distribution/storage in vine, 12–13
  photosynthesis and, 10–11, 43
  soluble solids content (SSC) and, 96
  See also starches; sugars
carbon dioxide
  in controlled atmosphere storage, 92–93, 111, 113, 119
  photosynthesis and, 10–11, 43
  postharvest disorders and, 92–93, 113
  respiration postharvest and, 89–90, 91, 92, 110, 111
  respiration preharvest and, 10, 11
  sensitivity to, 92–93, 113, 119
caterpillars, leaf-rolling, 77, 84–86
Central Coast, preharvest sprays, 120
Chico, USDA Plant Introduction Station at, 9
Chico Early variety, 9
Chico Extra Early variety, 9
Chile, 3, 4
chilling requirements, 9, 14–15, 18
China, 1, 10, 54
chloride
  accumulation in leaves, 58
  requirements, 58
  toxicity, 74, 75, 58, 60
chlorophyll, 10–11, 17, 43, 95
chlorosis
  heat stress and, 74
  illustrated, 74, 75
  iron chlorosis, 18, 74, 75, 58, 59–60
  manganese deficiency and, 74, 75
  nematode-induced, 70
  pH and, 59
  phytophthora root and crown rot and, 76, 80
  spider mites and, 86
Choristoneura rosaceana (Harris), 77, 85
citric acid, in fruit, 16, 94
cleaning
  crop residue, 18
  fruit, 102–102
  See also brushing fruit
climate requirements, 18
  See also frost; humidity; rain; temperature; wind
clipping canes to trellis wires, 32
clonal propagation, 21
cloudy conditions, frost and, 62
cold-hardiness, 13
  See also chilling requirements; cooling; frost; temperature
color (flesh)
  green, 9, 17, 94, 95
  pigments in, 9, 17, 95
  yellow, 9, 17, 74, 75, 95
columella, 88

commercial development, 1–2
  See also marketing
compensation point, 11
composition, of fruit, 94–95
compression bruising, 106
conduction, 62–63, 64
consumption per capita, in United States, 6
container-grown plants, 20, 22, 24
containers. See packing, containers
contours, 39, 42, 48–49
controlled-atmosphere storage, 91, 92–93, 111–113, 119
convection, 63, 65
cooling
  harvested fruit, 98, 100–101, 108–109, 110, 119
  vineyards, 36, 38, 40, 43, 69
  See also chilling requirements; cold; frost; temperature
copper, 58, 60
cordons
  defined, 30–31
  forming, 28–29
  maintaining, 32
  twisting causes stunting, 32
  whitewashing, 30, 32
cork cells, on wounds in fruit, 88
corrugated flats, 107, 108
costs, operating, 6–8
cover crops
  cleaning up crop residue, 18
  frost injury and, 12, 64, 68
  grains, 19, 72
  grasses, 72, 73
  nematode control and, 19, 72, 73
  rotation crops, 19
  weed control and, 68
  See also ground cover management; weed control
cracking
  crown gall and, 82
  in stored fruit, 78, 79, 109
crown gall, 76, 82–83
crown rots
  Armillaria root rot (oak root rot), 76, 80, 81–82
  irrigation and, 38
  phytophthora root and crown rot, 36, 38, 76, 80–81
  from storing bare-root plants, 24
culls
  fans (fasciated fruit), 17, 35
  flats, 17, 35
  soft fruit, 99, 101, 118
  sorting out, 103–104, 118
cultivation. Sees weed control; cover crops; ground cover management
cuticle, transpiration and, 11
cuttings, growing, 22

D

damping off, 22
defoliation
    spider mites and, 86
    toxic elements and, 60
density, of fruit, 88, 95
depreciation, 8
designing vineyards, 25–27
deterioration of fruit. *See* diseases (postharvest); disorders (postharvest); postharvest physiology
developing vineyards. *See* establishing vineyards
development
    of flowers, 14–16, 17, 18, 35
    of fruit, 14–17, 94
    of vines, 10–13
dewpoint temperature, frost and, 63, 66
diffusion porometers, 52
dimension sizers, 102, 104
diseases (postharvest), 78, 79, 93, 116–122
    Alternaria rot, 78, 79, 120–121
    blue mold, 78, 79, 121
    Botrytis rot (gray mold), 78, 79, 93, 110, 116–118, 119, 120
    buckshot rot, 78, 79, 122
    chemical controls, 120
    Dothiorella rot, 78, 79, 121
    ethylene and, 110, 119
    firmness of fruit at harvest and, 118–119
    fungicides and, 117–118, 120
    handling fruit of low firmness and, 119
    illustrated, 78, 79
    Mucor rot, 121
    Phoma rot, 78, 79, 121
    Phomopsis rot, 78, 79, 121
    Sclerotinia rot, 121
    softening of fruit and, 97, 118–119
    storage atmosphere and, 111, 119
    storage humidity and, 92, 98, 120, 121
    storage temperature and, 98, 117, 119
    sunburned fruit and, 93, 120
    sun-exposed vs. shade-exposed fruit and, 59, 118
    wounds and, 118, 119, 120, 121, 122
    See also disorders (postharvest)
diseases (preharvest), 76, 80–83
    Armillaria root rot (oak root rot), 76, 80, 81–82
    bacterial leafspot, 76, 83
    bactericides and, 80
    bleeding canker (Pseudomonas canker), 76, 82
    blossom blight, 76, 83, 118, 121
    causes, 80
    crown gall, 76, 82–83
    fungicides and, 80
    illustrated, 76
    managing, 37, 80
    phytophthora root and crown rot, 36, 38, 39, 76, 80–81
    from storing bare-root plants, 24
    See also crown rots; root rots
disking, 69
disorders (postharvest), 78, 79, 92–93, 112–113
    carbon dioxide and, 92–93, 113
    ethylene and, 92–93, 112–113
    hard-core, 92, 113
    illustrated, 78, 79
    ink staining, 78, 79, 101–102
    juice blotch, 78, 79, 121
    pericarp granulation, 78, 79, 92–93, 112, 113
    pericarp translucency, 78, 79, 92, 112, 113
    white-core inclusions, 78, 79, 93, 112–113
    See also diseases (postharvest)
distributing fruit. *See* transporting, fruit
dormant pruning. *See* pruning, dormant
Dothiorella rot, 78, 79, 121
drainage
    leveling and, 18
    phytophthora root and crown rot and, 80, 81
drip irrigation, 37–38, 40–41, 49
    advantages, 36, 37
    described, 37
    disadvantages, 37, 38, 41
    evaluating, 40–41
    frequency and quantity of irrigation, 6, 49
drop roll sizers, 102, 104
dry weight. *See* total solids content

E

electrical capacitance instruments, for measuring soil moisture content, 52
electrical conductivity (EC) of soil, 18
electrical resistance instruments, for measuring soil moisture content, 50–51, 52
electrothermal methods, for measuring soil moisture content, 52
Elmwood variety, chilling requirements, 9
energy transfer methods, 62–63
equipment
    costs, 6–8
    harvesting bins, 99–100
    picking bags, 99, 100
    psychrometers, 62, 66
    refractometers, 96
    in Sacramento Valley, 8
    sizers, 102, 104–105
    for soil moisture measurement, 50–52
    sorting equipment, 103–104
erosion, preventing, 69
establishing vineyards, 18–20, 72–73
    costs, 6, 7
    nematodes and, 71–73
    planning and design, 25–27
    planting and early care, 19–20, 73
    planting windbreaks, 27
    site preparation, 18–19, 72
    site selection, 18, 63–64, 67, 72
ethylene
    accelerating ripening with, 114–115
    in controlled atmosphere storage, 91, 92–93, 111, 112, 119
    harvest exposure to, 100
    packing exposure to, 101
    postharvest diseases and, 110, 119
    postharvest disorders and, 92–93, 112–113
    production of, 89, 90, 91, 92, 102, 110, 111, 114, 119
    sensitivity to, 88, 91, 92–93, 109, 110, 119
    softening of fruit and, 88, 89–91, 92, 101, 109–112, 119
    transport exposure to, 114
    wounds and, 90, 91, 92, 102
evaporation, 45, 64, 65
evaporation pans, 45–46
evaporative cooling, 43
evaporative deposits, on fruit, 38
evapotranspiration, 45–46, 47, 49
exports, worldwide, 3–5

F

fans (fasciated fruit), 17, 35
female flowers, 15, 53–54
female vines
    ratio of male-to-female vines, 25, 54
    varieties, 9
fertilizing
    boron, 18, 60
    burn avoidance, 59
    calcium, 60
    frequency, 6
    iron, 59–60
    magnesium, 60
    manganese, 60
    mature vines, 59
    necessity for, 58, 59
    new plantings, 19
    nitrogen, 58, 59, 118
    potassium, 60

root function and, 13
seed plantings, 21–22
toxic element correction, 60
young vines, 59
zinc, 60
See also nutrition; specific minerals
fiber, in fruit, 95
field capacity, 47
firmness
  ethylene production and, 89–90
  handling fruit of low firmness, 93, 119
  at harvest
    discarding soft fruit, 99, 101, 103–104
    postharvest diseases and, 97, 118–119
    recommended level, 92, 97, 118
  injury susceptibility and, 91–92
  nitrogen fertilization and, 59, 118
  respiratory activity and, 89–90
  retention of, early vs. late harvest and, 97
  See also softening process
flats (fruit shape), 17, 35
flats (packing), 3, 105–106, 107, 109
floor management. *See* cover crops; ground cover management; weed control
flowers
  abnormalities, 17
  abscission, 16
  bloom, 18
    delaying for frost protection, 64, 67
  blossom blight, 76, 83, 118, 121
  brown, blossom blight and, 76, 83
  budbreak, 10, 14, 15, 80
  development, 14–16, 17, 18, 35
  fan-producing, 17
  female flowers, 15, 53–54
  frost and, 15
  male flowers, 15, 53, 56
  structure, 15, 53–54
  thinning flower buds, 17, 35
  timing of, 9, 10
  wind and, 15
  See also pollination
fog
  frost and, 62
  low-lying areas and, 64
foggers, 65
forced-air cooling, 108–109, 114
France, 3, 4
freeze damage, from low-temperature storage, 78, 79, 109
freezing injury. *See* frost
freezing point, of stored fruit, 89, 109
frost, 61–67
  advection frosts, 61, 62, 67
  bacterial leafspot and, 83
  bleeding canker and, 82
  cloudy conditions and, 62
  container-grown plants and, 22
  crown gall and, 82
  dewpoint temperature and, 63, 66
  energy transfer and, 62–63
  fall frosts, 12, 18, 61
  flowering and, 15
  fog and, 62
  frost-free days requirement, 18
  location of frost injuries, 12, 18
  low-lying areas and, 63–64, 67
  National Weather Service and, 61, 62
  protection from
    active protection, 65–66
    chemical protection, 64
    delaying bloom, 64, 67
    flood irrigation, 65, 67
    foggers, 65
    ground cover management, 12, 64, 68
    heaters, 65, 67
    irrigation cut off, 12
    irrigation frequency, 6
    misters, 65
    multiple irrigation systems, 40
    overhead sprinklers, 36, 38, 65–66
    passive protection, 63–65
    pruning low branches, 12
    site selection, 63–64, 67
    soil moisture content and, 64, 67
    summary of recommendations, 67
    under-plant sprinklers, 65
    whitewash, 24
    windbreaks, 64–65, 67
    wind machines, 65, 67
    wrapping trunks, 12
    for young vines, 59
  radiation frosts, 61–62
  rapid temperature drop and, 12
  sensitivity of kiwifruit to, 61
  spring frosts, 18, 61
  sugar concentration and, 12–13
  temperature inversion and, 65, 67
  temperature minimums, predicting, 61–62, 63, 64
  temperature at which damage occurs, 12, 18, 89
  understanding frost events, 61–63
  wet-bulb temperature and, 66, 67
  wind and, 61, 62, 64, 65, 66, 67
frost-free days requirement, 18
fructose
  in fruit, 16, 94
  vine growth and, 43
fruit
  acids, 16–17, 90, 94, 95, 111
  actinidin (tenderizing enzyme) in, 95
  alternation between heavy crops and light crops, 31
  browning reaction, 91, 95
  bruising, 78, 79, 91–92, 100, 106, 113
  brushing, 88, 92, 101, 102, 120
  bud fruitfulness, factors affecting, 14–15, 33
  chlorophyll in, 17, 95
  chlorotic, 74, 75
  color (flesh)
    green, 9, 17, 94, 95
    pigments in, 9, 17, 95
    yellow, 9, 17, 74, 75, 95
  composition, 94–95
  cracking, 78, 79, 109
  deformed
    blossom blight and, 83
    boxelder bugs and, 87
    fans (fasciated fruit), 17, 35
    flats, 17, 35
    omnivorous leafroller and, 85
  density, 88, 95
  described, 9, 88–90
  development, 14–17, 94
  evaporative deposits on, 38
  fiber, 95
  firmness. *See* firmness
  freezing point in storage, 89, 109
  illustrated, 74, 75, 88
  ink staining (black surface marking), 78, 79, 101–102
  juice blotch, 78, 79, 121
  lipids, 95
  maturity measures, 88, 92, 94, 95–98
  moisture content, 16, 88–89
    postharvest water loss, 92, 108, 109, 114
  nitrogen and, 59, 118
  pectin, 95
  polyphenol oxidase activity, 91, 95
  polyphenols, 91, 95
  protecting
    at harvest, 100
    during pruning, 34
    during thinning, 35
    during transport, 100, 113–114, 115
  quality
    eating quality, 96, 97
    quality control, 103, 106–107
    quality standards, 5, 17, 98, 103
  ripening for early market, 114–115
  ripening process, 88, 89–91, 96, 97, 101, 108, 109–113, 119, 122
  scale damage, 77, 86
  scarring
    from omnivorous leafroller, 77, 85
    susceptibility to, 35
    from touching while pruning, 34

from touching while thinning, 35
from wind, 18, 27
seed number, 15, 16, 25, 54
shriveling, 92, 108, 109, 114
size
   blossom blight and, 83
   irrigation and, 60
   maximum, 88
   pollination and, 15, 54
   presizing, 101–102
   pruning and, 60
   seed number and, 25, 54
   sizing, 104–105
   species producing small fruit, 9
   sunlight exposure and, 16, 33
   thinning and, 35
   water stress and, 44
soluble solids content (SSC), 88, 89, 90, 95, 96, 97, 111
soluble sugars, 94
specific heat, 89
standard fruit prototype, 9
starch content, 16, 88, 89, 91, 95
structure, 88
sugar content, 16, 88, 89, 91, 94, 95
sunburned
   May pruning of male vines and, 30, 32
   postharvest diseases and, 93, 120
   water stress and, 44
tannin, 95
thermal conductivity, 89
thinning, 17, 35, 98
third-year, 29
total solids content (dry weight), 16, 94, 95, 97
trichomes (fuzz), 88, 89, 102
tunneling, by omnivorous leafroller, 77, 85
vitamin C in, 16, 94–95
water stains on, 38
See also diseases (postharvest); disorders (postharvest); harvesting; packing; postharvest physiology; storing, fruit; transporting, fruit; wounds, in fruit
fruit drop
   boxelder bugs and, 87
   omnivorous leafroller and, 85
fruitful canes, defined, 31
fruittree leafroller, 85
fumigating
   Armillaria root rot (oak root rot), 19, 81
   Botrytis rot (gray mold), 120
   crown gall, 83
   nematodes, 18, 19, 72–73
fungal diseases. See diseases (postharvest); diseases (preharvest)

fungicides
   for postharvest diseases, 117–118, 120
   for preharvest diseases, 80
furrow irrigation, 39, 42, 48–49
fuzz (fruit), 88, 89, 102
   See also brushing fruit

G

galls. See crown gall
germination, 21–22
gibberellic acid treatments, 21
glucose
   in fruit, 16, 94
   photosynthesis and, 43
grades, 5, 17, 98, 103
grafting
   described, 23
   as preferred propagation method, 21
   storing scion wood, 23
   xylem sap and, 13, 22
grain crops
   nematode control and, 19, 72
   as rotation crop, 19
granulation, pericarp, 78, 79, 92–93, 112, 113
grasses
   nematode control and, 72, 73
   See also bermudagrass; johnsongrass
gray mold. See Botrytis rot (gray mold)
Greece, 3, 4
greedy scale, 86
green color, of fruit, 9, 17, 94, 95
ground cover management
   frost and, 12, 64, 68
   methods, 69
   See also cover crops; weed control
growing season, 18
growth process. See development
growth rate, 25
gypsum blocks, 50–51, 52

H

hairs (fruit), 88, 89, 102
   See also brushing fruit
hard-core, 92, 113
hardening seedlings, 22
hardpan, ripping, 19
harvesting, 99–100
   bins, 99–100
   cooling harvested fruit, 98, 100, 108–109, 110, 119
   ethylene exposure during, 100
   firmness
      discarding soft fruit, 99, 101, 103–104
      postharvest diseases and, 97, 118–119
      recommended level, 92, 97, 118

   heat exposure during, 100
   maturity measures, 88, 92, 94, 95–98
   mechanical injuries to fruit, 100
   methods, 99–100
   picking bags, 99, 100
   protecting fruit, 100
   timing of
      in Australia, 5
      in Chile, 4
      flesh softening and, 91, 97
      in Japan, 5
      postharvest disorders and, 91, 97
   water loss after harvest, 108, 109
   See also diseases (postharvest); packing; postharvest physiology; storing, fruit; transporting, fruit
Hayward variety
   budbreak, 10
   chilling requirements, 9
   flower development, 14
   fruit development, 14–17
   fruit illustrated, 74, 75, 88
   fruit respiratory activity, 89
   as preferred variety, 2, 6
   propagating, 21–24
   sizers and, 102, 104
   as standard fruit prototype, 9
heading back. See pruning
heat
   protecting fruit from during harvest, 100, 108
   See also cooling; heat stress; temperature
heaters, 65, 67
heat stress
   chlorosis from, 74, 75
   stomates and, 43
   See also cooling; heat; temperature
heat transfer methods, 62–63
heavy yields, alternation with light yields, 31
heeling bare-root plants, 24
Heinke, John, 2
Hemiberlesia lataniae (Signoret), 77, 86
Hemiberlesia rapax (Comstock), 86
herbicides
   postemergence herbicides, 69
   for postplanting weed control, 6, 20, 74, 75, 68, 69
   preemergence herbicides, 69
   for preplanting weed control, 19
   protecting trunks from, 19–20
history, of *Actinidia deliciosa*, 1–2
hoeing, for weed control, 69
honey bees, 53, 54–56, 57
hooking of terminal growth, bleeding canker and, 82
hose-pull sprinklers, 39, 41–42, 48–49
humidity
   frost and, 61

photosynthesis and, 11
in storage, 92, 98, 108, 109, 120, 121
summer pruning and, 33
in transport, 98, 114
See also temperature; water
hydrocooling, 108
hypodermal cells, of fruit, 88

I

impact bruising, 78, 79, 91–92, 106, 113
imports, worldwide, 3–5
income, 6–9
infrared temperature probes, 52
Ingram, Judd, 2
injuries. *See* wounds
ink staining, 78, 79, 101–102
See also juice blotch
inositol, in fruit, 16
insects, 84–86, 87
    armored scales, 77, 86
    boxelder bugs, 77, 87
    controlling, 55, 56, 84
    illustrated, 77
    impact on California crops, 84
    leaf-rolling caterpillars, 77, 84–86
    pollination by, 53, 54–56, 57
    See also spider mites
instruments. *See* equipment
international marketing, 3–5
iron
    deficiency (iron chlorosis), 18, 74, 75, 58, 59–60
    requirements, 18, 58
    stability of leaf concentrations, 12
irrigating
    Armillaria root rot (oak root rot) and, 82
    boron toxicity and, 60
    chloride toxicity and, 60
    container-grown plants, 22, 24
    drainage, 18, 80, 81
    frost injury and, 12
    fruit size and, 60
    importance of proper design, 18
    leveling and, 18
    necessity for, 43
    new plants, 19, 20, 24, 74
    nursery plants, 22
    phytophthora root and crown rot and, 36, 38, 39, 80, 81
    root growth and, 13
    scheduling, 43–49
    seed plantings, 22
    spider mites and, 86
    water requirements, 18, 22, 43, 44–49
    windbreaks, 27
    young vines, 49

See also irrigation systems; water; water stress
irrigation systems, 36–42
    choosing a system, 36
    drip systems, 6, 36, 37–38, 40–41, 49
    evaluating efficiency/uniformity, 40–42
    frost protection and, 36, 38, 40, 65–66, 67
    goal of, 36
    low-volume systems, 6, 36–38, 40–41, 49
    microsprinkler systems, 37–38, 40–41, 49
    multiple systems, 40
    scheduling irrigation, 43–49
    sprinkler systems, 38–39, 41–42, 48–49, 65–66, 67
    surface systems, 39–40, 42, 48–49, 64, 67
    types, 36–37
    See also irrigating; water; water stress
Italy, 3, 4
ivy scale, 86

J

Japan, 3, 5
johnsongrass, 19, 68–69
juice blotch, 78, 79, 121
    See also ink staining

K

Kiwifruit Administrative Committee, 5
Kiwifruit Marketing Board (KFMB), 3–4
Kramer variety, chilling requirements, 9

L

latania scale, 77, 86
latent heat, 63, 65–66
laying out vineyards, 25
leaf burn
    boron toxicity and, 74, 75, 60
    chloride toxicity and, 74, 75, 60
    overhead sprinklers and, 38
    potassium deficiency and, 60
    salts excess and, 60
    stomates and, 43
    water stress and, 43, 74, 75, 60
leaf-rolling caterpillars, 77, 84–86
leafspot, bacterial, 76, 83
leaves
    abscission, 13
    bronzing, phytophthora root and crown rot and, 80
    bud development, 14, 15

    dark spots surrounded by yellow halos, bacterial leafspot and, 76, 83
    defoliation
        spider mites and, 86
        toxic elements and, 60
    dry, dead, spider mites and, 86
    herringbone appearance, manganese deficiency and, 74, 75
    necrosis of
        bacterial leafspot and, 76, 83
        boron toxicity and, 74, 75
        chloride toxicity and, 74, 75
    physiology, 10–12
    rolled
        leaf-rolling caterpillars and, 77, 84–86
        potassium deficiency and, 60
    scale damage, 86
    scorching, 43
    small
        crown gall and, 82
        phytophthora root and crown rot and, 76, 80
        water stress and, 44
    sparse
        crown gall and, 82
        phytophthora root and crown rot and, 76, 80–81
    sunlight and, 10, 14, 16, 33
    wilting
        bleeding canker and, 82
        permanent wilting point, 47
        phytophthora root and crown rot and, 80
        stomates and, 43, 44
        water stress and, 43, 44
    See also chlorosis; leaf burn
Leptocoris trivittatus (Say), 77, 87
leveling, 18
light yields, alternation with heavy yields, 31
lipids, in fruit, 95
loading fruit. *See* transporting, fruit
low-lying areas, frost and, 63–64, 67
low-volume irrigation systems
    described, 36–38
    evaluating, 40–41
    frequency and quantity of irrigation, 6, 49

M

M51 variety, 9
M52 variety, 9
M54 variety, 9
M56 variety, 9
magnesium
    accumulation in leaves, 58
    deficiency, 60
    in fruit, 95

requirements, 58
male flowers, 15, 53, 56
male vines
    planting, 20
    pruning
        dormant, 30, 32
        summer, 30, 32, 34
    ratio of male-to-female vines, 25, 54
    varieties, 9
malic acid, in fruit, 16, 94
manganese
    accumulation in leaves, 58
    deficiency, 74, 75, 60
    requirements, 58
manure, nematode control and, 73
marketing, 3–5
    See also commercial development
Matua variety, 9
maturity measures, 88, 92, 94, 95–98
McGregor, James, 1
measuring soil moisture, 44, 50–52
Meloidogyne. See nematodes
microsprinkler systems, 37–38, 40–41, 49
milk cartons, for trunk protection, 12, 19–20
minerals
    accumulation in leaves, 11–12, 58
    in fruit, 95
    recovery from senescing leaves, 13
    storage in wood and bark in winter, 13
    See also nutrition; *specific minerals*
minimum temperatures
    predicting, 61–62, 63, 64
    See also temperature
misters, 65
mites, 77, 86–87
    See also insects
moisture content. *See* water
Monty variety, chilling requirements, 9
moths, tortricid, 84–86
mowing, for weed control, 6, 74, 75, 69
Mucor rot, 121
mulching, for weed control, 68, 69
multi-layer packs, 3, 105–106, 107
mycelia, from Botrytis rot, 78, 79, 116–117

N

National Weather Service, minimum temperature forecasts, 61, 62
necrosis of leaves
    bacterial leafspot and, 76, 83
    boron toxicity and, 74, 75
    chloride toxicity and, 74, 75
nematicides, 73
nematodes, 70–73
    controlling, 19, 72–73
    damage caused by, 70
    defined, 70
    established vineyards and, 72, 73
    establishing vineyards and, 71–73
    laboratory analysis, 70, 72
    monitoring guidelines, 71–72
    overview, 70
    root knot nematodes, 70, 71
    soil sampling, 71–72
neutron probes, 52
New Zealand
    blossom blight, 118, 121
    Botrytis rot (gray mold), 118
    commercial cultivars from, 9
    commercial development of kiwifruit, 1
    Dothiorella rot, 121
    Phomopsis rot, 121
    production and trade, 3, 4
    soluble solids content (SSC) standard, 96
    white-core inclusions, 112
nitrate, absorption by roots, 13
nitrogen
    accumulation in leaves, 58
    in fruit, 95
    recovery from senescing leaves, 13
    requirements, 58, 59
    storage disorders and, 59, 118
    winter storage in wood and bark, 13
nursery stock, 21–24
    chronology, 22, 24
    digging, 24
    grafting, 23
    starting seedlings and cuttings, 21–22
    transplanting to field, 24
    transplanting to nursery, 22
    transporting to field, 24
nutrition, 58–60
    boron, 18, 74, 75, 58, 60
    calcium, 12, 58, 60, 95
    chloride, 74, 75, 58, 60
    chlorotic vines and, 59–60
    copper, 58, 60
    diagnosing disorders, 58–59
    iron, 12, 18, 74, 75, 58, 59–60
    magnesium, 58, 60, 95
    manganese, 74, 75, 58, 60
    mineral accumulation in leaves, 11–12, 58
    nitrogen, 13, 58, 59, 95, 118
    pH and, 58
    phosphorus, 13, 58, 60, 95
    potassium, 12, 13, 58, 60, 95
    requirements, 58
    salts, excess, 18, 60
    sulfur, 60
    toxic elements, 74, 75, 58, 60
    zinc, 22, 58, 60
    See also carbohydrates; fertilizing; starches; sugars

O

oak root rot. *See* Armillaria root rot (oak root rot)
obliquebanded leafroller, 77, 85
oleander scale, 86
omnivorous leafroller, 77, 84–85
operating costs, 6–9
optical sizers, 105
orange tortrixes, 77, 85–86
organic acids
    distribution in vine, 12
    in fruit, 16–17, 90, 94, 95, 111
Osmia lignaria, 54
overhead sprinklers, 36, 38, 41–42, 48–49, 65–66, 67
oxalic acid, in fruit, 16–17
oxygen
    in controlled atmosphere storage, 92–93, 111, 113
    photosynthesis and, 10, 43

P

packing, 100–107
    bin dumping, 101, 102
    brushing fruit, 88, 92, 101, 102, 120
    cleaning fruit, 101–102
    containers, 105–106, 107
        bags, 92, 105, 106, 107
        bulk bins, 3, 105–106
        in California, 5
        cooling and, 108–109
        corrugated flats and lugs, 107, 109
        multi-layer packs, 3, 105–106, 107
        polyethylene film, 92
        single-layer flats, 105, 106, 107
        tri-packs, 3, 105–106, 107
        types, 105
        volume-fill packs, 105–106, 107
        wood flats, 107, 109
    cooling considerations, 100–101, 108–109
    ethylene exposure during, 100, 101
    injury avoidance during, 106
    ink staining from juice, 101–102
    methods, 106–107
    palletizing, 107
    preparing for, 100–105
    presizing, 101–102
    quality control, 103, 106–107
    sizing, 104–105
    sorting, 101, 103–105, 106, 118
packing density, 88
painting. *See* whitewashing
palletizing, 107
pectin, in fruit, 95

penetrometers, 52
Penicillium expansum (Lk.) Thom, 78, 79, 121
per capita consumption, in United States, 6
pergola trellises
  described, 25–26
  pruning and, 32, 33, 34
pericarp, 88
pericarp granulation, 78, 79, 92–93, 112, 113
pericarp translucency, 78, 79, 92, 112, 113
periderm, 88
permanent wilting point, 47
pesticides
  bee colonies and, 55, 56
  for insect control, 84
pH
  iron chlorosis and, 59
  nutrient deficiencies and, 58
  requirements, 18
pheromone traps, tortricid moths and, 85, 86
Phoma rot, 78, 79, 121
Phomopsis rot, 78, 79, 121
phosphate, fumigation and, 22
phosphorus
  accumulation in leaves, 58
  deficiency, 60
  in fruit, 95
  recovery from senescing leaves, 13
  requirements, 58
  winter storage in wood and bark, 13
photosynthesis, 10–11, 43
physical injuries. *See* wounds
physiology, 10–13
  budbreak, 10
  cane growth, 10
  carbohydrate distribution/storage, 12–13
  mineral nutrient accumulation, 11–12
  photosynthesis, 10–11, 43
  rate of growth, 25
  root growth and function, 13
  shoot growth, 10, 13
  transpiration, 11–12
  See also postharvest physiology
phytophthora root and crown rot, 36, 38, 39, 76, 80–81
  See also crown rots; root rots
picking bags, 99, 100
pigments, in fruit, 9, 17, 95
planning vineyards, 25–27
planting
  bare root plants, 19–20, 24
  container-grown plants, 20, 24
  crown gall and, 82, 83
  mounds or berms reduce root rot, 19, 80
  new vineyards, 25–27, 71–73
  preparing for, 18–19
  seeds, 21–22
  spacing plants, 25
  transplanting nursery stock to field, 24
  transplanting seedlings to nursery, 22
  windbreaks, 27
Platynota stultana Walsingham, 77, 84–85
pollination, 15–16, 53–57
  achieving optimum, 54
  by atomizer, 57
  Chico male vines and, 9
  described, 15–16, 53–54
  by hand, 57
  by honey bees, 53, 54–56, 57
  period of, 9
  ratio of male-to-female plants and, 25, 54
  by spraying liquid suspensions of pollen, 57
  storing pollen, 56
  supplemental, 56–57
  wind vs. insect, 53
polyethylene film, 92
polyethylene tents, for controlled-atmosphere storage, 111
polyphenol oxidase activity, in fruit, 91, 95
polyphenols, in fruit, 91, 95
portable sprinklers, 38, 40–41, 48–49
postharvest diseases. *See* diseases (postharvest)
postharvest disorders. *See* disorders (postharvest)
postharvest physiology, 88–93
  carbon dioxide sensitivity, 92–93, 113, 119
  causes of deterioration, 91–93
  controlled atmosphere storage and, 91, 92–93, 111–113, 119
  ethylene production, 89, 90, 91, 92, 102, 110, 111, 114, 119
  ethylene sensitivity, 88, 91, 92–93, 109, 110, 119
  morphological characteristics, 88
  physical characteristics, 88–89
  physical injuries and, 91–92
  respiration, 89–90, 91, 92, 110, 111
  ripening for early market, 114–115
  ripening process, 88, 89–91, 96, 97, 101, 108, 109–113, 119, 122
  transpiration (water loss), 92, 108, 109, 114
  See also diseases (postharvest); disorders (postharvest); storing, fruit
potassium
  accumulation in leaves, 58
  deficiency, 60
  in fruit, 95
  instability of leaf concentrations, 12
  recovery from senescing leaves, 13
  requirements, 58
preparing
  for packing, 100–105
  for planting, 18–19
  sites for new vineyards, 18–19, 72
presizing fruit, 101–102
  See also sizing fruit
pressure bombs, 52
probes, for measuring soil moisture, 50
production
  per acre, 31
  costs, 6–8
  heavy yields alternate with light yields, 31
  per vine, 10, 31
  worldwide, 3–5
propagation, 21–24
  grafting, 13, 21, 22, 23
  methods, 21
  overview, 21
  starting seedlings and cuttings, 21–22
  transplanting nursery stock to fields, 24
  transplanting seedlings to nursery, 22
  xylem sap and, 13, 22
protecting fruit
  at harvest, 100
  during pruning, 34
  during thinning, 35
  during transport, 100, 113–114, 115
pruning
  bleeding canker and, 82
  budbreak and, 10
  crown gall and, 82
  dormant, 30–32
    fourth growing season, 29
    after heavy crops, 31
    after light crops, 31
    male vines, 30, 32
    mature vines, 31–32
    pergola pruning, 32
    second growing season, 28, 29
    T-bar pruning, 32
    third growing season, 29
    timing, 13, 30
    in warm-winter areas, 32
  frost injury prevention and, 12
  fruit size and, 60
  in May, male vines, 30, 32, 34
  new plants, 28
  purpose, 30, 98
  scarring of fruit from, 34
  summer, 33–34
    advantages, 33, 34
    fruit rot avoidance and, 118

heading back entwining shoots, 10
male vines, 30, 32, 34
methods, 33–34
pergola pruning, 33, 34
purpose, 33
T-bar pruning, 33–34
terminal shoots induced by, 10
terminology, 30–31
xylary sap from, 13, 30
See also thinning
Pseudomonas canker, 76, 82
Pseudomonas syringae, 76, 82
Pseudomonas viridiflava (Burkholder) Dowson
blossom blight, 76, 83, 118, 121
leafspot, 76, 83
psychrometers, 62, 66

Q

quality
eating quality, 96, 97
quality control, 103, 106–107
quality standards, 5, 17, 98, 103
quinic acid, in fruit, 16, 94

R

radiation, 62, 65
radiation frosts, 61–62
See also frost
rain, 43, 55
raised beds, for seedlings, 22
rate of growth, 25
ratio of male-to-female plants, 25, 54
reference crop water use, evapotranspiration based upon, 46
refractometers, 96
releveling, 18
replacement canes, defined, 31
resistance measuring devices, for measuring soil moisture content, 52
respiration
postharvest, 89–90, 91, 92, 110, 111
preharvest, 10, 11
ripening
for early market, 114–115
postharvest process, 88, 89–91, 96, 97, 101, 108, 109–113, 119, 122
ripping, 18–19
rodent damage, protecting trunks from, 19–20
rolled leaves
leaf-rolling caterpillars and, 77, 84–86
potassium deficiency and, 60
root knot nematodes. *See* nematodes
root rots

Armillaria root rot (oak root rot), 76, 80, 81–82
irrigation and, 38
phytophthora root and crown rot, 36, 38, 76, 80–81
planting on mounds or berms reduces, 19, 80
from storing bare-root plants, 24
waterlogged soils and, 19, 80, 81
young plant irrigation and, 20, 81
roots
container-grown plants, 22
depth estimation, 47–48
growth and function, 13
propagating from, 21
soil and, 13, 19
See also nematodes; root rots
rootstocks
age, 22
Bruno, 9, 21
improving, 9
propagating, 21–22
storing seeds for, 21
rotation crops. *See* cover crops
rototilling, 69
rots. *See* crown rots; diseases (postharvest); root rots
row spacing, 25

S

Sacramento Valley
commercial development of kiwifruit, 1–2
counties producing kiwifruit, 2
equipment and building list, 8
operating costs, 7
preharvest sprays, 120
See also California
salts
acceptable levels, 18
excess, 18, 60
San Diego
poor growing conditions in, 2
preharvest sprays, 120
See also California; Southern California
San Joaquin Valley
commercial development of kiwifruit, 1–2
counties producing kiwifruit, 2
nematodes, 71
preharvest sprays, 120
See also California
sap, 13, 22, 30
scales, armored, 77, 86
scarification, of seeds, 21
scarring (fruit)
from omnivorous leafroller, 85
susceptibility to, 35
from touching while pruning, 34

from touching while thinning, 35
from wind, 18, 27
scheduling irrigation, 43–49
sclerotia, from Botrytis-rot, 78, 79, 116
Sclerotinia rot, 121
scorching, 43
See also leaf burn
seedlings, 21–22
seeds
in fruit, 15, 16, 25, 54
planting, 21–22
storing, 21
sensible heat, 63
sex pheromone traps, tortricid moths and, 85, 86
shade
bud fruitfulness and, 14
eliminating with summer pruning, 33
evapotranspiration and, 49
fruit size and, 16
photosynthesis and, 11
storage of sun-exposed vs. shade-exposed fruit, 59, 92, 118
See also sunlight
shoots
defined, 31
growth, 10, 13
See also terminal growth
shovels, for measuring soil moisture, 50
shriveling, 92, 108, 109, 114
single-layer flats, 105, 106, 107
site preparation, 18–19, 72
site selection, 18, 63–64, 67, 72
sizing fruit, 101–102, 104–105
size of fruit
blossom blight and, 83
irrigation and, 60
maximum, 88
pollination and, 15, 54
presizing, 101–102
pruning and, 60
seed number and, 25
sizing, 104–105
species producing small fruit, 9
sunlight exposure and, 16, 33
thinning and, 35
water stress and, 44
slipplowing, 18–19
Smith, Robert, 1
sodium. *See* salts
softening process, postharvest, 88, 89–91, 96, 97, 101, 108, 109–113, 119, 122
soil
boron content, 18
for container-grown plants, 22
electrical conductivity (EC), 18
erosion prevention, 69
irrigation system selection and, 37

moisture content
   available water content, 47–48
   extractable moisture in root zone, 47–48
   frost protection and, 64, 67
   measuring, 44, 50–52
   permanent wilting point, 47
   yield threshold depletion, 47
nematodes and, 19, 71–72
pH, 18, 58, 59
phytophthora root and crown rot and, 36, 80, 81
preparing for planting, 18–19
requirements, 18
root growth and, 13, 19
rototilling damages, 69
sandy, fumigating, 19
sodium content, 18
temperature of
   for growing cuttings, 22
   for growing seedlings, 21
soil tubes, for measuring soil moisture, 50, 51
solid-set sprinklers, 38, 39, 40–41, 48–49
soluble solids content (SSC), 88, 89, 90, 95, 96, 97, 111
soluble sugars content, 94
sorbitol, vine growth and, 43
sorting, 101, 103–105, 106, 118
Southern California
   nematodes, 71
   poor growing conditions, 2, 32
   See also California; San Diego
spacing plants, 25
specific heat, of fruit, 89
spider mites, 86–87
sprinkler systems, 38–39
   advantages, 36, 39
   disadvantages, 39
   evaluating, 41–42
   frequency and quantity of irrigation, 48–49
   frost protection and, 36, 38, 65–66, 67
   hose-pull sprinklers, 39
   overhead sprinklers, 36, 38, 65–66, 67
   portable sprinklers, 38
   solid-set sprinklers, 38, 39
   under-vine sprinklers, 38, 65, 67
   See also microsprinklers
spurs, 31, 32
SSC (soluble solids content), 88, 89, 90, 95, 96, 97, 111
starches
   conversion to sugar, 12, 88, 89, 91, 96
   distribution/storage in vine, 12–13
   in harvested fruit, 88, 89, 91, 94
   in immature fruit, 16

photosynthesis and, 11
stomates
   photosynthesis and, 11
   transpiration and, 11, 43, 44
storing
   bare root plants, 24
   fruit, 109–113
      ascorbic acid levels and, 95
      boron toxicity and, 60
      bruising and, 78, 79, 91–92
      brushing and, 88, 92
      calcium deficiency and, 60
      controlled-atmosphere storage, 91, 92–93, 111–113, 119
      cooling immediately after harvest, 98, 100–101, 108–109, 110, 119
      cracking and, 78, 79, 109
      diseases in storage. See diseases (postharvest)
      disorders in storage, 78, 79, 92–93
         hard-core, 92, 113
         illustrated, 78, 79
         juice blotch, 121
         pericarp granulation, 78, 79, 92–93, 112, 113
         pericarp translucency, 78, 79, 92, 112, 113
         white-core inclusions, 78, 79, 93, 112–113
      ethylene and, 88, 90, 91, 92–93, 101, 109–111, 119
      firmness at harvest and, 97, 118–119
      freeze damage from, 78, 79, 109
      freezing point, 89, 109
      handling fruit of low firmness, 119
      harvest timing and, 91, 97
      humidity and, 92, 98, 108, 109, 120, 121
      nitrogen fertilization and, 59, 118
      physical injury and, 78, 79, 91–92, 118, 119
      respiration and, 89–90, 91, 92, 110, 111
      scales and, 86
      shriveling, 92, 108, 109, 114
      softening process in storage, 88, 89–91, 96, 97, 101, 108, 109–113, 119, 122
      soluble solids content (SSC) reduction, 97
      summer pruning and, 33
      sunburned fruit, 93, 120
      sun-exposed vs. shade-exposed fruit, 59, 92, 118
      temperature and, 92, 98, 108, 109–110, 112–113, 117, 119
      total solids content reduction, 97
      water contact avoidance, 108, 109
      water loss, 92, 108, 109, 114
      See also postharvest physiology

pollen, 56
scion wood, 23
seeds, 21
structure
   of flowers, 15, 53–54
   of fruit, 88
   of vines, 30–31
   See also physiology
stubs. See spurs
suckers, 22, 29, 82
sucrose
   in fruit, 16, 94
   vine growth and, 43
sudangrass, 72, 73
sugars
   conversion of starch to, 12, 88, 89, 91, 96
   distribution/storage in vine, 12–13
   frost injury and, 12–13
   in fruit, 16, 88, 89, 91, 94, 95
   photosynthesis and, 10–11, 43
sulfur deficiency, 60
sulfur dioxide, for postharvest diseases, 120
summer pruning. See pruning, summer
sunburn
   May pruning of male vines and, 30, 32
   postharvest diseases and, 93, 120
   protecting trunks from, 19
   water stress and, 44
sunlight
   bud fruitfulness and, 14
   fruit size and, 16
   maximizing exposure to, 10, 33
   rule of thumb, 33
   storage of sun-exposed vs. shade-exposed fruit, 59, 92, 118
   See also photosynthesis; shade
surface irrigation systems, 39–40, 42, 48–49, 65, 67
syrphid flies, 54

T

Tanimoto brothers, 1–2
tannin, in fruit, 95
taping canes, 32
T-bar trellises
   described, 25, 26
   pruning and, 32, 33–34
temperature
   bees and, 55
   chilling requirements, 9, 14–15, 18
   cold-hardiness, 13
   cooling harvested fruit, 98, 100–101, 108–109, 110, 119
   cooling vineyards, 36, 38, 40, 43, 69
   dewpoint temperature, 63, 66

freezing point of fruit in storage, 89, 109
frost injury and, 12, 18
grafting and, 23
heat stress, 43, 74, 75
high-temperature tolerance, 9
minimums, predicting, 61–62, 63, 64
photosynthesis and, 11
phytophthora root and crown rot and, 80
postharvest diseases and, 117, 120, 121
requirements preharvest, 18
for seed germination, 21–22
of soil
   for growing cuttings, 22
   for growing seedlings, 21
specific heat of fruit, 89
spider mites and, 86
in storage, 92, 98, 108, 109–110, 112–113, 117, 119
thermal conductivity of fruit, 89
in transport, 98, 113–114
wet-bulb temperature, 66, 67
winter-hardy varieties, 9
See also frost; humidity
temperature inversion, frost and, 65, 67
tenderizing enzyme, in fruit, 95
tensiometers, 50, 51–52
terminal growth
   bleeding canker and, 82
   crown gall and, 82
   phytophthora root and crown rot, 76, 80
   water stress and, 44
   See also shoots
Tetranychus urticae Koch, 86–87
Tewi variety, chilling requirements, 9
thermal conductivity, of fruit, 89
thinning, 17, 35, 98
timing of
   dormant pruning, 13, 30
   flowering, 9, 10
   harvest
     in Australia, 5
     in Chile, 4
     flesh softening and, 91, 97
     in Japan, 5
     postharvest disorders and, 91, 97
   irrigation, 43–49
   nursery stock stages, 22, 24
   thinning, 35
tissue culture propagation techniques, 21
Tomuri variety, 9
tonnage, worldwide, 3
tortricid moths, 77, 84–86
total solids content, 16, 94, 95, 97
toxic elements, 74, 75, 58, 60

trade, 3–5
training young vines, 28–29
translucency, pericarp, 78, 79, 92, 112, 113
transpiration
   postharvest fruit, 92, 108, 109, 114
   vine, 11–12, 43–44, 45, 64
   See also evapotranspiration
transplanting
   crown gall and, 82, 83
   nursery stock to fields, 24
   seedlings to nursery, 22
   See also planting
transporting
   bare-root plants to field, 24
   fruit, 113–115
     ethylene exposure during, 114
     injuries sustained during, 78, 79, 91–92, 100, 113
     protection measures, 100, 113–114, 115
     removing injured or infected fruit prior to transport, 113
     ripening for early market, 114–115
     temperature and humidity management, 98, 113–114
     water loss avoidance, 114
trellising
   end posts, 26
   end support braces, 26
   importance of proper design, 18
   pergola trellises, 25, 32, 33, 34
   pruning and, 32, 33–34
   purpose, 10
   T-bar trellises, 25, 26, 32, 33–34
   training young vines on, 28–29
   weight-bearing requirements, 26
   wire tension, 26
trichomes, 88, 89, 102
   See also brushing fruit
tri-packs, 3, 105–106, 107
trunks
   establishing in new plants, 28–29
   milk carton protection, 19–20
   whitewashing, 19, 24
   wrapping, 12, 19–20
tunneling in fruit, by omnivorous leafroller, 77, 85
twospotted spider mites, 86–87
tying canes, 32
Typhula spp. See buckshot rot

U

under-vine sprinklers, 38, 40–41, 48–49, 65, 67
United States
   acreage, 1, 2, 3, 4
   per capita consumption, 6

   production and trade, 3, 4
   See also California; worldwide acreage; worldwide production and trade
USDA Plant Introduction Station at Chico, 9

V

vegetative canes, defined, 31
vibration bruising, 78, 79, 91–92, 100, 113
Vincent variety, chilling requirements, 9
Vinclozolin, 117
vines
   development, 10–13
   parts, 30–31
   water movement in, 43–44
   See also young vines; specific parts of vines
vineyards
   cooling, 36, 38, 40, 43, 69
   developing, 18–20, 72–73
   costs, 6, 7
   nematodes and, 71–73
   planning and designing, 25–27
   planting and early care, 19–20, 73
   planting windbreaks, 27
   site preparation, 18–19, 72
   site selection, 18, 63–64, 67, 72
   floor management. *See* cover crops; ground cover management; weed control
   operating costs, 6–8
   water's role in, 43
vitamin B1 dips, 19
vitamin C, in fruit, 16, 94–95
volume-fill packs, 105–106, 107

W

water
   in fruit, 16, 88–89
     postharvest water loss, 92, 108, 109, 114
   movement in vines, 43–44
   photosynthesis and, 10–11, 43
   requirements, 18, 22, 43, 44–49
   role of, 43
   in soil
     available water content, 47–48
     extractable moisture in root zone, 47–48
     frost protection and, 64, 67
     measuring, 44, 50–52
     permanent wilting point, 47
     yield threshold depletion, 47
   in storage, avoiding contact with, 108, 109
   See also humidity; irrigating; irrigation systems; rain; transpiration

water budget (water balance) method, 44–45, 47
waterlogging
   Armillaria root rot (oak root rot) and, 82
   phytophthora root and crown rot and, 36, 38, 39, 80, 81
   root sensitivity to, 13
watersprouts, 22
water stains, on fruit, 38
water stress
   humidity and, 11
   symptoms, 43, 44, 74, 75, 60
   yield threshold depletion and, 47
weather. *See* climate requirements; frost; humidity; rain; temperature; wind
webbing
   omnivorous leafroller and, 84
   orange tortrix and, 85
   spider mites and, 86
weed control, 74, 75, 68–69
   crown gall and, 82, 83
   frost and, 64, 67
   herbicides, 6, 19–20, 74, 75, 68, 69
   identifying weeds, 69
   illustrated, 74, 75
   methods, 74, 75, 68, 69
   necessity for, 18, 68
   omnivorous leafroller and, 84, 85
   postplanting control, 6, 20, 74, 75, 68–69
   preplanting eradication, 19, 68–69
   prevention, 68–69
   species of weeds, 68
   under-vine sprinklers and, 38
   See also cover crops; ground cover management
weight sizers, 104–105
wet-bulb temperature, 66, 67
whip grafting, 23
   See also grafting
white-core inclusions, 78, 79, 93, 112–113
whitewashing
   cordons, 30, 32

trunks, 19, 24
wilting
   bleeding canker and, 82
   permanent wilting point, 47
   phytophthora root and crown rot and, 80
   stomates and, 43, 44
   water stress and, 43, 44
wind
   bees and, 55
   damage caused by, 18, 27
   flowering and, 15
   frost and, 61, 62, 64, 65, 66, 67
   pollination by, 53
   preventing damage to new plants, 28
windbreaks
   caring for, 27
   frost protection and, 64, 67
   illustrated, 26
   necessity for, 18, 27
   types of, 27
wind machines, 65, 67
winter chilling requirements. *See* chilling requirements
winter-hardy varieties, 9
winter pruning. *See* pruning, dormant
wire tension, for trellising, 26
wood flats, 107, 108
wood tissues
   mineral storage in, 13
   starch storage in, 12
   See also bark
worldwide acreage, 1, 2, 3
worldwide production and trade, 3–5
wounds
   in fruit
      bruising, 78, 79, 91–92, 100, 106, 113
      cork cells covering, 88
      ethylene production stimulated by, 90, 91, 92, 102
      firmness and susceptibility to, 91–92
      from harvesting, 100
      postharvest disease susceptibility and, 118, 119, 120, 121, 122

      from pruning, 34
      from thinning, 35
      from transport, 78, 79, 91–92, 100, 113
      from wind, 18, 27
   in vines
      causes of, 82
      preharvest disease susceptibility and, 82
wrapping trunks, 12, 19–20

X

xylary sap, 13, 22, 30
xylem, water movement in, 44

Y

yellow fruit
   from iron chlorosis, 74, 75
   yellow carotenoid pigments, 9, 17, 95
yellow leaves. *See* chlorosis
yield
   per acre, 31
   heavy yields alternate with light yields, 31
   per vine, 10, 31
   worldwide, 3–5
yield threshold depletion, 47
young vines
   fertilizing, 59
   frost damage prevention, 59
   irrigating, 49
   training, 28–29

Z

zinc
   accumulation in leaves, 58
   deficiency, 60
   fumigation and, 22
   requirements, 58